KINGDOMS OF THE YORUBA

Kingdoms
of the Yoruba

ROBERT SMITH

Third Edition

The University of Wisconsin Press

Published in the United States of America by
The University of Wisconsin Press
114 North Murray Street
Madison, Wisconsin 53715

Published in Great Britain by
James Currey Ltd
54b Thornhill Square, Islington
London, N1 1BE

Library of Congress Cataloging-in-Publication Data
Smith, Robert Sydney.
Kingdoms of the Yoruba.
Bibliography: pp. 156–164.
Includes index.
1. Yorubas——History. I. Title.
DT515.45.Y67S65 1988   966.9'2   87-40516
ISBN 0–299–11600–X
ISBN 0–299–11604–2 (pbk.)

Typeset in 10/11½ pt Palatino
by Colset Private Limited, Singapore
Printed in Great Britain

'*Every effort at synthesis, however premature it may seem, cannot fail to react usefully on investigations, provided one offers it in all frankness for what it is.*'

Henri Pirenne

CONTENTS

LIST OF ILLUSTRATIONS

LIST OF ABBREVIATIONS

C.M.S.	Church Missionary Society
J.A.H.	Journal of African History
J.H.S.N.	Journal of the Historical Society of Nigeria
J.R.A.S.	Journal of the Royal African Society
L.N.R.	Lagos Notes and Records
N.G.J.	Nigerian Geographical Journal
P.P.	Parliamentary Papers
P.R.O.	Public Record Office
W.A.J.A.	West African Journal of Archaeology

PREFACE TO FIRST EDITION

The history of tropical Africa, whose sources are largely unwritten even for periods quite near in time to our own and whose study has been undertaken systematically only in late years, bears the marks of its necessarily provisional character. But in fact any history of any area or any people, however rich in primary and secondary material, shares this character. In any study of the past, whether near in time or remote, there are always new ways of looking at the material and new evidence to be adduced. History can never be more than a selection, both deliberate and fortuitous, of the factors in a situation. 'Ultimate history', which would need no addition, correction, or modification, and which to Acton seemed to lie only just beyond the reach of his generation, is an elusive, unattainable – though always attractive – goal.

The past of the Yoruba of West Africa, who form the population of the Western State of Nigeria, must be reconstructed, so far as the period preceding the penetration of their country by Europeans from about the mid-nineteenth century is concerned, almost wholly from tradition, or 'oral evidence' in the cumbersome phrase, a method which is only now achieving respectability among historians. As J. D. Fage pointed out in his inaugural lecture at Birmingham in 1965, 'The sense of history, the need for history can be quite independent of the ability to write'; many African societies in the absence of writing 'developed formal oral records of their past and elaborate methods of maintaining these records for their posterity'. In the case of the Yoruba, the historian who is prepared to use such material is fortunate, since they are a people unusually rich in tradition, expressed and conserved in many ways. Their country is made up of different kingdoms all having specific and complex traditions about their origins and subsequent history, preserved deliberately and ritually by officials who bear almost the character of professional historians. Although these traditions are often of a legendary and miraculous kind, they may be sifted, correlated, and cross-checked as any other evidence until a residuum is obtained which is acceptable as 'truth'. Moreover, such accounts can usually be supplemented in other ways: from ceremonies recalling and re-enacting the past which are performed on public occasions, from place and proper names and titles, from a treasury of proverbial and epigrammatic phrases (called *owe*). All these preserve, although often enigmatically, fragments of the past.

Unhappily, as new forms of society impose new ways of thought and new conventions, much of this repository of knowledge is being lost. Within a generation tradition may be so weakened among the Yoruba as to cease to be an important source of new information for the historian.

To supplement tradition and to correct, corroborate, or confirm it, there are few other sources. Barely a dozen unambiguous references to the Yoruba in written material before the nineteenth century are known, and these throw only a fitful light on their circumstances. But while it is unlikely that much new written evidence will be discovered, there is greater hope of obtaining information from archaeology. This is still a rather neglected field in West Africa, but it is probably here that the greatest advances in early Yoruba historical studies can be expected, in conjunction with such newer ancillary studies as comparative linguistics and the analysis of the distribution of blood-groups.

The construction of a coherent narrative of the past, which must precede any attempt at interpretation, provides as great a problem for the historian of the Yoruba as the recovery of his material. It is a platitude that oral tradition must be treated with caution and reserve – as must all evidence – and that precision is needed in the use of terms and the indication of sources. Since a supernatural element frequently intrudes into tradition, especially (but not exclusively) into tradition about earliest times, it is useful to distinguish between 'myth', in which the supernatural plays a large part, and 'legend', which strains credulity less or not at all. A further distinction may be made (and is made in this book) between 'legend', which is tradition related by word of mouth, and 'tradition', which is a wider term and embraces all methods of recording the past – re-enactment ceremonies, for example – which are not ultimately based on contemporary written material or on archaeology. Again, tradition is subject to falsification in several well-known ways: for example, to what has been called 'legendary elision' (the suppression of the 'middle ages' in a people's history by assigning all events to either the period of the origin of their society or to recent times) and 'legendary stereotyping' (the compression of a narrative by reducing and stereotyping the names of persons and places), or to the production of official, often justificatory accounts of the past by means of 'Authorized' and then 'Revised' versions of events. Moreover, among the Yoruba tradition is closely concerned with title to land, and this often leads to the production by different towns or different families of rival 'Authorized Versions' and to competition based on these accounts for precedence and chieftaincies. The difficulties which beset the historian working from tradition are indeed many, and they differ at many points from the difficulties which arise in connection with other kinds of evidence. Yet, as Vansina has shown, there is no priority among classes of historical material. All evidence must be subjected to rigorous, even sceptical, examination, and in using tradition the historian must strive to apply the same standards, if not the same criteria, as he applies in the use of other sources.

The Yoruba awareness of their past, expressed in the abundance of their tradition, has led over the last half-century to an increasing flow of historical publications. Many local histories have been produced, in both Yoruba and English. These are of varying standard, and nearly all lack a critical basis, but in every case they contribute in some degree to the recovery and understanding of the history of the Yoruba in the wider national sense as well as locally. More recently, academically trained Nigerians, and a few expatriate historians, have been producing books, articles, and theses which deal with Yoruba history analytically and according to modern techniques of research and presentation. Most of these latter, however, have concentrated on the last hundred or so years, avoiding thereby heavy dependence on tradition. Both groups are dominated by a figure who stands midway between them: the Reverend Samuel Johnson, a Yoruba and an Anglican priest of Oyo, whose *History* of his own people constitutes a masterly narrative based on tradition and related in majestic English prose. Johnson's work lacks the references to sources which would have trebled its value to later historians and is handicapped by his preoccupation with the affairs of Oyo and by his religious determinism. Nevertheless, the *History of the Yorubas* is a classic to which resort will always be made. The present writer's first acknowledgement must therefore be to the Reverend Samuel Johnson.

Meanwhile the process of reconstructing the Yoruba past is gaining momentum, even though at present hypotheses predominate over established fact. An attempt, such as this book, to give a general account of the major Yoruba kingdoms, is likely to be overtaken within a very short time by new evidence and reinterpretations. The writer still hopes that his work may serve as a summary of knowledge and current theories and perhaps also provide for those working in this field an indication of points where their efforts are most needed. His thanks are now most sincerely rendered to his many helpers. In particular, he expresses his gratitude to the great number of local rulers (the *oba*), their chiefs and officials, and other residents of their towns, who have patiently answered his many and importunate questions about the days of their ancestors. His thanks are due to his colleagues in the Universities of Lagos and Ife for help in various ways; he owes special gratitude to Mr R. C. C. Law, who read his manuscript and made many useful suggestions, generously sharing his deep knowledge of West African written sources. He also benefited greatly from the advice of Mr Festus Adetula. Finally, he acknowledges his debt to the students of Lagos and Ife, many of whom gave their time to interpreting for him their history and customs, as well as their language.

Lagos
1969

PREFACE TO SECOND EDITION

During the five years since this book was first published, the impetus towards the recovery and writing of Yoruba history has gained pace. A measure of this is the list of over eighty books and articles, nearly all of recent date, which have been added to the Sources and Bibliography section of this second edition. In the first Preface, it was forecast that 'new evidence and reinterpretations' were likely to overtake the book very shortly. The appearance of much new material has made it desirable even sooner than was expected that a new synthesis of Yoruba history should be attempted, and the writer is grateful to the publishers for making this possible. The main changes and additions to the original text will be found in Chapter 2, on Ife, to take account of recent archaeological discoveries, Chapter 4, where the omission of any consideration of the history of the Igbomina and other north-eastern Yoruba has been remedied, and Chapter 10, on the reasons for and chronology of the decline and fall of Old Oyo, but numerous minor amendments have been made throughout the work. To the writer's surprise (and somewhat to his disappointment), the general structure of the book escaped criticism, and has therefore been retained.

Once again many thanks are due to Dr R. C. C. Law, now of the University of Stirling, for his helpful comments on the text. The writer also expresses his gratitude to the authorities of the University of Aberdeen for appointing him to a Research and Teaching Fellowship in 1973–4, during the latter part of which this revision was carried out, and to Professor J. D. Hargreaves of Aberdeen for much help and constant encouragement.

Aberdeen
May 1974

Note: Under the administrative re-arrangements in early 1976, the Western State of Nigeria (constituted in 1967 from the former Western Region) was divided into three states: Ondo, with its capital at Akure, Oyo, with its capital at Ibadan, and Ogun, with its capital at Abeokuta. Lagos remained a state, its capital being removed to Ikeja, its northern suburb on the mainland, but was to be replaced as Federal capital.

PREFACE TO THIRD EDITION

The last ten years have seen important advances in the study of the pre-colonial history of the Yoruba, and the present third edition of this book now attempts to take these into account in numerous additions and amendments. There has also been growing scepticism about the status and interpretation of oral tradition in general, which is reflected in recent writing about the past of the Yoruba, heavily dependent as this has been on such tradition. This development has especially influenced the treatment throughout Part I and in Chapter 7 of this edition of the traditional accounts of the origins and early histories of the Yoruba kingdoms. Nevertheless, the writer has been unable to accept the more radical reinterpretations which dismiss the traditions as little more than legitimizing and propaganda devices evolved consciously or half-consciously to meet particular situations. He still believes that, except where supernatural and irrational elements are introduced, oral tradition can be weighed, sifted and assessed to suggest serious answers as to 'what really happened' in Yorubaland during the pre-colonial centuries.

Kew
1987

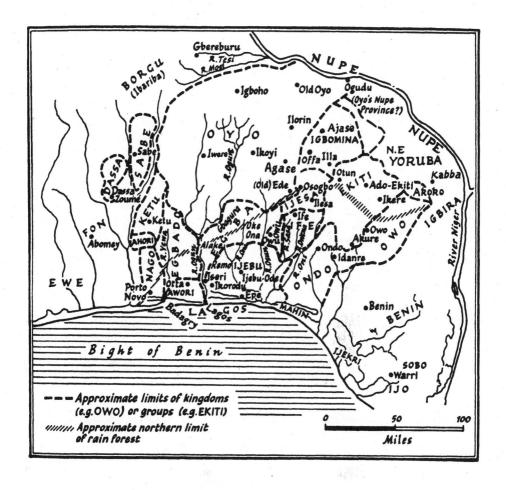

Map 1. The Yoruba Kingdoms and their Neighbours

This map is intended to illustrate the political divisions of the Yoruba between the foundation of the kingdoms and *c.* 1830. The limits shown for the kingdoms and groups are extremely tentative. They are mainly based on the 'cultural groups' shown on the map attached to Forde (1951); important exceptions are in the northward extension of the Egba before *c.* 1830 and the inclusion of the Ife, Ijesha, Owo, and Owu kingdoms. The Oyo kingdom at its zenith probably extended on the north-east as far as the Niger between Ogudu and the junction of the Moshi with the Niger, an area now mainly inhabited by Nupe.

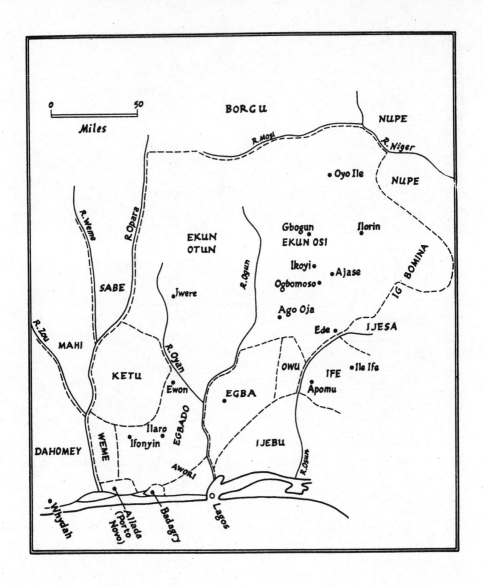

Map 2. The Kingdom and Empire of Oyo in the Later Eighteenth Century

This map has been taken, with permission, from Law (1971), p. 26.

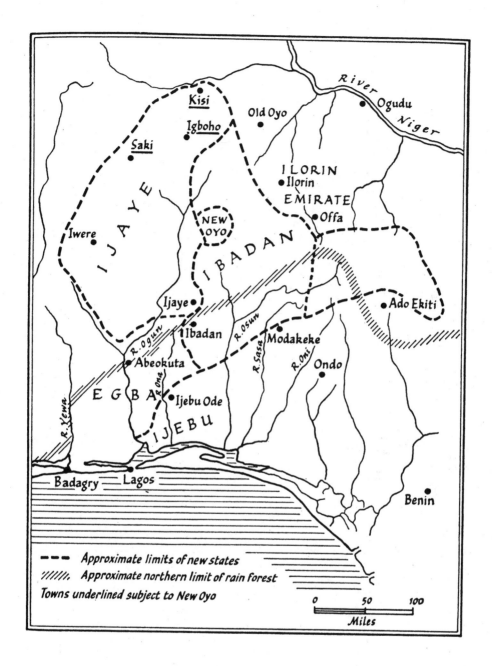

Map 3. The New States, c. 1836–62

This map is intended to illustrate the rearrangement of the Yoruba provinces under Alafin Atiba, with Ijaye preponderant in the western Ekun and Ibadan in the eastern, as shown on the map in Morton-Williams (1967), p. 47. The eastern extension of Ibadan dates only from the 1850s. The regrouping of the Egba, both shifting southward and extending west across the river Ogun, with their new capital at Abeokuta, should also be noted.

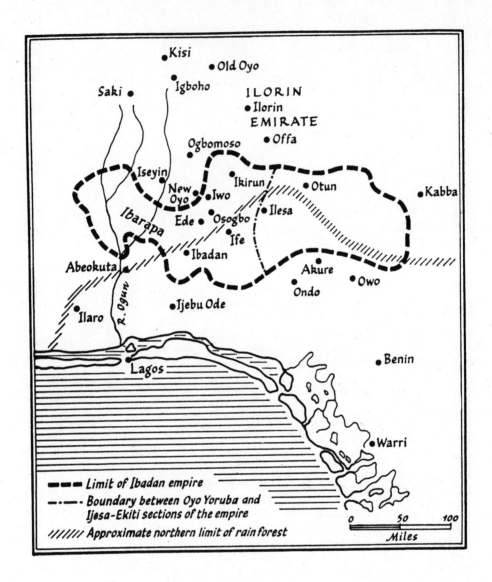

Map 4. Ibadan and its Neighbours, 1862–86

This map is based on that in Awe (1964b), p. 60. It will be seen that from 1862 Ibadan absorbed the southern part of the former Ijaye territory and also Ibarapa in the upper Ogun. On the other hand, towns such as Shaki and Iseyin in the former western provinces (*ekun etan*) of the old Oyo kingdom were independent of Ibadan and remained only loosely subject to the Alafin at New Oyo.

KINGDOMS OF THE YORUBA

PART I

ONE
THE YORUBA AND THEIR HOMELAND

The political structure of West Africa in the twentieth century tends to cut across the history both of the peoples living there and of their earliest contacts with the world beyond. This is partly the result of the drawing of frontiers by the European empire-builders of the last century in such a way that in places they divided a people between two or even more states. The extent to which this was done has sometimes been exaggerated. A more important factor is that the countries which have developed from the coastal annexations of the British, French, and Germans are all based upon that 'penetration of the interior' which was a prominent object of European missionaries, traders, and officials alike; thus they group together peoples whose disparate histories, cultures, and languages reflect the different worlds of the Guinea forestlands and the savannah.

Nigeria exemplifies this contrast. Its ten northern states (until 1967 the vast Northern Region) consist almost entirely of open countryside, of the type known as savannah (either grassland or woodland), whereas the states to the south are much more thickly wooded, especially within a hundred miles of the coast, where the forest is dense. The contrast is repeated in the social organization and history of these regions. Until the conquest of the whole country by the British at the end of the last century, the north was dominated by the Hausa (or, from early in the same century, Hausa–Fulani) and Borno emirates, which have their place in the history of the empires of the West Sudan, while to the south-east the Igbo and, farther south again, the Efik, Ibibio, and other peoples of the Niger Delta preserved a society which was highly fragmented.

The Yoruba in the south-west, and also their neighbours to the east, the Bini or Edo of Benin (now the Bendel State), make a transition and a link between these extremes. Much of their homeland lies in the forest, while the rest can be described as woodland savannah, and yet states developed here which, although generally on a smaller territorial scale than the states to the north, evolved forms of government which could be adapted to areas far beyond the founding metropolis and to situations involving a form of international relations between themselves and with other peoples. It can also be claimed that the Yoruba and Bini kingdoms were, as Michael Crowder puts it,[1] 'purely African states whose growth was stimulated neither by contact with Islam nor Europe'. They preserved their government,

3

religion, and ways of life in this relative isolation until the Europeans, who had been trading on the coast from the fifteenth century onwards, changed their role in the nineteenth century and became proselytizers of their religion, their economy, their culture, and finally their political forms.

It is not difficult to explain the rise of states in the West Sudan, where lateral communications across the savannah are relatively easy, as the pilgrimage routes to Mecca show; even the great Sahara was traversed by caravan trails leading to the Barbary ports, and an almost ideal vehicle for the desert had been available since Roman times in the camel. But in the Guinea forest the position was different. Here, climate, disease, and limiting agricultural conditions made life hazardous, while the dense undergrowth hindered communications. The coast was forbidding: the beaches beaten with surf, and beyond them the intricacies of the mangrove swamps. Such conditions would seem to combine to hinder the rise of organized communities on a scale which could be dignified by the term 'state', much less 'empire'. Yet, despite these unfavourable conditions, such states as Abomey, Asante (Ashanti), Benin, and the Yoruba kingdoms arose both in the forest depths and on its fringes. Although they seem to have emerged somewhat later and more slowly than the better-known states of the grasslands, their polities and cultures were no less distinguished than those of, for example, Ghana, Mali, Songhay, Hausa or Borno.

The origins of the Guinea states are likely to have been as varied as their subsequent histories and institutions. Though the evidence is still meagre, increasing light is gradually being thrown on early times by the work of archaeologists. Thurstan Shaw's discovery of a Stone Age habitation at Iwo Ileru near Akure has yielded radiocarbon dates showing occupation there between the tenth and second millennia B.C., while dates from Ife indicate that there was a substantial settlement on the site as early as the ninth century A.D.[2] By the end of the first millennium A.D. this part of the rain forest was clearly supporting a fairly extensive population who were living in permanent agricultural settlements and smelting their own iron.

A number of factors which must have been important in the formation of states can now be isolated. The first is the development in the Guinea forest of a type of food production capable of supporting an organized society. This depended upon the presence of suitable crops and of metal tools for their efficient cultivation. The dating of this development for any part of Guinea is still a matter of controversy. Among the most important food crops the common yam (*Dioscorea*), the cocoyam (*Colocasia esculenta*), plantain, and banana seem to have been introduced from Malaysia about the beginning of the Christian era, while maize was probably brought to West Africa from South America about the sixteenth century and cassava from the same source a century later. But several species of yam, as well as the kola tree and the oil-palm, are now known to be indigenous to West Africa, and the theory that the forest and humid zone could not be inhabited to any significant extent until after the introduction from outside the continent of new crops is no longer tenable; it has been claimed, for example, that 'there was already an ancient province of yam culture, extending over the whole forest and woodland zone of Africa', before the coming of the Malaysian plants. On the other hand, the use of iron apparently did not spread into the forest until about A.D. 300–500, so that cultivation and population must have been restricted until well after that time.[3]

The next factor is trade. Here two distinct sets of trade relations and movements must be considered. On the coast there were the European traders, drawn there from the late fifteenth century in search of the reputed gold of Guinea and then of such tropical products as pepper and other spices, but for whom the slave trade came all too soon to predominate. For the most part, however, contact between these Europeans and the West Africans was limited, and in any case almost entirely confined to the coast, the Africans there jealously guarding their control of the trade with the interior. More important in this connection than the seaborne trade was the trade between the forest and the savannah. The kola nut, indigenous to the Guinea forest, was in great demand in the Sudan, especially after the spread of Islam, as it was one of the few stimulants allowed by that religion. But at first it had been gold for which Guinea was chiefly famed; reports of this trade stimulated the Moorish conquest of Songhay at the end of the sixteenth century, just as over a century earlier it had lured the Portuguese explorers ever farther south in their West Coast voyages. Ivory was produced from the elephant herds, and there was some trade in slaves, although this does not seem to have been on any considerable scale until the nineteenth century. The forest products travelled across the lagoons, up the river highways and along intricate tracks through the bush until they reached the Sudan, and not only the Sudan, since, through the markets of Kano, Timbuktu, and lesser centres, they were brought across the desert to Barbary and the Mediterranean. The widespread use of cowries on the West Coast, which has so far been traced back to the early sixteenth century,[4] is evidence both of the extent to which communications had developed in Africa – cowries were imported via Egypt from the Indian Ocean – and of the existence of a form of money economy which was independent of European contact.

The third factor which seems likely to have affected the rise of the older Guinea states is the influence of the states of the West Sudan. In these latter, indigenous concepts of government fused, in proportions which are controversial and must have varied from place to place, with Islamic concepts. They may also have been influenced by remoter ideas from the Nile Valley transmitting, perhaps via Meroe, a distant echo of the Pharaohs of Ancient Egypt and a knowledge of iron-working which may have been evolved in Meroe itself – though this last speculation has recently been challenged; iron-working in the area of the Nok culture to the north-east of the Yoruba seems to be contemporary with, or even earlier than, the large-scale industry of Meroe. The degree to which the idea of the Sudanic state and its civilization and techniques influenced Africa south of the savannah is a live question for historians, and perhaps the recent tendency has been to exaggerate it.[5] But it is credible that events such as the decline of Ghana (in the late eleventh and twelfth centuries) and its supersession by Mali, the decline in turn of Mali (in the late fifteenth century), and the fall of Songhay (in 1591) affected societies several hundred miles to the south of their area.

The last factor to be considered here is a more remote one, and more difficult to trace: the influence of the Mediterranean and Near Eastern worlds, an influence which, though tentative, often interrupted, and relayed at third or fourth hand, was of great antiquity. The Moors of North Africa were interested not only in the products of the West Sudan but also in those of Guinea farther to the south, and above all its gold, obtained through the markets of the Sudan but derived from the alluvia of the upper Senegal and Niger valleys. The word 'Guinea' itself almost certainly derives from the Berber word for black people, as in, for example, the Bab Aguinaou ('Gate of the Black') in Marrakesh and in the Berber word for the Sudan, Akal n-Iguinawen.[6] Until the Moroccan invasion of the Sudan, the caravan trade across the Sahara had a continuous history of at least fifteen hundred years, and thus political, cultural, and economic developments on the Mediterranean coast two thousand miles away were liable eventually to affect the peoples of Guinea. The Arab conquest of North Africa in the seventh century, for example, is likely to have had repercussions far to the south, and it has even been suggested that either this or perhaps the later movement up the Nile and then westward across North Africa of those turbulent Beduin tribes, the Beni Hillal and Beni Sulleim, may have brought about the move either of the Yoruba people or of a group of conquerors who later became assimilated with them in the present Yoruba homeland. Again, it seems possible that the knowledge of iron-working came to the Yoruba from the Mediterranean area, since the type of furnace used by them is similar to Roman furnaces found in Europe.[7]

The states which arose in the Guinea forest and immediately to its north all seem to have owed something to the preceding factors, though in greatly varying degrees. Not unexpectedly, therefore, they had in common certain characteristics. At the centre, and usually as the outstanding political phenomenon, was a divine king with whose well-being the well-being of the whole people was identified and who either claimed descent from a god or himself personified a god. This institution may account for a second important attribute of many of these states, the prevalence of towns on a scale unusual in Africa, since such conglomerations of people probably took their rise from the settlement of a divine ruler. With this urbanization there developed an emphasis on internal trade. The Guinea state was a commercial emporium; sometimes the king himself had a kind of monopoly over all trading, the article most vigorously dealt in being cloth, whether imported or manufactured at home. Oliver and Fage write:[8] 'It was this universality of trade in cloth and other luxuries [in beads, for example] which, together with the largely urban pattern of settlement, chiefly distinguished the Guinea region from all other parts of Africa south of the "Sudanic" savanna belt, at least during late medieval and early modern times.' Security along the trade-routes, combined with specialization in agriculture and crafts, led to the development of markets on a greater scale than elsewhere in Africa. It contributed also to the last, and best-known, of the characteristics of the Guinea states to be noted here. This was the high degree of skill attained by many of the peoples, and notably the Yoruba, in the plastic arts: wood, stone, and ivory carving, sculpture cast in bronze or brass, terracottas, and the rarer mud sculptures and wall paintings. This art of Guinea must in many cases be the product of specialists and is an index of the social and economic conditions prevailing there. Sometimes, too, it provides the historian with more direct evidence, as in the case of the mud reliefs in the palace at Abomey, which depict incidents in the wars between the Dahomeans and the Yoruba in the nineteenth century.

The Yoruba of West Africa are a numerous people with many kings, among whom some twenty or more are rulers over what were formerly distinct and independent states (or sub-ethnic groups), while the rest, amounting in one list to over 1,000, are subordinate rulers whose territories consisted of single towns and groups of villages.[9] They form the third largest ethnic group in Africa's most populous country, some 15 million of them (at least) living in the rich forest and farmland of south-western Nigeria; there is also a Yoruba irredenta in the republics of Bénin (formerly Dahomey) and Togo, cut off from their brethren by the European frontier makers in the Scramble for Africa at the end of the nineteenth century, while a diaspora, derived partly from their trading operations and partly consisting of Muslims who have failed to return home from the pilgrimage to Mecca, is found over a wide area stretching from the Senegal to the Nile. They are a black people whose language belongs to the Kwa group (within the Niger–Congo family of languages) which predominates in West Africa; though it remained unwritten until the 1840s, Yoruba is rich in oral literature, and there are many dialects. Primarily they are a farming people, cultivating their family lands in individual holdings. At the same time they have many ancient towns, so that they appear to be the most urbanized of the people of tropical Africa; today Ibadan, the capital of Oyo state, and Lagos, the present Federal capital but Yoruba in its origin and the bulk of its population, each have several million inhabitants. Their art and culture are being increasingly studied; the incomparable 'bronzes' of Ife, for example, are no longer seen as isolated and enigmatic phenomena, but are now confidently interpreted as testimony to the greatness of the Yoruba past and to its continuity.

The homeland of the Yoruba – *ile Yoruba* – stretches from the swamps and lagoons of the coast across the rain forests, rising gradually towards the oil-palm bush and woodland savannah and the distant bend of the Niger. For the most part it is a fertile and verdant country, watered by many rivers and streams, and with a landscape which varies from the gloom and mystery of the swamps and high forest to the exhilarating panorama of the northern uplands, where rocky hills stud a park-like scene which recalls the paintings of the Romantic School in Europe. It was in the extreme north of this area that was founded the great city and capital of the Oyo, while Ile Ife, the traditional cradle of the race and their spiritual centre, lies in the forest over a hundred miles to the south. When in the early years of the last century Old Oyo was overthrown by the Hausa–Fulani armies a great migration southwards followed, swelling the towns in the forest and on its edge. Today the boundary of the northern states of Nigeria with the south-western states cuts through the northern edge of the historic homeland, leaving many Yoruba in the districts of Ilorin and Kabba.

The Yoruba have undoubtedly occupied this homeland (as big as England) for many centuries. When the Portuguese first arrived on the coast in the fifteenth century their political organization into a number of major and minor states had already been evolved, and may well have been in existence for several hundred years, as an examination of their king-lists and other data suggests. For the period preceding the formation of the states almost nothing is known. But the Yoruba seem never to have constituted a single political entity; their very name was one not used originally by themselves but by their Hausa neighbours with reference to the northern group among them, the Oyo (from whose own name it perhaps derives), and then given a wider application by the Christian missionaries in the nineteenth century. Even today they more often speak of themselves as members of the different kingdoms and towns than as Yoruba. Their language, despite its many dialects, provides the main evidence of a common origin and cultural

Plate 1　River scene in Yorubaland. From the *Church Missionary Intelligencer*, volume 10, 1859.

heritage; the name sometimes applied to this language, *anago*, has been used by their neighbours, especially the Dahomeans, to describe the people, while another name, or nickname, was Olukumi ('my friend'). (See Appendix II.)

A second pointer to a common origin of the Yoruba kingdoms is the existence over the whole country of a cycle of myths and legend which purports to describe the creation of the world and its people and the foundation at Ile Ife, the world's centre, of the first kingdoms.[10] Into these myths are woven the names of the heroes whom the Yoruba regard as their founding ancestors. A commonly found version[11] tells how Olorun, owner of the sky, let down from heaven a chain by which Oduduwa, father of all the original Yoruba kings, descended to the primordial ocean below. Oduduwa threw into the waters a handful of soil, and on this he placed a cock and a palm nut. The cock scratched at the earth, which became land, and the nut grew to a tree with sixteen branches, symbolizing the crowned rulers of Oduduwa's house. The political counterpart to this story relates, on the other hand, that Oduduwa was a son of Lamurudu, King of Mecca, who migrated westwards until he came to Ife and settled there. From Ife his children and grandchildren went forth to become the founders of kingdoms and royal dynasties in all parts of Yorubaland.[12] These stories of the creation of man – the myths – and of the foundation of the Yoruba polity – the legends – are found in all the kingdoms, and most of the royal houses trace their descent to Ife. They vary considerably in detail and rarely have the coherence of, for example, the myths of Ancient Greece. Nevertheless, they remain recognizably the same in essentials, and their prevalence among almost all the Yoruba, and perhaps too their very incoherence, support the claims of a common origin and a shared Yoruba past.

It is hazardous to attempt to trace the evolution of these traditions – myth and legend – although (as will be seen in Chapter 2) they do not appear to be of great antiquity. While some remote factual basis remains likely, their literal acceptance would strain credulity too far. It seems best, for the present at least, to follow those historians of oral tradition who in general connect such stories with a people's need under differing circumstances (for example, threats from newcomers or when themselves arriving from elsewhere) to legitimize possession of land or other forms of wealth and power.

There has been much speculation about the origins and prehistory of the peoples of West Africa. The growing appreciation of black art stimulated this, and in particular the discovery of the art of Ife led to numerous, sometimes fantastic, hypotheses to account for objects whose artistic value was so high (and which seemed to resemble and equal the classical art of Europe) that they could not, it was said, have been in any way connected with the present inhabitants.[13] Anthropologists propounded the 'Hamitic theory', according to which the black populations of Africa were conquered at some remote period by a 'white people', the Hamites, who brought with them from the north of the continent a superior culture from which derives any cultural and technical achievement of the blacks of West Africa in the centuries preceding European contact. This theory has been subject in the last few years to devastating criticism[14] and is no longer tenable.

The Yoruba legends relating how their ancestors 'came from the east' are by no means peculiar to them: indeed, they are found among many other West African peoples. These legends are often interpreted to imply an Egyptian origin, and this view, despite the naming of a 'King of Mecca' in one version of their legend of origin, has been enthusiastically propounded by some Yoruba historians.[15] This interpretation may seem to some extent supported by the possibility that certain of their techniques, for example, iron-working and the *cire-perdue* (lost-wax) method of casting metal objects, and forms of government, in particular the 'Sudanic state' and the divine kingship, may have been diffused from the Nile Valley. But these possibilities are far from justifying the acceptance of the Egyptian theory, while other parts of the argument, especially the supposed resemblance in language between ancient Egyptian and Yoruba, can be dismissed. As to 'Lamurudu', he undoubtedly represents the Namrud or Nimrud of Arabic and Muslim legend and also of the Old Testament, and it is probable that this part of the tradition derives from the account of Yoruba origins which occurs in a writing of Muhammad Bello of Sokoto in about 1812.[16]

A recent theory concerning the origin of the Yoruba state demands more serious attention. Ade Obayemi makes a distinction between 'mega-states' and 'mini-states', the latter being those which lack powerful royal dynasties and urban capitals and are small in population and territory. He points out that mini-states exist in some numbers in the area surrounding Yorubaland and also among those living within but at the extremities of the Yoruba language area, and then argues that such small but adaptable polities are 'representative of basic patterns of social organisations from which all the great states in the region must have developed'.[17] From one point of view, an objection to this theory is that it seems to postulate an extraordinary degree of changelessness among the mini-states. On the other hand it suggests a parallel with state evolution from smaller to larger units which can be demonstrated in many parts of the world where often mini-states continue to exist as agreeable anomalies alongside much greater neighbours. But in the case of the Yoruba kingdoms there exists little firm evidence to trace such a process and it remains an attractive speculation.

The best hope of throwing light upon the earliest times of the Yoruba seems to lie now with archaeology. New techniques, which are already adding to the depth of historical knowledge of West Africa as of other parts of the world, may be important here, and methods of excavation suitable to the physical conditions are being worked out.[18] Yet in this field, too, the difficulties are immense. The characteristic building materials of West Africa, mud and bamboo, are notoriously impermanent, especially in a climate noted for the violence of its rainstorms. Again, little more than a beginning has been made in dating such artifacts as the metal and terracotta sculptures of the classical period at Ife and the pottery fragments which abound on sites such as Old Oyo.

Finally, there are two other, relatively new, sources from which help may be sought in this problem. The first is serology, or the compiling and interpretation of the distribution of blood groups among the population. So far, however, little useful information is available from this about West Africa.[19] Linguistic data, on the other hand, have already produced interesting, though very general, findings. These are mostly based upon glottochronology, the rebarbative name given to the analysis of relations between languages, especially their pace of change, which leads to inferences about their respective ages. Christopher Wrigley has deduced from 'the general linguistic configuration of Africa' that the Niger–Congo group of languages, which includes Yoruba, must have separated from one another at a period very much more distant than 1,500 years, his minimum for the differentiation of the Bantu languages, and he concludes that 'unless we posit a large number of separate but parallel migrations into West Africa' the present inhabitants 'must have been living in that region for several thousand years'.[20] It has been tentatively suggested elsewhere, on the basis of comparative word-lists, that Yoruba separated from Edo, Igbo, and Ijo about 5,000 years ago, from Idoma 6,000 years ago, and from Igala 2,000 years ago.[21] (See Appendix II.)

If the broad conclusion from the linguistic evidence is accepted, then the traditions of origin which are preserved by the Yoruba seem to refer to movements over only comparatively short distances or, less probably, to the advent of a small group of conquerors who quickly became assimilated with their new subjects. It seems likely that in either case movement was from the grassland, where cultivation was earlier advanced and where there might be some population pressure, into the forest, and the legend of Oduduwa and the royal progeny of Ife may be a distant memory of such a movement.

To speculate beyond this point is hazardous, since new myths are all too easily created. There has, for example, been a tendency in recent writing about African history to attribute the orgin of most states to the conquest of the people of one culture by people of another, postulating a sharp distinction between the rulers and the ruled. Stereotyping of this kind usually results in over-simplification and other distortions, for, while most states in the world develop under the stimulus of older states, their origins are many and diverse.[22] Meanwhile, new material on the subsequent history of the Yoruba is being uncovered, and, as more is established about what may be called their 'middle ages', this should in turn shed light on earlier times. But this kind of reconstruction has especial dangers for the historians, whose study permits generalizations but has no laws and whose material is unpredictable humanity; extrapolation unsupported by evidence should usually be left to scientists and mathematicians. Early Yoruba history now waits, not over-hopefully, upon archaeology and its ancillary sciences.

NOTES

1. Crowder (1966), p. 65.
2. Shaw (1978), p. 47, who considers that the skeleton found here is 'probably the oldest recognizable negroid yet found in Africa'; Willett (1971). pp. 345, 365–7. For a warning against over-dependence on radiocarbon dating, see H. Barker (1972).
3. Wrigley (1960), p. 199; Denis Williams in Biobaku (1973), pp. 142–4.
4. M. Johnson (1970), p. 18 and *passim*.
5. Shaw (1978), pp. 85–6. Shaw follows Williams (1974), pp. 62, 106, in suggesting a Carthaginian origin (via the Berbers of the Sahara) for iron-working in Nigeria. For discussion of the 'Sudanic state', see Omer-Cooper (1964), especially pp. 105–8.
6. Bovill, p. 119; Fage, p. 13. John II of Portugal was allowed by the Pope in 1481 to style himself 'Lord of Guinea'.
7. See note 5 above.
8. Oliver and Fage, p. 110.

9. Kenyo, Chs. 1–3.
10. For an introduction to the oral history of the Yoruba and its problems, see Biobaku (1956a).
11. This version of the myth may well qualify as the type of 'Authorized Version' whose very coherence and wide acceptance are suspect; see p. x above.
12. These legends are given according to an Oyo version, in S. Johnson (1921), Chs. I and II. But the Ife account of the Creation is that a 'priest' named Ojuma threw down earth which was spread by a fowl (Aderemi, p. 3: Ademakinwa, p. 14), while Idowu (p. 19) records a tradition that it was Orisha-nla who wrought the earth.
13. Such views were first propagated by Leo Frobenius who early in the twentieth century drew attention to the art of Ife.
14. For example, by Omer-Cooper (1964), p. 104.
15. S. Johnson (1921) briefly discusses the possibility of an Egyptian origin (pp. 6–7), but it is most fully developed and argued by J. Olumide Lucas (1948).
16. R. W. Wescott, review of Lucas in *JAH*, II, 2 (1961), pp. 311–15, and also 'Did the Yoruba Come from Egypt?' *Odu*, 4 (n.d.); Shaw (1964), pp. 20, 23–4; Law (1984), pp. 199–205. For the relevant extract from Bello's *Infaq al-maisur*, see Hodgkin (1975), pp. 78–9.
17. Obayemi in Ajayi and Crowder, vol. 1 (1976, 2nd ed.), pp. 201–209.
18. For example by Thurstan Shaw and G. Connah.
19. Blood-group maps of Africa are given, with important reservations, by J. P. Garlick (1962), pp. 297–300.
20. C. Wrigley (1962). pp. 269–70.
21. R. Armstrong, public lecture, University of Ife, 1962.
22. Lewis (1966), pp. 402–5.

TWO

THE PRIMACY OF IFE

At the heart of the life of all the Yoruba lies Ile Ife. All roads in their religion, history, government, and art seem to lead there. Some contend that the whole people should properly be called 'Ife' rather than 'Yoruba', a name which originally applied to the powerful Oyo alone and only in the nineteenth century was given, first apparently by the Christian missionaries, to the subjects of all the kingdoms and to their common language. The traditions of the creation of the world and of the orgins of the peoples and their states centre on Ife, the source whence all the major rulers derive the sanctions of their kingship and which, burdened with gods and their shrines and festivals, is the centre of religion.[1]

This primacy of Ife is nearly everywhere admitted among the Yoruba,[2] but it is not easily defined. Until recently historians adhered to the theory, on the authority of Johnson, that there was a kind of Gelasian duality in the Yoruba polity, with the Alafin of Oyo as the paramount political ruler and the Oni of Ife as spiritual head.[3] This conception even affected the application of Lugardian indirect rule to Yorubaland by the British in the first part of this century. But it is open to question on two grounds. First, it is evident that the political ascendancy of Oyo for long periods over much of Yorubaland, including possibly Ife itself, never led to the assimilation of the component kingdoms of this empire, which retained their identities, politically and culturally, and reasserted their independence whenever possible. Secondly, it has been claimed that the influence, spiritual and political, of the Oni was not confined to his own kingdom but was also exercised over the other Yoruba through the sanctions of kinship and by ancient constitutional devices.[4] This contention, which would rarely find acceptance beyond Ife itself, is discussed in Chapter 8 below. But an interesting demonstration of the veneration felt for the ruler of Ife took place in 1903, when the British Governor of Lagos invited the Oni to pronounce upon the claim of an Ijebu oba, the Elepe of Epe, to wear a beaded and fringed crown, a type deriving from Ife. The Elepe's pretension had been bitterly contested by another Ijebu ruler, the Akarigbo of Shagamu. The Oni travelled to Lagos for a meeting with the Governor and the Lagos chiefs and there ruled that only twenty-one of the oba of Yorubaland were entitled to wear such crowns, and these did not include the Elepe, who was thereupon fined £100 by the Governor, Sir William MacGregor. This visit in itself marked a breach with tradition, however, since no previous Oni had been known to leave his palace (*afin*) after his accession except for religious and state ceremonies within the capital, and his journey caused consternation in the land. A contemporary account of this even claims that during the Oni's absence from the Afin Ife many other Yoruba oba, including the Alafin, left their palaces and dwelt outside their walls until they were assured of the Oni's safe return. But no confirmation of this picturesque detail can now be obtained.[5]

Oduduwa, sent from heaven by the Creator Olodumare (called also Olorun, 'Owner of the sky') to establish land upon the surface of the waters, was both first ruler of Ife and ancestor of the royal dynasties in the other principal kingdoms of the Yoruba. This much of the myth is common to most of the country, but thereafter the accounts diverge considerably. The historians of Ife add many details about subsequent events, but agree about these neither among themselves nor with the historians of other kingdoms.[6] Paradoxically, such divergence is in an important sense reassuring, since it shows that an 'Authorized Version' has not yet been established. Moreover, while it is useful to try to identify and then knit together common factors in the differing accounts, it must be remembered that the reconciliation of conflicting tradition, a process which often leads to its rationalization, can provide no more than a hypothesis. Nor can the antiquity of the myth be established since it was not recorded until the nineteenth century.

The Ife accounts agree in describing the descent of Oduduwa from heaven upon the Ora hill with sixteen companions to share in his task of colonizing the earth. From the Oke Ora the party moved a short distance to settle on the place where the Afin Ife still stands at the centre of the town. But dissension soon broke out between Oduduwa and Obatala, one of the foremost of his followers. To Obatala, as to Oduduwa, both divine and material functions are attributed. On the one hand, it was he to whom Olodumare entrusted the fashioning of men out of clay, into which models the Creator breathed life, and on the other, he is described as one of Oduduwa's subordinate rulers at Ife. In this latter capacity he rebelled against the authority of Oduduwa, who, with the help of Obameri (sometimes described as the first among the sixteen and sometimes as Obduduwa's eldest son) drove him from the town. The quarrel was composed, but Obatala retained leadership of the people whom he had met in the surrounding forest. These, known as the Igbo or Ubo (possibly after a variety of bird), (and not to be confused with the Igbo of Eastern Nigeria)[7] have been held to be the indigenous people whom Oduduwa and his followers had found already dwelling at Ife. After his death Obatala was venerated as 'the great god' (*Orisha-nla*), and his festival is one of the most important events in the Ife year.[8]

Myth now shades into legend, and all versions of the Oduduwa cycle – again, not recorded until the last century or later – give prominence to the dispersal from Ife at some point in Oduduwa's lifetime of the princes of the royal family, who travelled away from their home in all directions to found new kingdoms and dynasties. This exodus has been ascribed in one account to a drought, a feasible enough occurrence towards the end of a long dry season in Yorubaland. The tradition further suggests that a decision to extend the scope of the Yoruba settlement may have been precipitated by the pressure of a growing population towards the end of a long and successful reign, combined with an impetus similar to that which had led Oduduwa and his original followers to Ife – more probably, as has been suggested earlier, from the savannah lands to the north than direct from heaven to the Ora hill. The place in Ife at which the dispersal was decided upon is still known as 'the place of conference', Itajero. Here the children of Oduduwa (or, in other accounts, his grandchildren by his son Akanbi) were given crowns and sent away to found kingdoms. Sometimes the number of these princes is given as sixteen, elsewhere as only seven. One of the princes founded a new dynasty in the already established kingdom of Benin,[9] and another (who cannot be traced further) ruled over Popo, an indeterminate area stretching from Badagry along the coast into modern Togo, while the rest became rulers of the major kingdoms of the Yoruba. According to the Oni's ruling at Lagos in 1903, the number of crowns conferred by Ife amounted to twenty-one, some, perhaps the majority, on this occasion and the rest presumably by Oduduwa's successors on the throne. This story of the dispersal is told in all the major kingdoms whose oba claim descent from Oduduwa, varying widely in its details but always recognizable in its principal elements.

It was apparently at some time after the dispersal that the people of Ife began to suffer from the depredations of the Igbo from the nearby forest. The unearthly appearance of these people filled them with such terror that they were unable to offer any resistance. Thus the town was several times burnt to the ground by the raiders before salvation came through the heroism of Moremi. This was a local woman who, after sacrificing and making promises to the *orisha* (god or goddess) of a stream near the town, allowed herself to be taken captive by the Igbo. Because of her beauty she became the favourite of their king, and from him she learnt that the fearful Igbo were simply ordinary humans who disguised themselves for war in all-concealing garments of raffia fibre. Then she succeeded in escaping, and on her return to Ife taught the people to defend themselves against the Igbo by setting fire to their costumes with lighted torches. By these means the Ife were at last able to overcome their enemies. But when Moremi repaired to the stream to express her gratitude her gifts were all rejected by the orisha until she was brought to offer her only son, Ela Olorugbo. The defeat of the Igbo and Moremi's terrible sacrifice are commemorated at Ife in the annual Edi festival,[10] while the episode has been interpreted both as an encounter between the aboriginal inhabitants of the forest and the newcomers led by Oduduwa and as a clash between rival factions within the town.[11]

Tradition is silent about the death of Oduduwa. His twofold role as emissary of the Creator and as leader of a migration is reflected in the reverence paid to him both as a principal member of the Yoruba pantheon, a god of indeterminate sex who is nearly everywhere worshipped either under this name or as Olofin, and who is widely regarded as a symbol of Yoruba unity, and also as first oba of Ife, the Oni or Onife. There are differing accounts of his successors in the latter role. Some say that his son Obalufon reigned as second Oni, then his youngest son (or grandson) Oranyan, who is also remembered as founder of Oyo, the most powerful and extensive of the Yoruba kingdoms but who even in Oyo tradition is believed to have died and been buried at Ife, and next, as fourth Oni, Alaiyemore or Obalufon II, son of Obalufon I. Other versions describe Obatala as either second, third, or fourth Oni. At Oyo it is related that it was Oranyan who succeeded Oduduwa and that before he left Ife for Oyo he appointed one of his father's former slaves, the son of a woman who had been condemned to death for some crime, to take charge of the royal treasures remaining there. This man, Adimu, became the founder of the present kingship of Ife and ancestor of subsequent Oni, whose title, according to Johnson, is a contraction of the phrase *omo oluwoni*, 'the son of a sacrificial victim'.[12] But this is rejected at Ife itself, where the succession of their oba from Oduduwa the national hero, and thus his seniority among all the oba of Yorubaland, is naturally preferred.

Obayemi, in his recent account of the Yoruba people before 1600, has postulated that ancient Ife, beginning as a 'mini-state' comprising several distinct settlements, was transformed into a 'mega-state' in a 'revolutionary phase' which he links, following tradition, with Oduduwa; this mega-state, he thinks, was flourishing well before Europeans arrived on the coast in the mid-fifteenth century. He considers that the Oduduwa dynasty was at some subsequent time supplanted by the present dynasty of rulers, and this he links with the Oyo tradition cited above about Adimu.[13] But this remains highly speculative.

The names of many subsequent Oni are recalled at Ife, but there seems to have been no practice there (as elsewhere in Yorubaland) of reciting these names formally at installation ceremonies or other times, and no complete or chronological list has been compiled. The last oba was described as the 47th,[14] but this is derided in Ife as far too low a number, and those associated with the court speak of over four hundred Oni having reigned – though this sounds like a formula to be interpreted simply as 'many'. There are two royal graveyards in Ife, but these have not been excavated, and they do not shed much light on the present problem; the first, at Lafogido near the Afin, has been much built over, while the second, in the forest outside the walls at Igbo Odi, described as the burial place for those oba whose reigns were not markedly successful, contains some thirty or forty mounds, some or all of which may be graves of Oni. An Ife historian, J. A. Ademakinwa, has recorded the names of forty-five Oni following Alaiyemore, belonging to four different royal compounds (or houses where the families are regarded as of royal descent and eligible in their turn for the succession). He could not indicate the order in which these oba reigned, and he added that there were five other compounds in the town from which had come Oni whose names he was unable to supply.[15]

No documentary record of Ife earlier than the mid-nineteenth century is known, nor does it seem likely that any such record was ever made. But it has been suggested that two Portuguese writers of the early sixteenth century refer incidentally to Ife in the course of their descriptions of the contacts between their countrymen and the kingdom of Benin. The earlier is Duarte Pacheco, who in describing the slave trade from the West Coast writes:

> To the East of this Kingdom of Beny, 100 leagues inland, there is known to be a country which has at this time a King called Licasaguou. He is said to be lord of many peoples and to possess great power. Near there is another great lord, who has the name 'Hooguanee'. He is considered among the Negroes as the Pope is among us.[16]

The second possible reference occurs in *Da Asia* by De Barros:

> Among the many things which the King Dom Joao learnt from the ambassador of the King of Beny, and also from Joao Afonso de Aveiro, of what they had been told by the inhabitants of those regions, was that to the east of the King of Beny at twenty moons'

journey – which according to their account, and the slow pace at which they travel, would be about two hundred and fifty of our leagues – there lived the most powerful monarch of those parts whom they called Ogane. Among the pagan princes of the territories of Beny he was held in as great veneration as are the Supreme Pontiffs with us. In accordance with a very ancient custom, the Kings of Beny, on ascending the throne, sent ambassadors to him with rich gifts to inform him that by the decease of their predecessor they had succeeded to the Kingdom of Beny, and to request him to confirm them in the same. . . . All the time this ambassador was at the court of the Ogane he never saw him, but only some silk curtains behind which he was placed, like some sacred object.[17]

In these accounts, 'Licasaguou' has been identified with the Alafin and 'Hooguanee' and 'Ogane' with the Oni. But difficulty immediately arises from the directions which are given, since both Oyo and Ife lie to the north-west, not east, of Benin. The identification of the Ogane with the Oni has been discussed by A. F. C. Ryder, who concludes that the Ogane is more likely to have been a ruler in the Nupe–Igala area straddling the Niger–Benue confluence than the Oni of Ife. Ryder has also cast doubts on the widely accepted theory of the derivation of both the dynasty and also the associated lost-wax technique of brass-casting at Benin from Ife, showing them to be based on traditions which in Benin can be traced no further than records made after the British occupation in 1897.[18] Nevertheless, the description in De Barros of the Pope-like ruler hidden behind silk curtains and his relationship with the Benin kingship accord so well with the veneration with which the Oni is still regarded in both Yorubaland and Benin and with the traditions as recorded by the local historians in both places that the debate on these enigmatic texts is not closed.

Difficulties in establishing a coherent account of the past of Ife have led to the suggestion that the present town does not stand upon its original site. This would be far from surprising, since many, perhaps most, Yoruba towns have traditions of migration; Ifa verse is said to refer to six different Ife, and it is known that in the nineteenth century the present Ife was twice abandoned for short periods. J. O. George wrote at the end of the last century that 'the old Ile Ife was much farther in the interior', but he cited no authority or evidence for this, while Ryder has recently suggested that the ruling dynasty may have removed to the present site at some time after the sixteenth century.[19] For some years since the Second World War archaeological investigations have been carried on at Ife, though intermittently. Important results have been obtained by the method of radiocarbon dating. In particular, material from the traditional burial place of the heads of the Oba of Benin (Orun Oba Ado) has given four dates ranging from the sixth to the late tenth centuries A.D.; material excavated below potsherd pavements has given two dates of the tenth and twelfth centuries A.D. Willett adds to this last information that 'The seven brass castings from this site were in a corresponding stratigraphic position'. He concludes that 'There can be no doubt that the modern city of Ife is on the site of Ile–Ife', that 'a settlement of substantial size' existed there between the ninth and twelfth centuries, and that 'terracotta sculptures and *cire-perdue* castings were made there from early in the present millennium'.[20]

The present Ife, with its population of some 150,000, is contained within a double circuit of the earthen walls which are characteristic of Yoruba towns, covering here an area of somewhat over two miles. The outer wall is apparently that built by Oni Abeweila between the collapse of Old Oyo about 1835 and his own death in 1849, while an inner and older wall runs at a radius of about one mile from the centrally placed Afin. It is evident that the ancient town occupied a considerably greater extent than the present enclosure, since several of the sacred groves associated with the town lie well beyond the outer walls; moreover, pavements made of potsherds placed edgewise, which are found in palaces and large compounds in several parts of Yorubaland, have been discovered at distances up to four miles from the Afin in several directions. Pavements have also been uncovered under both town walls, which suggests that the walls were built long after the disappearance of the buildings associated with these particular pavements. Ife tradition is said to assign the first making of these pavements to the reign of Luwo Gbagida, a female ruler who has been listed as sixteenth or nineteenth Oni in the Oduduwa dynasty. Finally, Ozanne has detected a complex system of older, or 'medieval', town walls which underlie and extend beyond the nineteenth-century defences; he also reports traces of an outermost wall of much greater extent.[21]

Presumably all buildings of ancient Ife, like many of those of the present day, were constructed by puddling mud on the site, and it is impossible by present archaeological techniques to establish either the dates of surviving walls or even to distinguish confidently between collapsed buildings and the surrounding soil. Willett has written that, 'The "pavement period" is in part, if not entirely, later than the introduction of maize into West Africa at the beginning of the sixteenth century, for pottery decorated with the impressions of maize cobs has been found beneath at least one pavement.'[22] But this is far from conclusive since no starting or terminal points have been suggested for a pavement period, and indeed the making of pavements in the more important compounds seems never to have entirely died out.[23]

In the absence of other evidence, it seems reasonable to assume, as do the inhabitants of Ife and indeed all Yoruba, that the present town both represents the 'cradle of the Yoruba', as it is so often called, and also that it stands on or very near to its original site. That the town has contracted at some period is clear from its archaeology. Local historians, in particular the present Oni himself, have referred to traditions of a drawing together of the people after the dispersal of the princes and their followers. But it seems more likely that the contractions indicated by the relation between the existing town walls and the groves and pavements were a consequence of forgotten wars, perhaps arising from the restless ambition of the Oyo. Indeed Shaw has postulated that the decline of Ife was due to the related causes of the rise of Oyo and the inability of the Ife to take a part in the lucrative slave trade on the coast. Whereas Oyo had gained an access to the sea at Badagry, the Ife were 'hemmed in' by the Ijebu to the south and by Benin to the east.[24]

It is not the central position of Ife in the history of the Yoruba which has given the town its wider fame but the incomparable 'bronze' and terracotta sculptures, mostly human figures, which have been discovered there during the present century. The art of Ife is now known throughout the world. Attention was first called to it by the German anthropologist Leo Frobenius, who spent some weeks investigating the sacred groves and shrines of Ife in 1910 and 1911. During these visits he was shown the bronze head known from the grove where it had been buried as Olokun, the sea-god of the Yoruba,[25] and collected a number of terracotta heads

Plate 2   Crowned head of an Oni. Zinc brass. Probably cast between the twelfth and fifteenth centuries A.D. From the Wunmonije compound, Ife. Photograph by Dirk Bakker from Ekpo Eyo and Frank Willett, *Treasures of Ancient Nigeria*, London, 1982.

and fragments. He also recorded many of the stone monuments which he saw in various parts of the town. His publication of these unexpected finds caused excitement, and some understandable scepticism, in Europe, and aroused the interest which has led to the many later discoveries. In 1919 the existence in the Afin of the bronze Obalufon mask (reputed to represent Obalufon II, the third or fourth Oni) and the large terracotta head called Lajuwa (after a palace official said to have attempted to usurp the Oni's throne) was disclosed to the public, and then in 1938–9 seventeen bronze heads and the upper part of a male figure were found buried in the Wunmonije compound, one of the royal houses of Ife. A number of small bronzes and terracottas were next discovered in 1957 during excavations at Ita Yemoo on the eastern side of the town. Since then there have been many other

Plate 3 Standing figure of an Oni. Zinc brass. Probably fourteenth or early fifteenth century. From Ita Yemoo, Ife. Photograph by Dirk Bakker from Ekpo Eyo and Frank Willett, *Treasures of Ancient Nigeria*, London, 1982.

finds, though of nothing so spectacular as those from Wunmonije.[26]

The twenty major figures now known, unlike most African sculpture, are all in a naturalistic style, and are apparently somewhat idealized portraits of individuals; sixteen of them are near life-size. Of the heads it has been written that 'they would stand comparison with anything which Ancient Egypt, Classical Greece and Rome, or Renaissance Europe had to offer'.[27] The smaller bronzes, four of which represent full-length standing figures, are of almost equal excellence. Like the larger heads, they were made by the lost-wax method of casting and are in much the same style, though the full-length figures have heads which occupy a quarter of the overall height, a proportion characteristic of African art. To quote Willett again, these 'show a broader range of subject [than the heads] . . . and a humour which was quite unsuspected'.[28] The terracottas form a much larger and more varied body of work and, since the majority are in the same naturalistic style as the bronzes, make it almost impossible that Ife art should represent the output of one isolated genius (as was once suggested) or even one generation. They consist of fragments of full-length figures and of heads, at least some of which appear to be portraits, and there is even a full-size stool in this material whose making must have required as much skill as did the casting of the bronzes.

In addition there remain in and around Ife a number of stone monuments and other objects which have no discernible stylistic connection with the bronzes and are usually held to be anterior to them. These consist of monoliths, crudely carved figures of humans and animals, and decorated stools, and are found mostly near the centre of the town, especially in the area of the palace, and in the groves and shrines. Since they seem in most cases to occupy their original positions, whatever their purpose, they are classified, unlike the bronzes and terracottas, as primary material. The most notable is the eighteen foot-high granite column known as the Opa Oranyan, or 'staff of Oranyan', studded with a mysterious pattern of 123 nails. The Opa is said to mark the grave of Oranyan, but no burial pit has been found in the vicinity, and it has been alternatively suggested that it was originally dedicated to Ogun, the god of iron and war. Equally interesting are several elaborate quartz stools, objects which (alone among the stone carvings) provide a link with what Willett has called the 'Classical Period' of Ife, since similar representations are found in bronze and terracotta.

Although radiocarbon dating has revealed that the art of Ife is likely to have flourished before, as well as possibly after, the arrival of Europeans on the West African coast in the late fifteenth century, and therefore to be of a considerably greater antiquity than was thought only a few years ago, major questions remain for the historian. Who were the artists? Were they ancestors of the present inhabitants of Ife, or did they belong to quite another people? When and precisely where did this art flourish, and if at Ife itself, did it precede or follow the establishment of the dynasty of Oduduwa? What was the purpose of the sculptors and what kind of society produced and nourished this school of artists? And what is the relationship between this art, the art of the Yoruba in general, and the art of neighbours of the Yoruba in West Africa? Unhappily, to none of these can answers be confidently returned, and the historian must speculate against a background even more puzzling than in the case of the political origins of the Yoruba kingdoms. Apart from the stone monuments, the terracottas excavated by Ekpo Eyo from the shrine of Lafogido (an early Oni), and perhaps the so-called Obalufon mask and Lajuwa head, all these antiquities have been discovered on secondary sites, that is, they seem to have been brought from elsewhere and to have been *in situ* at the place of discovery for only a comparatively short time.[29] Moreover, they seem to have been neither understood nor much valued at Ife before the present century, and to bear no real relationship to the myths and legends associated with the Oduduwa dynasty or Yoruba religion, despite some rather suspect attributions. An added difficulty is that the art of Ife, and indeed Yoruba art in general, unlike that of, for example Dahomey, does not seem to depict actual events.[30] Again, no recollection exists in Ife today of the intricate lost-wax technique by which all the bronzes were cast, and tradition throws no light upon its introduction nor whence it came. Another mystery lies in the source of the materials used in the bronzes. These are in

Plate 4 The Staff of Oranyan (Opa Oranyan), Ife. This monolith is reputed to mark the grave of Oranyan. The pattern of nails hammered into the stone is probably decorative. From Frank Willett, *Ife in the History of West African Sculpture*, London, 1967

Plate 5 Terracotta head from Nok, c. 500 B.C./c. A.D. 200. Photograph by Frank Willett

fact not really bronzes (though it is convenient to continue to call them so), since they contain little tin and are either of brass or, in a few cases, of almost pure copper. Since copper is not now found in Nigeria, it is generally assumed that it must have been imported from far afield – though the American missionary, Bowen, was told in the mid-nineteenth century of copper-mining by the Efon of Ekitiland.[31] Finally, the naturalism characteristic of this art, which is naturalism of the highest order, remote from experiment, distinguishes it sharply from almost all other African sculpture, including that of other Yoruba schools.

These challenging difficulties have led to a wealth of speculation, ranging from the theories of Frobenius, who thought that he had discovered the traces of a Greek colony on the Atlantic coast, to almost equally unlikely suggestions about wandering Roman or Renaissance artists or the ubiquitous Portuguese. But as archaeological investigation and comparative studies continue, more rational interpretations emerge. In the first place, it has been realized that the facial characters of most of the sculptures are undoubtedly negroid, and indeed striking similarities to the modern inhabitants of Ife can sometimes be detected, as well as family resemblances between different groups of the sculptures. The striations, or skin scarifications, which appear prominently on some of the faces, and in the large bronze figure on the abdomen, probably represent tribal marks, though most are in a form not used by the Yoruba within recent times.[32] An important development has been the discovery of a number of terracottas in the naturalistic or classical Ife style in association with others which are non-representational and immediately recognizable as 'African'. These finds, at the small village of Abiri near Ife, at Obgon Oya near the Oni's palace, and on a farm along the Ondo road, reveal, in Willett's words, that 'beside the naturalistic art of Ife, and almost certainly contemporary with it, there was a freely imaginative style as well'.[33] Moreover, since attention was first drawn to the antiquities of Ife, finds have continued apace, and excavations in and around the town produce a flow of objects. Thus the theories of a non-African origin for the art become ever more unlikely, and in their place it is reasonable to assume that these antiquities were the product of a civilization in Ife itself which was ancestral to the present culture of the Yoruba, and that both the artists and their human subjects were the ancestors of the Ife of the present day.

The isolation of the art is now beginning to break down. As Yoruba art as a whole is subjected to study, links, both iconographical and technical, with classical Ife are observed. Many centres of bronze-casting, using the lost-wax method as at Ife, existed, and indeed still exist, in the rest of Yorubaland, and also elsewhere in Nigeria.[34] The nine bronze figures from Tada and Jebba in Nupe country show striking affinities in style and technique with the Ife sculptures – indeed, one of them, the famous seated figure from Tada, has been claimed by Willett as belonging to the Ife corpus.[35] At Benin tradition relates that the art of bronze-casting was brought there from Ife. Denis Williams has, however, pointed out a small but significant technical difference in the preparation of the Benin and Ife bronzes. Moreover, Benin art is stylistically very different from that of Ife, especially in its comparative lack of naturalism, and it has been suggested that it was evolved in other materials than bronze, such as wood, terracotta, and ivory.[36] Finally, the revelation in recent years of the Nok art and culture, covering a wide area of north-eastern Nigeria, has seemed to provide both Ife and Benin with a

Plate 6 Memorial head from Benin. Bronze. Fifteenth/early sixteenth century (early period). Photograph by Dirk Bakker from Ekpo Eyo and Frank Willett, *Treasures of Ancient Nigeria*, London, 1982.

remote ancestry, since the objects found on the Nok sites (mostly terracotta figures of humans and animals in varying degrees of semi-naturalism) show stylistic affinities with the sculptures from both places, as well as with other West African art. But these objects have been ascribed by radiocarbon tests to a period between *c.* 900 B.C. and *c.* A.D. 200, and thus there is a gap of several hundred years between the latest date for the Nok culture and the earliest date which could be envisaged for the Ife bronzes and terracottas.

Perhaps the most intractable problem presented by the art of Ife, as by the art of much of West Africa, is that of the origin of the lost-wax (*cire-perdue*) technique used in the metal casting. A possible solution is suggested by study of the secondary problem concerning the source of the copper which forms a major part of the castings. It seems probable, despite the possibility of some local mining mentioned on page 23 above, that the bulk of this came from outside the region, North-West Mauretania, Southern Morocco, the Byzantine Empire, and Central Europe all being likely sources.[37] There is evidence of trade between the forest regions and the Arab/Islamic world of North Africa from the end of the first millennium A.D., and of trade in copper and brass from the eleventh century onwards. Thurstan Shaw has drawn attention to the strategic advantage which Ife, and later Oyo Ile, enjoyed in their proximity to the Niger, which may have enabled them to exercise control over the trade between north and south. On this basis he speculates that 'the introduction of the technique of *cire-perdue* metal-casting into West Africa followed the import of actual bronze or brass objects from the Arab/Islamic world' and was made possible by the import also of copper from the same source. He suggests, furthermore, that 'when introduced the technique was applied to the existing art canon' in terracotta.[38]

As to the purpose and the subjects of the Ife sculptures, the suggestion has been advanced that the major heads are portraits of the Oni and of leading members of his court for use in the ceremonies for the dead which are still held by the Yoruba, and other West African people, at an interval of usually about a year after the hasty burial of the corpse necessary in a tropical climate. Willett has pointed out that in the second funeral ceremonies at Owo, called *ako*, effigies of the dead, with naturalistic heads mounted on roughly carved bodies, were carried in procession and subsequently buried. He concludes that the bronze heads of Ife were used in the same way, the small holes in the tops of the heads being intended for the attachment of crowns (rather than for hair, as has also been suggested).[39] Resemblances between the symbols of authority still used by the Oni and his chiefs and those depicted on the sculptures increase the likelihood that the heads were portraits of rulers and of their courtiers, probably those required to follow the king to his grave. This explanation applies equally to the near life-size heads and full-length figures in terracotta, but the majority of the terracotta heads and the smaller bronzes must have had a different purpose. Most probably these latter were produced for the shrines of the numerous cults of Ife, on whose altars they were placed, or in commemoration of sacrificial victims, human and animal, at these shrines.[40]

The ever-growing quantity and variety of the sculptures from Ife and the evidence of links between the art of Ife and that of its neighbours make it clear that this was the production of a whole school of artists working within a tradition. On the basis of his view that the heads were effigies of the dead, Willett has advanced alternative theories about the duration of the classical period. If the nineteen major bronze heads (to which possibly the half-length figure should be added) are all portraits of Oni, then, allowing about twenty years for each reign, they would seem to have been produced over a period of some 300 or 400 years. But if they represent not only the kings but also members of the court (as seems more likely), then the great period may have covered only a couple of generations.[41] The stylistic homogeneity of the major works suggests, indeed, that they were all produced within one or at most two hundred years, but African art is in general so conservative that this can only be tentatively advanced.

The dating of any part of Ife art provides the greatest problem of all. In 1967 Willett's view was that the art of Ife probably reached its aesthetic peak in the thirteenth or fourteenth century and that the stone and terracotta sculptures, with their greater variety of style, flourished considerably longer, both before and after the bronze or classical period. The end of bronze-casting in Ife may then have been due to the cessation of supplies of metal farther north, perhaps because of the spread of Islam in the fifteenth and sixteenth centuries.[42] The field has subsequently been further narrowed. Posnansky and McIntosh conclude on the basis of new radiocarbon dates that 'the "classic" terracotta period, and also the pottery pavements' at Ife 'belong to the twelfth to the fourteenth centuries', while thermoluminescent dating carried out on some of the bronzes by Willett and Fleming places them in the fourteenth to fifteenth centuries.[43] The extinction of the art at Ife might then be explained by the unrecorded factors, whether catastrophe or decline, which accounted for the contraction of the town at some time before the building of its present older (and inner) wall, and which, as suggested above, could have been a consequence of the depredations of the powerful Oyo.

As to the society which produced the art of Ife, nothing is known, since the antiquities include almost no objects of everyday use. Yet such art presupposes a setting of sophistication. The inspiration and aesthetic judgement which enabled the artists to create their sculpture must have been rooted in a culture of distinction and maturity, which in turn could only have evolved against a background of a sufficient political stability. Modern analogies among the Yoruba suggest that the sculptors were also the craftsmen who cast the bronzes and fired the terracottas, but whether or not these functions were performed by the same men, considerable technical knowledge and skill were required. These artists and craftsmen, from the quality of their work, must have been professionals whose activities were only possible in a society where economic life had attained a high degree of organization and differentiation.

There are few facts in this account of the history of Ife. The traditions and the antiquities, with the findings of the archaeologists, can be put together to form hypotheses, and though those now current are more acceptable to both the historian and the local patriot than the prejudiced speculations of Frobenius and others at the beginning of this century, they do not at best amount to more than probabilities. The search for new evidence continues in the realization that present theories, like those of Frobenius, may have to be abandoned in the light of discoveries to come. But the primacy of Ife in the life of the Yoruba – their religion, their political system, their culture – is unlikely ever to be contested. Until now, Ife preserves its major mysteries inviolate: its kingship, gods and shrines, its incomparable sculptures, cannot as yet be placed confidently in any coherent pattern. For the Yoruba, all this is seen through the eye of faith. Ife remains the centre of his universe: *Ife ondaiye, ibi oju ti imo wa*, 'Ife, the creator of the world, whence comes the light.'

NOTES

1. The words *Ile Ife* have been translated as 'the spreading of earth'. But Idowu (p. 20) writes that Ife means 'that which is wide' and the prefix Ile (or suffix, as in Oyo Ile and many other place-names) signifies 'original home'. Both versions could refer here to the creation of the world at Ife.
2. For exceptions to this, especially the interesting case of Oba, a small town near Akure, see H. U. Beier (n.d.) and Idowu, 15–17.
3. For example, see Burns, p. 25. R. E. Dennett, in *Nigerian Studies* (London, 1910), p. 19, describes the Oni as being 'in much the same position as the Archbishop of Canterbury in England'.
4. Akinjogbin (1965), p. 32. For a discussion of this view, see pp. 87–91 below.
5. Editor, *JRAS*, 2 (1902–3), pp. 312–15. See also Appendix I below. According to a chief at Ijebu Ode in February 1968 it is unthinkable that the Awujale should have left his palace for this reason.
6. See especially the article by the late Oni of Ife, Sir Adesoji Aderemi, and also J. A. Ademakinwa, *passim*. Idowu (pp. 23–7) gives an account of these myths which differs in several respects. For example, he writes that Oduduwa was preceded from heaven by Oreluere, whom he later found living in Ife as leader of 'a community of aboriginal people'. For yet another account, see Fabunmi (1969).
7. Ademakinwa, Part II, p. 34. Willett (1967), pp. 210–11, n. 114, does, however, suggest that the Igbo (formerly spelt Ibo) of Eastern Nigeria, 'retain the name of the original population of Southern Nigeria'.
8. Beier (1956b); Stevens (1978).
9. The late Oni (Aderemi, 1937) writes that the first Oba of Benin from the Ife dynasty was Eweka, son of Oranyan and grandson of Oduduwa. This agrees with Benin tradition as related by Egharevba, pp. 6–9. S. Johnson (1970, p .7), however, describes this first Oba as the third son of Oduduwa, without giving his name.
10. Walsh.
11. Beier (n.d.); Akinjogbin (1967b.).
12. S. Johnson (1921), pp. 11, 24–5. This is supported by similar traditions in Ketu (Parrinder (1956), p. 12, quoting Crowther) and Ijebu Ode (Olotufore, informant, February 1968). For a full discussion, see Law (1973a).
13. Obayemi in Ajayi and Crowder, II (1976, 2nd ed.), pp. 210–15, 256, 261.
14. Kenyo, p. 9.
15. Personal communication from Mr J. A. Ademakinwa, March 1967. See also Akinjogbin (1967b).
16. *Esmeraldo de Situ Orbis*, quoted by Hodgkin, p. 94.
17. Quoted by Hodgkin, p. 96.
18. Ryder (1965), pp. 25–8. Ryder mentions that 'west' and 'east' to the Bini meant respectively 'seaward' – where the sun sets – and 'inland'. But it is unlikely that De Barros would use 'east' in this way.
19. Abimbola, p. 21; George, p. 28; Ryder (1965), pp. 36–7.

20. Willett (1967), p. 103; Willett (1971), pp. 365–7.
21. Willett (1960b), p. 244; Akinjogbin and Ayandele in Ikime (ed.), p. 125; Ozanne (1969), *passim*.
22. Willett (1967), p. 108.
23. G. J. A. Ojo (1966b), pp. 61, 90, 91.
24. Aderemi, p. 4; Shaw (1978), p. 164.
25. There is a mystery about this head, since in 1950 it was discovered to be a copy made by modern methods. Willett (1960b) asserts (p. 238, n. 34) that the substitution must have taken place between 1910 and 1934 when the head was brought into the palace.
26. Willett (1967), *passim*.
27. Willett (1960b). An interesting comparison is made by John Crook in 'Ife Portraits and Roman Portraits', *Ibadan*, 17 (1963).
28. Willett (1958), p. 33.
29. Fagg and Willett (1960), p. 21; *Sunday Times* (Lagos), 27 April 1969; Eyo (1974), pp. 99–109. When Oliver Myers of the University of Ife excavated the Obameri shrine in the town in 1965 he found a number of terracottas of the classical period which had apparently been buried on this site only some hundred years previously.
30. Willett (1960b), p. 233; Ryder (1965), p. 30; Biobaku (1973), pp. 7, 165.
31. Bowen (1857), p. 253; Bowen (1858), pp. x, xii. I am grateful to Mr P.H. Gilliland for these references.
32. Willett (1967), pp. 22–3, 28–9, Plates 32, 33.
33. Willett (1967), pp. 64–6; Willett (1960b), pp. 239–40.
34. See Willett (1967), Chs. XIII and XIV, and Williams (1965).
35. Willett (1967), Plate 8 and pp. 51, 169, 172. See also Shaw (1973), who suggests that the bronzes at Tada, Jebba and Giragi were 'left behind' when Oyo ceased to control the west bank of the Niger.
36. Willett (1967), pp. 154–5; Williams (1967b), pp. 27–8. The Ife casters prepared their cores and moulds with an admixture of charcoal, whereas the Benin and also other non-Ife Yoruba casters added dung.
37. Herbert, pp. 179–80.
38. Shaw (1973), pp. 233–8.
39. Willett (1967), pp. 20–1, 26–8, and Plate 2; also see Willett (1966).
40. Willett (1967), pp. 50, 58, 68–9.
41. Ibid., pp. 130–1.
42. Ibid., pp. 132, 149–51.
43. Posnansky and McIntosh, pp. 169–70, 195; Shaw (1978), p. 162. For the Egbejodu terracottas, see Eluyemi (1976, 1977).

THREE

THE RISE OF OYO

In the remote north-eastern corner of the Oyo State of Nigeria are the remains of a great city: Oyo Ile ('home Oyo'), now usually called Old Oyo to distinguish it from its successor town some ninety miles to the south, and known to the Hausa and Nupe and to its first European visitors as Katunga. Here was the capital of the kingdom and empire of the Oyo, ruled by the Alafin, said to descend from Oranyan, the youngest son (or, in another account, the grandson) of Oduduwa. The Alafin's title describes him simply as Lord of the Palace, but his authority was that of king (oba) of the Oyo people, and he was also 'Lord of the World and of Life' (Alaiyeluwa), 'Owner of the Land' (Onile), and 'Companion of the Gods' (Ekeji Orisa).

The site of Oyo Ile is on the edge of the Yoruba highlands, which here slope towards the River Niger; from this area streams flow north to the River Moshi and south to the Ogun. This is a gently undulating country covered with low savannah woodland, diversified by frequent rocky hills and outcrops and by the giant baobab (the characteristic tree of the West Sudan, and perhaps deliberately planted here for its supposed benign influences). Some fifteen to twenty square miles were enclosed by the earthen walls encircling the town, which may still be traced, while the remains of compound walls, numerous grinding holes in the rocks (for the crushing of maize, cassava, and yams), and the abundance of pottery fragments on the surface testify to the large population which lived here before the abandonment of the town in the first part of the last century. Today the site is deserted and thickly overgrown; lying twenty miles from a motorable road and ten miles from the nearest village, it is rarely visited.[1]

Tradition relates that Oyo was founded by Oranyan as part of the great dispersal of princes from Ife. The account given by Johnson, the Oyo historian, claims that on Oduduwa's death Oranyan succeeded to the throne of Ife and was entitled Alafin there. The dispersal was occasioned by a military expedition against 'Mecca', an explanation which perhaps reflects a fanning-out over the land of a dominant group of conquerors, though not necessarily men of a different race. The story continues that the royal brothers quarrelled and that Oranyan with his followers made his way through Nupe country into the land of the Borgu, or Ibariba as the Yoruba call them. Here Oranyan consulted the king about where he should settle and was then guided by a serpent, on which the king had fixed a charm, to a hill called Ajaka where the serpent halted. Still following the instructions which he had received from the king, Oranyan built his town here, calling it Oyo, meaning the 'slippery place' where his horse had slid and stumbled on the hillside.

It must be interpolated here that a Yoruba historian, B. A. Agiri, explains the story of the Oranyan migration to Oyo in a way very different from the literal acceptance of either the Oyo (as related by Johnson) or the Ife tradition. According to Agiri, far from being an historical narrative of the spreading power of an Ife-based dynasty, this is a myth which disguises the conquest of an already Yoruba-speaking region by neighbouring Borgu (Ibariba) – a myth 'into which accounts of Nupe influence have been woven'. This thesis, which will be adverted to elsewhere in this book, does explain a number of puzzling features in Oyo tradition, yet remains entirely speculative. It has been broadly accepted by Law who makes use of a little-known traditional account published in 1914 by Michael Adeyemi which is independent of and at variance with Johnson. Law suggests that a Nupe dynasty was first established in the Oyo region of north-eastern Yorubaland and that this was overrun by an 'intrusive group from the Bariba country' which had settled at Igboho to the west.[2]

After establishing the settlement at Oyo (Johnson's account continues) Oranyan next removed to Oko (whose site has not been identified), where he remained for several years. But at the end of his life he is believed to have returned to Ife, where he died and was buried. Meanwhile his elder son, Ajaka, ruled at Oyo as his father's regent and successor until eventually he ceded the throne to his more vigorous brother, Shango. The new oba's first act was to refuse tribute which the ruler of Owu had demanded from Ajaka. After routing the army which the Olowu had sent against him, Shango proceeded to remove the government from Oko to Oyo, recovering the latter town by a trick from Egboro, the Oloyokoro, a prince who ruled over a people living at Oyo before the arrival of Oranyan and his followers from Ife.

Shango was equally reputed as a warrior and a magician. But the exercise of his magical powers was to have a tragic result, for one day when demonstrating to his courtiers his power to call down lightning, he accidentally destroyed his palace and whole household. After this disaster, either in despair or in order to escape the hostility of his people, he hanged himself on an *ayan* tree. The gentler Ajaka then resumed his reign, while Shango entered the Yoruba pantheon as god of thunder and lightning.

Johnson writes that with the next reign, that of Aganju, Ajaka's son, the period of the 'historical kings' begins, after that of the legendary first three rulers. Although Crowder comments here that 'we are still very much in the land of legend',[3] Johnson's distinction is useful since from this point there is a decline in the miraculous content of the traditional accounts. The picture is still shadowy, but certain features can be discerned. It seems clear that the Alafin's kingdom was only one among a number of Yoruba states which were already in existence and had sprung like Oyo from the womb of Ife, and that it was by no means the most important. It is significant that Oranyan, Oyo's founder, is described as the youngest either of Oduduwa's sons or grandsons and that Ajaka was compelled to pay tribute to the ruler of Owu (a town about 125 miles to the south and only about twenty miles from Ife itself). The very site of Oyo on the extreme edge of Yoruba country suggests that its founder was forced by his junior status to settle farthest from the base at Ife. This site, moreover, was dangerously near to two difficult neighbouring people: to the north and west, across the River Moshi – which provided an effective barrier only in the wet season – lived the Borgu, renowned as warriors, and across the Niger, some thirty to forty miles to the north-east, were the Nupe, who controlled the river crossing at Jebba island. But this situation proved to have advantages. The town lay under a range of low, rocky hills which ran from north to south down the western walls and formed an extended acropolis. It was strategically placed athwart the tracks which led from the southern forests and across the nearby Niger towards the markets of the West Sudan. Most important, it lay within the savannah, where lateral communications were far easier than in the dense forests to the south and where horses could range comparatively freely and also be maintained, and occasionally bred and reared, without succumbing to the tsetse fly as in the south. Thus the Oyo were enabled to raise a cavalry force as an important, probably predominant, element in their army, and one which distinguished them from the other Yoruba kingdoms and which probably made possible their imperial expansion. There is an apparent reference to the Oyo cavalry by a Dutch writer of the late seventeenth century, Bosman, who describes the army of an unnamed inland power which had overrun the kingdom of Ardra (or Allada) as 'all Horsed' and adds that 'This Nation strikes Terror into all the circumjacent *Negroes*'.[4] Finally, the traditions indicate that Oyo maintained close relations – which might frequently become hostile – with its northerly non-Yoruba neighbours, the Hausa, Nupe, and Borgu, the first of whom, at least, were in turn in touch with the distant Arab and Berber across the Sahara. This must have been as much a stimulus as a danger; both trade and warfare would serve to bring the political, military, and technical ideas of the Sudan and even beyond to the Oyo and through them to the other Yoruba.

Thus the state of Oyo came to be firmly established as a power in northern Yorubaland, at a period which can be provisionally and tentatively assigned to the fourteenth century. The names of two early Alafin (if the title was used then), Aganju and Oluasho, are recalled as long-lived and strong rulers. Between their reigns came that of Kori, who is believed to have established a subordinate king at Ede, on the frontiers of the growing Oyo influence and nearly 100 miles to the south. The duty of this ruler, entitled the Timi, was to protect the kingdom against the neighbouring Ijesha, or, in another tradition, against the Nupe.

Under Onigbogi, Oluasho's son (so Johnson's narrative continues), a time of troubles began. There was discontent both in the capital and in the subordinate towns. While the army was dealing with rebellion by one of these towns, Oyo itself was attacked by Nupe from across the Niger. Onigbogi was forced to flee from his capital, making his way north-west into the country of the Borgu, a people who, like the Yoruba, were divided among a number of kingdoms. Here he might expect to find friends and allies; not only was his wife, the Iyalagbon (mother of the Aremo or eldest prince), a woman of Borgu but also the senior of the Borgu rulers, the King of Bussa (farther up the Niger), claimed a common ancestry with the Alafin, since according to the tradition of his country both descended from Kisra – that elusive hero who figures in Nigerian legend as an ancestor also of the Hausa and who, like Oduduwa, entered West Africa 'from the east'.

Relations between Onigbogi and his Borgu host – who was more likely to have been the ruler of Nikki than of Bussa – were apparently cordial, for Onigbogi was allowed to settle with his followers at a place called Gbere, apparently a few miles north of the Moshi, the river which formed the boundary between the Borgu and the Oyo. Here Onigbogi died, to be succeeded by his eldest son Ofinran. But now relations between the exiled Oyo and the Borgu began to deteriorate, and eventually Ofinran decided to return to his own land. According to a story preserved by the Bada of Shaki,[5] he was opposed in this by the Borgu, and the escape had to be accomplished by a ruse, a Nupe man in Ofinran's party carving models of archers which were placed in the bush to cover the withdrawal of the Oyo.

From Gbere the Alafin travelled some fifty miles to the south into his own country, halting eventually at Kushu on the banks of the Okin stream. Here the court remained for some years, during which, it is said, the Ifa and Egungun mysteries were introduced among them. At last Ofinran was ready to set out again for the old capital, but he died before he could leave, being succeeded by his son the Aremo Egunoju. His *oriki*, or praise words, describe him as one 'not fearing a fight' (*Ofinran ko ko 'ja*). The new Alafin now left Kushu, but before he turned in the direction of Oyo Ile he settled for some years in the town of Shaki. Eventually, after disagreements with the Shaki people, he set out towards Oyo. But about halfway along his path he came to a hilly place where two streams flowed together; here, propitious omens suggested that a halt should be made and a town established. Thus it came about that a new capital, called Oyo Igboho, was founded, destined to be occupied by Egunoju for the rest of his reign and by three of his successors.

Igboho offered security to the court after its long wanderings and its natural defences were presumably soon strengthened (it became famous for its triple walls), so that the Oyo were enabled to resist the continued menace from the Nupe and now also from the Borgu, dangers which, it may be assumed, made hazardous the reoccupation of the ruined and more exposed former capital. Egunoju's reign was followed by that of Orompoto, who, according to tradition in Igboho (though not in New Oyo), was a woman ruler (*oba obinrin*), but who in any case is remembered as having formed a large army whose rearguard alone consisted of 1,000 horsemen and 1,000 foot soldiers.

Orompoto was succeeded by Ajiboyede, called also Shopasan, whose stern character is recalled by his *oriki*: '. . . the world complained to God, and God gave them oba Shopasan who flogged many of them to death.' During this reign the Nupe sent yet another expedition against the Oyo, which penetrated as far as Igboho itself. The counter-attacks of the Esho, the Alafin's Noble Guard of seventy leading warriors, had failed to halt the enemy when the tide of battle was turned by a curious episode. In order to protect the Alafin, a warrior named Ajanlapa exchanged clothes with him and drew on himself the concentrated fire of the Nupe bowmen. His dead body, transfixed by their arrows, remained upright, his teeth set as in a grin. The Nupe, supposing themselves to be opposed by a supernatural being, fled in terror from the field, leaving their king a prisoner of the Oyo. Ajanlapa's son was later honoured with the right of intimate attendance on the Alafin and of deputizing for him on certain public occasions. This office, whose holder was called the *Osi 'efa* ('the deputy on the left hand'), has continued at Oyo to this day.

The last of the Igboho Alafin was Abipa, said to have been born to one of Egunoju's queens as the royal party was aproaching Igboho from Shaki (his name is a contraction of *a bi si ipa* – 'one born on the wayside'). The menace from the Nupe had now been contained, and Abipa determined to carry out the return to Oyo Ile. His leading nobles, unwilling to abandon their farms and houses at Igboho, tried to frustrate his decision by a trick. Hearing that the Alafin had decided to send an advance party to reconnoitre the site of the old city, each dispatched there one of those unfortunates called *enia orisha*, 'people of the gods': the Bashorun sent a hunchback, the Asipa a leper, the Alapini an albino, the Shamu a man with a projecting jaw, and the Akiniku a cripple. When the royal messengers arrived at the site of the former palace, where they were to offer sacrifices, these odd creatures roamed all night over the nearby Ajaka hill with torches in their hands, hooting and shrieking '*ko si aiye, ko si aiye*' ('no room, no room'). The terrified messengers hastened back to tell the Alafin of their adventure, but Abipa soon learnt what had happened and sent six hunters to round up the bogus phantoms. From this episode he received the attributive name by which he is often referred to in Oyo, *Oba m'oro*, 'the king who caught ghosts', and Old Oyo itself is often called Oyo Oro, 'Oyo of the ghosts'. The story is still re-enacted during annual festivals at Oyo and on the installation of a new Alafin (and in recent years has provided a plot for one of Duro Ladipo's folk operas).

Oyo Ile was re-occupied, so it seems from Johnson's account, only towards the end of Abipa's reign, a halt being made for some time at an intermediate place known as Kogbaye ('not room enough'), perhaps while the former capital was being repaired or rebuilt. When at last the royal party re-entered Oyo, sacrifices were offered by the palace priests, and the Alafin gained further honour with his people by handing over for this purpose a son newly born to one of his wives. His oriki refers to him as '. . . the royal catcher of ghosts who sacrificed his son for the peace of the world' (. . . *oba moro ti o fi 'omo re tun 'le nitori ki aiye le roju*). The return was marred, however, by a quarrel with the Ijesha, who had been absent from the delegations sent from other parts of Yorubaland to congratulate the Alafin. Subsequently the Oyo army set out to punish the Ijesha, but was forced to retreat with the loss of many warriors.

Igboho continued to be a place of importance, and in the early nineteenth century it was accounted by Lander, the Cornish traveller, as 'the second town in the kingdom' of Oyo.[6] Despite the stormy events of that century and the movement southwards into the forests of much of the population of northern Yorubaland, the town survived, and today the Alafin's representatives still rule there, the remains of its three lines of massive earthen ramparts can be seen, and four graves, said to be those of Alafin Ofinran, Egunoju, Orompoto and Ajiboyede, are tended by an official established there for that purpose, the Are.

To some extent, recent investigations at both New Oyo and at Igboho support the traditions retailed by the *Aroken*, or court historians, of Oyo to Johnson and to subsequent inquirers. Thus earlier editions of this book accepted, albeit provisionally, the accounts of Johnson and other local historians about both the origin of the kingdom and the sojourn of the Alafin at Igboho. Indeed, it seemed that it was during the exile of the court from Oyo Ile that the foundations of later greatness were laid. However, growing scepticism about the oral traditions, stressing in particular their comparative modernity, their repetition of earlier incidents and events in different settings, and the suspiciously convenient support which they seemed to give to vested political interests, has demanded a re-assessment of Johnson's account, despite (or, indeed, perhaps because of) its acceptance by the Oyo authorities as almost the official version of the past.

In an article published in 1985, Law argues that the story of the abandonment of Oyo Ile, the temporary occupation of Igboho by five Alafin, and the return to the old capital were all put forward as a 'traditional stereotype' to legitimize the re-establishment of Oyo on a new site by Alafin Atiba in the early nineteenth century. He suggests instead that there was a Nupe state in the area of Oyo Ile which was 'symbolized in the traditions by Sango', that Igboho was the seat of an 'essentially Yoruba' group under a ruling dynasty of Borgu origin, and that the latter overran and superimposed itself upon the original Nupe kingdom at or in the area of Oyo Ile. Furthermore, in his view, 'The claim of origin from Ife' by the Alafin 'probably reflects no more than that Ife was known to have been the earliest kingdom in the Yoruba area'.[7]

The best hope of arriving at a conclusion as to the relative degrees of truth in the various traditions and theories which have now been advanced about the origins and early years of the Oyo kingdom seems to lie with archaeology. Excavations were conducted on the site of Oyo Ile by Willett in 1956–7 and by Soper between 1973 and 1979. Apart from evidence of Stone Age occupation of the Mejiro cave on the site, pottery fragments from the area of the city itself indicated a long and possibly continuous occupation. This (following Law's summary) was apparently in two phases, the first being associated with a style of pottery known (from a local hill) as 'Diogun and with settlement in round buildings in the northern and western parts of the large site, and the second characterized by pottery similar to modern Yoruba (especially Ilorin) pottery, rectangular buildings like modern Yoruba compounds, and the building of the city walls; this second phase continued until the abandonment of the site in the 1830s. For 'Diogun pottery a radiocarbon dating of the eleventh/twelfth century was obtained, and for the later pottery a date of the thirteenth/fourteenth century. Law then concludes that the site was clearly occupied long before the arrival of Abipa and his followers from Igboho and that the cultural transition indicated above 'is in fact a reflection of' that arrival.[8]

Whatever its antecedents, the establishment, or re-establishment, of the Yoruba kingdom at Oyo Ile under a dynasty of either Borgu or Ife origin was followed by an assertion, or perhaps a re-assertion, of its authority over the country to the south of the capital, extending roughly to where the present New Oyo lies on the edge of the forest. Here, in the Oyo kingdom, or 'Yoruba Proper' as it was called in the last century, are still found many old towns, such as Shaki, Iseyin, Igbetti, and Kishi, all owing allegiance to the Alafin but ruled by their own oba. Until the Muslim 'holy war' against the Oyo by the Fulani in the nineteenth century, this northern part of Yorubaland seems to have been more prosperous and populous, and certainly contained many more towns and villages, than today.

Even so, until about 1600, Oyo was probably a state of only minor importance. Then, traditionally during the reigns of Alafin Obalokun and Ajagbo, the Oyo began to extend their influence over the other Yoruba kingdoms. It is difficult to determine the full extent to which they were successful in this, and tradition is silent about the process of expansion. The strong Owu kingdom seems certainly to have become their vassal state in the south, while Ede protected them on the south-east. But they were now entering a region where the forests hampered the effectiveness of their cavalry, and Johnson's only reference to Oyo's wars against her sister-states of the Ife tradition is his account of how the army, unaccustomed to fighting in the bush, was defeated by the Ijesha in the reign of Alafin Obalokun (this seems to be the invasion referred to above, prompted by the Ijesha refusal to pay tribute in the reign of Abipa, Obalokun's predecessor). It seems likely that the Oyo never succeeded in controlling either the Ijebu or the southern Ekiti; the hills and forests of the latter would have constituted an especially formidable obstacle, and it has been suggested that this area was regarded in Oyo as a reservoir where captives could be taken for the slave trade which came to play a large part in their economy from the latter part of the seventeenth century. This was also an area where expansion was checked by the powerful Edo kingdom of Benin. The traditions of the latter relate that war occurred between Oyo and Benin in the time of the warrior Oba Ehengbuda, who is believed to have reigned in the last quarter of the sixteenth century.[9] At the end of this war the armies of the Oba and the Alafin are said to have planted trees at Otun in the savannah of northern Ekiti to demarcate the frontier between their kingdoms.[10] Though it is impossible to substantiate the claim that Ife and Ijesha were brought within the 'empire' of Oyo (either as semi-independent provinces or merely as tributaries), there is no doubt that the extensive countries of the Egba and the Egbado were subject to Oyo, and it was through the latter's territory that ran Oyo's vital south-western trade-routes to the coast.

The growth of Oyo was by no means confined to Yorubaland (and it is unlikely that any distinction was made or felt between Yoruba and non-Yoruba before the nineteenth century). To the east and north of the capital respectively, parts of the territories of their old enemies and neighbours, the Nupe (called 'Tapa' by them) and the Borgu ('Ibariba'), were conquered by the Alafin's armies, a development which probably preceded the extension of the power of Oyo to the south and south-west. These areas, as far as the Niger on the north-east,[11] probably remained tributary to Oyo until quite late in the eighteenth century. That the Alafin had confidence in the loyalty of his non-Yoruba subjects is shown by the appointment of Nupe as his representatives in the client kingdom of Ijanna in south-western Yorubaland[12] and by the Borgu origin of the ruling families of several towns in Yoruba Proper, notably Shaki, Kishi, and Ogbomosho.

But it was in the economically important south-west that Oyo's expansion was most marked. In the reign of the warrior king Ajagbo (probably about the middle of the seventeenth century), 'Iweme in the Popo country' (the small state of Weme on the Nokwe coastal lagoon) was destroyed by the Alafin's army,[13] which implies that the Oyo had already brought under control the intervening territories of Ketu, Egba, and Egbado. Then in 1698 they overran the kingdom of Allada, some twenty-five miles inland, probably still the most important of the Aja states.[14] During the first half of the eighteenth century, a period which has been described as Oyo's 'golden age of imperial conquest', the Oyo succeeded in imposing their authority over the emergent Fon kingdom of Dahomey (sometimes known after its capital as 'Abomey'), farther inland from Allada, and the coastal area which was the home of the Ewe and Aja people (who, it has been claimed, are related to the

Yoruba and orginally migrated from their country). Between 1726 and 1730 the Oyo army undertook four expeditions against Dahomey, the first being a consequence of an invasion in 1724 of Allada, now tributary to Oyo, by Agaja, the Dahomean king, and the subsequent ones being occasioned by Agaja's invasion in 1727 of Whydah, which, with Weme and Allada, sent messengers to Oyo imploring the Alafin's help. In 1730 the Oyo reached an important agreement with the Dahomeans under which the latter were to pay an annual tribute to the Alafin and to respect the independence of the surrounding states.[15] These expeditions took place during the reign at Oyo of Ojigi, one of the most successful Alafin and a ruler who could rely on the support of such prominent men among his chiefs as Bashorun Yau Yamba and Gbonka (general) Latoyo, and seem to have consisted mainly, perhaps wholly, of cavalry. After Ojigi's death about 1735 the Dahomeans broke the agreement of 1730, and the Oyo army was twice dispatched against them, until in 1748 Tegbesu, Agaja's successor, agreed to a re-imposition of the 1730 terms, said to require an annual payment of forty men, forty women, forty guns, and 400 loads of cowries and corals. This tribute was paid each November to Oyo representatives at Kana (or Calamina), a few miles south-west of Abomey. In addition, the Oyo ambassadors were to keep the Alafin informed of events in the Dahomey kingdom.[16]

Johnson records that the glories of Ojigi's reign were consummated by a military expedition which encircled the Alafin's domain, first going north to the Niger, proceeding south along the west bank until the coast was reached, then west to the country of the Popo, and returning north-eastwards to the capital. This demonstrated, Johnson writes, the 'sovereignty' of Oyo over a vast area which, he adds, even included Benin.[17] The account seems exaggerated. As suggested above, it is unlikely that the authority of Oyo was ever a continuing reality in south-eastern Yorubaland, and it is even more unlikely that Benin was subject to Oyo, though there was debatable territory between them. Nevertheless, the tradition of this great sweep through the land by the Alafin's army indicates that at this time Oyo power was felt from the coast to the Niger bend, and that the empire in this reign stood at the zenith of its power and its greatest territorial extent.

At the centre of this formidable state of Guinea was its divine king, the Alafin. Oyo history is mainly recollected according to the Alafin in whose reign occurred memorable events. This, although a convenient and natural method for the *aroken* (the court drummers and official historians) to follow, does not imply that the Alafin was always a dominant figure or that he wielded autocratic power; he was in fact subject, like all Yoruba oba, to elaborate restraints embedded in the custom (which can justifiably be called the constitution) of the kingdom. He had to submit his decisions in the first place to his council of seven notables, the Oyo Mesi, whose principal officer was the Bashorun, a chief whose lineage suggests to Agiri that he represents 'an extinct (and probably Yoruba) dynasty' of rulers.[18] An Alafin of strong and resolute character could initiate and carry through a policy, obtaining the support and perhaps on occasions overruling the opposition of his counsellors. But not all Alafin were of this calibre, and the constitutional restraints on them were stringent. The Oyo Mesi were even entitled (or had come to be entitled) to pronounce a sentence of rejection on an Alafin, upon whose receipt (it was sometimes tactfully conveyed by a symbolic gift of parrots' eggs) the king was bound to commit suicide. The first recorded rejection and suicide seems to be that of Alafin Odarawu.[19] Another rule, apparently established during the reign of Ojigi (or at his death, probably in the 1730s), provided that the Aremo, the Alafin's eldest son, should take poison on his father's death, the intention being doubtless to protect the oba and his officers against the possible ambitions of a prince who was usually associated with his father in the government.[20]

The system of government of the capital was repeated on a smaller scale in the provincial towns of the kingdom, and paralleled also in the subject kingdoms. There are many indications that these latter were allowed by Oyo to retain a large measure of independence, although regular tribute had to be paid and the Alafin sometimes assumed the right to nominate a new ruler, and his confirmation of one was required. Oyo authority was expressed in a form of indirect rule by the stationing all over the empire of resident political representatives known as *ajele* (also called *asoju oba*, 'the eyes of the king') who in turn were supervised by the *ilari*, the royal messengers from Oyo. But in some places client kingdoms or towns were founded, as was the case at Ede or among the Egbado on the road to the sea.

The military strength of the Oyo goes far to explain their predominance over their neighbours. Another factor underlying the growth of Oyo's power, and also its expansion south-westwards, was the capital's position as a commercial centre. Oyo Ile was so situated that it linked together the trade of the coast, where from the late fifteenth century European traders had been active, with that of the cities of the West Sudan. There is said, for example, to have been a colony of traders from the Oyo town of Ogbomosho in eighteenth century Kano.[21] Most important, the Oyo had become by the late seventeenth century exporters on a large scale of slaves for the Atlantic trade. In return they received iron, salt, cutlasses, and such luxuries as cloth and mirrors; rather oddly, firearms do not seem to have featured among their imports (except for the tribute from the Dahomeans) until the early nineteenth century.

The earliest route for Oyo's south-western trade seems to have led through the territories of Ketu, then round the Kumi swamps to Allada, and thence to the port of Whydah (or Ouidah), a distance of over 200 miles.[22] The route ran through country where a break in the forest belt would have enabled the Oyo cavalry to give protection to the caravans almost as far as the coast. But the rise of Dahomey towards the end of the seventeenth century threatened this access to the sea, while in the same century the westward expansion of Benin, which had already set up a number of subject towns or camps on or near to the coast, including Lagos and Ado, posed a similar threat. Probably as a result, the trade route was shifted to the east and passed through the vassal kingdom of Ifonyin and its three offshoots, Ihumbo, Ilashe, and Ikolaje, which were founded by the Oyo on Egbado or perhaps Ketu territory about 1700.[23] For greater security, however, the route was later moved still farther to the east, leading to the development of Badagry and Porto Novo (Ajashe), both of which were tributary to Oyo, as the principal outlets for Oyo trade. This easternmost route – the 'Egbado trade corridor' – was protected by a series of towns, notably Ilaro, Ijanna, and Jiga. The development of this route, beginning with the establishment of a war camp which soon grew into the town of Ijanna, may be ascribed to the long reign of Alafin Abiodun (about 1770–89).[24]

Oyo's northern trade was almost certainly of greater antiquity than its connections with the coast. Probably the main routes were two: one towards the Niger at Bussa, where there was a ford, and the other to the Niger crossing at Jebba island on the edge of Nupe country. The most important items sent northwards seem to have been kola nuts from the forests to the south-west, peppers grown near the coast, cloth, and marine or European salt. Possibly slaves were sent from or through Oyo to the northern markets, but there are no indications of such a trade on a large scale. In return, many different items were imported, deriving either from the West Sudan itself or from the trans-Saharan trade, in particular horses, natron, swords and knives, leather, beads, unwrought silk, and in early times probably Saharan salt (Johnson records that salt was first introduced into Oyo during the reign of Obalokun, the first Alafin after the return from Igboho, but he does not indicate its provenance).[25] The Oyo probably purchased slaves as well as horses from the Nupe, since in the late eighteenth century they were supplying Hausa slaves to Porto Novo.[26]

Oyo's great age of conquest, initiated traditionally under Alafin Obalokun and Ajagbo in the seventeenth century, continued during the reigns of Ojigi and his second and third successors, Amuniwaiye and Onishile, in the first part of the eighteenth century. It was followed by 'the age of Gaha' – to use Akinjogbin's terminology – which lasted from 1754 to 1774. The beginning of the reign of Labisi saw the advent to power of Gaha, a son of the former Bashorun Yamba, who succeeded to his father's office and then subjected both the crown and government of Oyo to his personal rule. Johnson summarizes his career thus: 'He lived to a good old age, and wielded his power ruthlessly. He was noted for having raised five kings to the throne, of whom he murdered four, and was himself murdered by the fifth.'[27]

The ascendancy of Gaha and the violent deaths of the four Alafin have reasonably been interpreted as symptoms of the approaching decline of Oyo. But Akinjogbin argues that the primary significance of the Bashorun's career was that it reflected a dilemma which now confronted the government of Oyo: whether to continue on the path of territorial expansion or whether to consolidate and concentrate on the economic opportunities which had been opened up, especially the ever increasing trade in slaves through Badagry and Porto Novo.[28] He claims that it was the Alafin who were anxious to preserve peace and expand trade, while the Bashorun stood for a forward military policy. In the event neither policy could be carried out consistently. Although Gaha succeeded in imposing his will in internal matters, he could make no major war, since under the constitution only the Alafin could give the order for a military expedition (although on one occasion Gaha did insist on war being waged against the Elehin-Odo, the Ifonyin vassal king whose display of wealth when on a visit to Alafin Agboluaje at Oyo had angered him). Akinjogbin concludes: 'The only possible achievement was to maintain a *status quo* and this Gaha did, to his eternal credit . . . : he kept the boundaries of the Empire intact and completely inviolate.' Perhaps, however, he did more than that, since a trader's report of 1764 suggests that an Oyo army stationed – or at any rate, operating – as far west as Atakpame had in that year defeated an Asante army there.[29] That the power of the Oyo continued to impress their neighbours is confirmed by what Robert Norris heard of them in Dahomey. 'The Dahomeans may possibly exaggerate,' he wrote, 'but the Eyeos are certainly a very populous, warlike and powerful nation.'[30]

During the reign of Majeogbe, Gaha's power was at its zenith. According to

Johnson, he had stationed his sons as his agents in every part of the kingdom, and it was to them instead of to the Alafin that tribute was paid. Meanwhile Majeogbe, who was living in constant fear for his life, attempted to rid himself of the Bashorun by magic (or poison?) and had so far succeeded that Gaha was disabled in both his legs. But Gaha resorted to still more powerful magic by which he finally encompassed the Alafin's death, an event which apparently occurred in about 1770.[31] By now the Bashorun's physical powers were waning, and Abiodun, the new Alafin, was content to bide his time until in 1774 he felt strong enough to challenge him. He negotiated through an intermediary with the Kakamfo Oyabi (commander of the frontier army), who at this time was stationed at Ajashe, a town to the north-east of Ogbomosho,[32] and who agreed to lead his troops to Oyo to support the Alafin. There ensued a short, sharp struggle inside the capital between the Kakamfo's men and Gaha's family and supporters. After a desperate resistance the Bashorun's compound was entered and put to fire, and Gaha himself was taken captive. His end was violent. Johnson writes that he was ceremonially burnt, but another account is that his body was cut in pieces and distributed over the empire.[33]

Akinjogbin maintains that the overthrow of Gaha was 'no more than the usual power tussle in the capital' and did not imply any weakening in the empire. Indeed, Abiodun's success greatly strengthened his personal authority. Yet the career of Gaha, with its defiance of the hallowed institutions of the kingdom, must in the long run have diminished the prestige of the Alafinate and set an example of disloyalty in high places to future generations.

Abiodun now proved himself a strong and capable ruler, and his reign is still remembered as an age of peace and prosperity before the storm. The kingdom of Dahomey, for example, was so firmly under the sway of Oyo that the Alafin was apparently able to use its army (perhaps to the disadvantage of his own forces) to carry out his policies in the south-west. In 1784 a strong Dahomean army, joined by contingents from the western Yoruba and supported by Lagos, attacked Badagry; according to Dalzel, 'The operations of the Dahoman army were directed by the Eyeo messengers, who had conducted them hither: and nothing of importance was undertaken without their concurrence.'[34] In 1786, again apparently at the suggestion of Oyo, the Dahomeans took Weme, but when they proposed to follow this up by an attack on Ardra and Porto Novo the Alafin forbade the enterprise: 'Ardrah was Eyeo's calabash out of which nobody should be permitted to eat but himself.'[35]

Yet it is evident that during Abiodun's reign the army, on which the power and wealth of the kingdom depended, declined in effectiveness. The reasons for this are not clear. Akinjogbin surmises that the very nature of the Alafin's victory over Gaha involved a diminution in the influence of the military leaders and thus, he implies, an eventual lowering of the efficiency of the army.[36] This is not wholly convincing, especially as it was the co-operation of the army and its general which had enabled the Alafin to triumph in this crisis. Possibly the sense of security which he felt after ridding the kingdom of its over-mighty Bashorun led Abiodun to neglect his military forces, or possibly the inactivity of the first peaceful years of the reign after 1774 diminished the capacity of the Oyo for waging war. Whatever the explanation, the Oyo army was heavily defeated by the Borgu in 1783, six years before Abiodun's death in (probably) 1789, and in 1790, during the reign of his successor, the unfortunate Awole, the Nupe inflicted a similar blow on the kingdom.[37]

By the end of the century the influence of the Oyo to the north and east of their capital, across the Moshi and to the Niger, had been overthrown, despite the fact that this was an area within which their cavalry operated under favourable physical conditions. It even seems (if credence can be given to a contemporary report in Dahomey[38]) that in the late eighteenth century the Nupe were exacting tribute from the Oyo and that the Oyo expedition of 1791, so far from being an attempt to reassert ascendancy over the Nupe, was designed to end their own subjection. Still more serious, at about this time the Egba of the southern forest rose in revolt against the Oyo ajele stationed in their towns and gained their independence, an event which seems to have taken place about 1796. This had two dire consequences for the Oyo: first, it endangered their important trade route to the coast, and secondly, it set an example of rebellion to the other Yoruba states under their control. Thus the eighteenth century saw both the apotheosis of the empire of Oyo and the first stages of what was to be a swift decline.

NOTES

1. For the traditions and history of Oyo, see S. Johnson (1921), *passim*. The name 'Katunga' possibly derives from the Hausa *katanga* for a compound wall or the Nupe *tanga* for a hamlet. For a visit to the site of Oyo Ile and a summary of information about it, see Robert Smith and Denis Williams (1966). Frank Willett (1960a) has described his archaeological investigations there in 1956–7. He concludes that the site traditionally known as Oyo Ile is the same as the Oyo visited by Clapperton and the Landers in the first part of the nineteenth century, despite a slip in Clapperton's account of its longitude. The 1:50,000 Federal Survey map of Nigeria, sheet 201 NE (Igbetti), 1966, based on air photographs taken in 1962, shows the southern part of an extensive walled area. In the early 1970s an annual training camp by the Archaeology Department of the University of Ibadan carried out investigations on the site (Soper, 1973–77). According to Law ('Problems of plagiarism . . .' *Paideuma*, 33, 1987. p. 346) the earliest mention in any extant source of Oyo ('Oyeo') occurs in D'Elbée (1671), *Journal* (continuation), ed. de Clodoré, Paris, II, pp. 557–8.
2. Agiri (1975), p. 8; Law (1985b), *passim*.
3. Crowder (1966), p. 60.
4. Bosman, Letter XX, pp. 397–8.
5. Notes in the files of the Yoruba Historical Research Scheme (Oyo/1).
6. R. L. and J. Lander, pp. 78–9. The American Baptist missionary W. H. Clarke gives an interesting account of his visit to Igboho in 1855 in his *Travels and Explorations*.
7. Law (1985b), pp. 41, 46–8.
8. Ibid., pp. 48–9.
9. See Bradbury, pp. 274–6, and Law (1977), pp. 129–30, for the suggestion that Dapper's 'Isago' refers to Oyo. (Dapper, p. 505, describes a cavalry attack by 'Isago' on Benin.) Alternatively, 'Isago' may refer to the Nupe: Ryder (1969), p. 15.
10. Egharevba, p. 32; Weir, *Akure Intelligence Report* (1934); Bradbury, p. 276.
11. Law (1973c) examines, sceptically, the claim that Oyo exacted tribute from Nupe and Borgu, which derives from Johnson, pp. 41, 187. However, the oriki of Ajibesin, who

ruled Ikoyi in the reigns of Alafin Abipa and Obalokun, refers to the Oyo army under his command as chasing the Nupe to the banks of the Niger: Babeyemi (1974).

12. S. Johnson (1921), p. 168, assigns the appointment of this official, called the Onishare, to the reign of Obalokun, which immediately followed that of Abipa who brought back the Oyo from Igboho. Morton-Williams (1964a), p. 38, and Folayan (1967b), p. 25, place it much later, in the reign of Abiodun in the late eighteenth century.
13. S. Johnson (1921), p. 169.
14. Akinjogbin (1966b), p. 451, citing Bosman, p. 396, and Barbot, p. 352.
15. Dalzel, p. 59; Akinjogbin (1963), pp. 562-3; Law (1977), pp. 160-1.
16. Parrinder (1956), p. 28; Argyle, p. 25; Norris, quoted by Hodgkin p. 169.
17. S. Johnson (1921), p. 174.
18. Agiri (1975), p. 8.
19. S. Johnson (1921), pp. 169-70; Law (1982), p. 389.
20. S. Johnson (1921), p. 174; Law (1982), pp. 389-90.
21. Adeleye in Ajayi and Crowder (1974), Vol. I, p. 592. See also Agiri (1976) and (1977).
22. Morton-Williams (1964a), pp. 29, 40.
23. Ibid., pp. 30-1.
24. Morton-Williams (1964a), pp. 38-9; Folayan (1967b), pp. 15-25. See also note 12 above.
25. S. Johnson (1921), p. 168. See also Clapperton's description, pp. 135-8, of the market at 'Koolfo'.
26. Adams, pp. 221-2.
27. S. Johnson (1921), p. 178 and pp. 178-85 for the whole career of Gaha. Akinjogbin (1966b), p. 454, n. 4, adduces documentary evidence for dating Gaha's advent to power as 1754.
28. Akinjogbin (1966b), pp. 453-5.
29. William Mutter to African Committee, 27 May 1764 (T 70/31), quoted by Akinjogbin (1966b), p. 455.
30. Quoted by Hodgkin, p. 167.
31. Dalzel, p. 157; Akinjogbin (1966b), p. 455.
32. This Ajashe is not to be confused with Porto Novo, also called Ajashe by the Yoruba, nor with the Ajashe of the Igbomina. The writer thanks Dr R. C. C. Law for information about the Kakamfo's Ajashe, which derives from Oyerinde, *Iwe Itan Ogbomoso*. See also Law (1977), p. 194, note 88.
33. The second version is quoted by Akinjogbin (1966b) from A. L. Hethersett, *Iwe Kika Ekerin*, pp. 63-4. The date of the overthrow of Gaha by Abiodun is established from Dalzel (quoted by Hodgkin, p. 170), who refers tó Gaha as 'Ochenoo, the prime minister' (a garbled form of Oshorun, an alternative form for Bashorun).
34. Dalzel, p. 183.
35. Ibid.
36. Akinjogbin (1966b), p. 458.
37. Akinjogbin (1965), p. 30; Law 1973e, *passim*. Dalzel, p. 229.
38. Dalzel, p. 229.

FOUR

KINGDOMS OF THE EAST
Ijesha, Ekiti, Igbomina, Owo, and Ondo

Ile Ife, the historic centre of the Yoruba, lies in an undulating land of tall and dense forest, a closed landscape befitting its many mysteries. But east from Ife the scene changes as the wooded hills of Ilesha are reached and then the rocky summits of Ekiti. Here, in an Arcadian country where gods and goddesses abound in the rivers and on the hilltops, kingdoms proliferate. They range in size from Ijesha, Ondo, and Owo, each occupying something like the area of an English county, to the miniature states of Ekiti and Igbomina.

Ijesha

The Ijesha have sometimes been grouped by writers about the Yoruba with the Ife,[1] but their political and cultural traditions, history, and dialect all emphasize their separateness. Their kingship is held to derive from Ife, and their ruler, the Owa, wears a beaded crown. Ilesha, his capital, is the centre of a district of some forty square miles, the heart of the former kingdom, which stretches from Ife and Oshogbo on the west to Ekiti on the east; it is bounded on the north by the little-known Igbomina kingdoms, and on the south by Ondo, ruled by the Oshemawe. Writing about the origin of the Ijesha, Johnson suggests that their name is a contraction from *ije orisha*, 'the food of the gods', and refers to that part of the people already living in the area before the arrival of the founder of the present kingship from Ife, and who were looked upon by their neighbours as potential sacrificial victims – hence their name – and slaves.[2] He adds that until the abolition of human sacrifice by the British at the end of the last century, the Ijesha continued to be preferred, especially by the Ife, to other victims.

Ajaka (alternatively Ajibogun), the founder of the Ijesha kingdom, is described in local tradition as a son of Oduduwa by the sister of one of his wives.[3] The legend relates that as Oduduwa grew old his eyes dimmed, so that at last he was advised by an Ifa priest to send for sea-water to bathe them. But the princes held back from making the long and hazardous journey to the coast, until finally Ajaka, youngest or (from the circumstances of his birth) lowest-ranking among them, offered to perform this service. After many adventures and the passage of years, Ajaka returned to his father's court at Ife. When he entered the market-place the people there, astonished to see him after so long an absence, called out *O wa!* ('So you are back') – from which the title of Ilesha's oba, the Owa, derives; he replied *Mo b'okun* ('I have the sea-water') – and was thereafter called Obokun. Then he gave the water to Oduduwa, who (the story contains no more surprises) regained his sight.

During Obokun's long absence Oduduwa's two eldest sons had died, and the other princes, taking with them their inheritance from their father, had left Ife to found their own kingdoms. The only reward for Obokun was a sword, *ida ajashe*, 'the sword of victory'. With this he angrily pursued his brothers, seized from them a share of the family treasure, and returned to Ife. As he entered the Court he mistook his father, whose face was hidden by the beaded fringe of his crown, for one of his brothers and raised his sword against him. Slicing off the fringe of the crown, he realized, just in time, his dreadful error. Soon after this he left Ife to found his own kingdom and was given by his father a crown which was like that of his brothers except in one particular, that it had no fringe at the front, a peculiarity still preserved in the crowns worn by the Owa Obokun of Ijesha. The event is described in an Ijesha song:

The ebon rider,	*Okunrin dudu ori eshin,*
The lord who was given beads for propitiating the earth,	*Oluwa Okile gb'okun,*
Ajaka, master of the sharp sword,	*Ajaka onida arara,*
He fought the sea,	*O b'okun ja,*
He danced home with the sea.	*O bokun jo r'ele.*

Armed with his sword, Obokun led his followers to a place known as Igbadaye,[4] where they settled. It is said that he alone of Oduduwa's sons returned to Ife (no great journey for him) to attend the ceremonies which followed his father's death. He himself died at Igbadaye, and his son, Owa Oke Okile, resumed the migration, leaving in charge of Obokun's grave a follower whose descendants still rule there with the title of Agbadaye. The next settlement was at Ilowa ('the Owa's town'), and then in the next reign the Owa and his people removed yet again to Ilemure, renamed Ibokun, where the Owa displaced the Ita, a king whom he found already installed there. During their sojourn in Ibokun the Owa brought under his control the town of Ilare, whose ruler, the Alare, claimed (like the Owa and even the Ita) to have received a crown from Ife. Then from Ibokun the next Owa, Owari, removed to Ilaje, four miles distant, called after his death Ipole Ijesha. Finally, in the fifth reign, that of Owa Oge, the town of Ilesha was chosen as capital. Tradition relates that it was already famous for the water-pots made by its women, a circumstance from which its name may derive: *ile isha*, 'the town of water-pots', though it may also mean 'town of the gods'. It was already ruled by a king, the Onila (the 'king of the okro planters', who had built the town), who now became deputy to the Owa and whose successor, the Obala, still ranks second in Ilesha. According to Johnson, the town was rebuilt, and for this the Ijesha called on the help of a prince from the Alafin's family so that it could be laid out on the same plan as that of Oyo Ile.

A list has been preserved of the names of thirty-eight predecessors to the present oba; it is alleged that in addition the names of nine Owa have been lost, five of these having died before their coronation.[5] Of those named, five are said to have been women, but there has been no female ruler since Yeyeori, the eighteenth Owa. Little is recalled about the history of the Ijesha in early times. A derisory epithet sometimes applied to them, 'children of sticks' (*omo igi*), is explained by the myth that Obokun, the first Owa, found himself short of subjects and by magic converted bundles of sticks into human beings – which may reflect the thinness of the population in these forests at the period. Johnson adds unkindly that the epithet may instead be accounted for by the nature of the Ijesha, who are 'as proverbially deficient in wit as they are remarkably distinguished for brute strength'.[6] At all events, the Ijesha, as *omo Obokun*, were famous warriors, and in their heyday (which may have preceded the rise of the Oyo empire but more probably came during Oyo's decline at the end of the eighteenth century) their kingdom evidently occupied a considerably greater extent than the present boundaries of Ijeshaland, since Ijesha communities are found in the Oshun area to the north-west (usually accounted a part of Oyo), and to the east among the Ekiti, Akoko, and Owo.

Over many of the places conquered or settled by his warriors, it was the Owa's custom to place as ruler one of his sons. Descendants of these princes are known in the kingdom by the title of Loja. There are now seventeen Loja among the minor rulers of Ijeshaland, and every new Owa is required to have served as a Loja in the provinces before becoming eligible for the throne.[7]

At some time, probably in the seventeenth century, a group of Ijesha founded the now-important town of Oshogbo on the River Oshun, some twenty miles to the north-west of Ilesha. This may have been intended, as Johnson suggests, as an outpost against the Oyo and an answer to the establishment by them of the warrior Timi as ruler at nearby Ede.[8] Apart from this, there are no indications in Ijesha tradition about relations with their powerful Oyo neighbours. Nothing is heard, for example, of the stationing in the kingdom of the Alafin's ajele nor of the visits with presents which, Johnson alleges,[9] were made annually by the Owa to the Alafin. This is not surprising, since tradition tends to suppress the disagreeable – though on the part of the Oyo, Johnson does record the defeat of an expedition sent by Alafin Obalokun into Ijesha country, 'the Oyos being then unaccustomed to bush fighting'.[10] On balance, the claim by Oyo to have achieved political hegemony over eastern Yorubaland seems likely to allude to no more than the occasional exaction of tribute.

Oyo was not the Ijesha's only powerful and ambitious neighbour. To the east lay the kingdom of Benin and though the Ekiti provided a buffer between them, Benin seems at times to have exercised some influence at Ilesha. It is related that the seventh Owa, Atakunmasa, spent a number of years in exile in Benin. During his absence the throne was occupied by two women rulers, also styled Owa. Kenyo's version of the legend is that the purpose of the oba's sojourn in Benin was 'to study effective medicine . . . in order that his wives might begin to bring forth male children'. The Benin account is that after an already long reign the Owa's restless subjects wanted a change of ruler, and so sent Atakunmasa into exile; the Oba of Benin eventually summoned their elders and persuaded them to allow the Owa to return. Finally, tradition also recounts that the Ijesha have twice suffered invasion by Nupe armies.[11]

Ekiti

The Ekiti and Owo form the marches of the Yoruba with the Igbira, Afenmai, and Edo or Bini of the Benin kingdom. There are many recollections of incursions here by the Benin army, and it seems that at times parts of the area were subject to the rule of Benin. At least one of the Ekiti dynasties, that of Ikere, was established by Benin, and in some towns there are groups who, though they are now Yoruba-speaking, trace their descent from Bini settlers there – for example, the Ado living in the Igiso, Eyinke, and Oritogun wards of Akure. Little is recorded about relations between the Oyo and the people of this area, and Ekiti traditions are silent on the subject. As suggested in the last chapter,[12] Ekiti may have been looked upon by the Oyo as too difficult and rugged a terrain to control politically, and convenient therefore to be left for slave-raiding. The establishment of the Oyo–Benin frontier at Otun does, however, imply that the northern part of Ekiti was regarded as within the sphere of Oyo.

The name 'Ekiti' denotes a country of hills, and it is perhaps this physical feature which, more than any other factor, accounts for its division into a number of small kingdoms or city states, all centring on towns which are in the traditional definition *ilu alade*, 'towns with crowned oba'. There has long been uncertainty as to which towns can properly be considered as belonging to Ekiti. Usually sixteen oba are named, and from 1900 a sort of federal assembly of these rulers has met; this, the Pelu-pelu (from *pe olu*, 'to call the lords together'), was based on the military league of the late nineteenth century known as the Ekiti Parapo. All authorities seem to agree that the four leading rulers are: the Ore or Owore of Otun, the Ajero of Ijero, the Elewi or Ewi of Ado, and the Elekole of Ikole. About the others there is less agreement, but the rulers of the following sixteen towns have been included in different lists: Efon Alaye, Ogotun Iddo, Aiyede, Igbara Odo, Oye, Omuwo, Ire, Ishe, Itaji, Ikerre, Ishan, Emure, Aramoko, Oke-Messi, Osi and Akure.[13] Most of these claim to derive their crowns and dynasties from Ife.

Between the four leading *ilu alade* there has been controversy about precedence. When the Pelu-pelu first met in 1900 the presidency was given to the Ore of Otun, but after the administrative separation of Otun from the other Ekiti towns leadership passed to the Ewi of Ado-Ekiti, who represented the Ekiti oba at the conference of Yoruba rulers held at Ibadan in 1939. The Ewi claimed, indeed, that his being placed third in rank at the 1900 convention was a mistake, arising in part from his deference to the Elekole (placed second) as his senior by age. But more probably Ado had lost prestige with the other Ekiti through having held aloof from the Parapo and not having taken part in the Kiriji war fought by the Parapo at the end of the last century.

The history and legends of Ado have been recorded by a local historian, the Rev. A. Oguntuyi. The legend of origin which he recounts follows a familiar pattern. The ancestor of the present ruler of Ado was one of Oduduwa's sixteen sons, known from his talent as an orator as *Ewi*, 'the speaker'. He left Ife at the time of the dispersal of princes in the company of the prince who was destined to found a new dynasty at Benin. For a time these two settled side by side at Benin, but eventually they quarrelled, and Ewi with his followers returned westwards. The party halted in various places, and at length Ewi died, to be succeeded by an unrecorded number of rulers, now called 'Ewi' after him. Finally, they came to the site of Ado, where they made their home among the hills. The Ewi at this time was named Awamaro ('the restless one'), and the present oba, his descendant, is enumerated from him as the twenty-first, though Fr Oguntuyi thinks that a number of names of additional Ewi have been forgotten.[14]

As in many other places, Ado tradition records that the emigrants from Ife found on their arrival that there was already an organized settlement of people living there who, it seems, spoke either the same language as themselves or one similar enough to be understood without difficulty. In this case the earlier settlers were known as the Ilesun and their ruler as the Elesun. They received the newcomers kindly, but a subsequent struggle for power led to their overthrow and to the execution of the Elesun. At the grave in the Erekesan market where Awamaro buried the Elesun's head, all subsequent Ewi have carried out propitiatory ceremonies as part of their installation rites.

Oguntuyi suggests that the settlement by Awamaro at Ado was made at the end of the fourteenth or early in the fifteenth century. His precise dating for all subsequent reigns seems to have been calculated from the number of years traditionally ascribed to each reign. It can hardly be more than an approximation, but by no means a far-fetched one. During the first three or four centuries of Ado history two themes predominated. The first was the gradual expansion of the Ewi's rule over the surrounding district so that today, in addition to Ado, the Ewi rules over seventeen subordinate towns, of which Igede is the largest. The second major theme consisted in a series of defensive wars which Ado fought with Benin. It was the expansion of Ado which apparently brought about the intervention in the area of Benin, since Ikere, a town some ten miles to the south of Ado which had formerly been subject to the Elesin, invited the Oba of Benin to send his troops there. According to Oguntuyi, this occurred during the reigns at Ado of Ata, the first oba after Awamaro whose name is recalled, and at Benin of Ewuare, and if this association with Ewuare is correct it can be ascribed to the middle or second half of the fifteenth century.[15] During the ensuing war Ekiti was overrun by the Bini, while the ruler of Ikere, the Olukere, was himself replaced by a Bini whose title was the Ogoga.[16] The Ewi survived, but the Bini seem to have acquired a form of suzerainty over Ado, probably expressed by the payment of tribute. Thenceforth Ikere under its Benin dynasty was to be a rival and a threat to Ado.

A second war between Ado and Benin took place during the reign of Ewi Obakunrin. It was again occasioned by an appeal for help to Benin by the Ikere, who were protesting against the Ado's attempts to enlarge the area under their control. The Ado say that in this Oluponnokusuponno ('let everyone die in front of his own house') war, the Bini for the first time had firearms, but they merely discharged them into the air to cause terror – perhaps the most effective use of the primitive muskets which these must have been. Once again Ado submitted to Benin and affirmed its loyalty.

Another town in this region whose history is bound up with Benin is Akure (now the capital of Ondo state).[17] Although it has not always been accounted an Ekiti town, lying on the southern edge of the area, its ruler, the Deji, sat among the Ekiti oba in the local administrative council formed in this century, occupying fifth place, until a reorganization in 1946. Accounts of the origin of the town are contradictory. S. O. Arifalo has pointed out that the people in two sections of the town, the Isikan and the Isolo, have traditions which are distinct from those of the majority of the inhabitants, and that the former claim to be the original owners of the land. Both these groups seem to represent earlier settlers on the site of Akure. As to the present kingship, Arifalo has examined six different accounts.[18] The official version, not unexpectedly, traces the origin of the kingship to Ife, describing how the first oba, Asodeboyede, received the crown from Oduduwa, his grandfather. The original title of these Akure kings was Ajapada, said to mean 'one who kills a rat with a rattle', derived from an endurance test which Oduduwa forced his grandson to undergo before he left Ife and which is still commemorated at Akure in the annual Ifunta festival when the oba withdraws into an inner part of the *afin* for seven days. The majority of accounts agree that the present title of Deji arises from an episode which links the dynasty with that of Ilesha. As related above, Owa Atakunmasa, seventh ruler of the Ijesha, journeyed to Benin, where he spent some years in exile. On his way he passed through Akure, and later a son was born there, either to one of the Owa's wives or (the story has, of course, fissiparated) to one of his daughters given in marriage to the Ajapada. When the Owa returned, again passing through Akure, he saw this child, named Ogunja, and joyfully placed him on his knee, conferring on him a crown and the additional name of Olufadeji. When Ogunja came to the throne of Akure he preferred to use the shortened form of his new name, 'Deji', as his title, and it is thus that his successors are usually known to this day.[19]

The presence in Akure of a sizeable population of Bini origin, known as the Ado-Akure, living in the Igiso, Eyinke, and Oritagun quarters of the town and subject to a chief known as the Olotu-Ekiran,[20] is evidence of the close relations which have existed between the two kingdoms. Akure was the main base for Benin's trade in this area and, indeed, was apparently regarded at times as being within the western frontiers of that kingdom. The Ado-Akure may have constituted a kind of colony like those established by Benin in the south-west, and the name 'Ado' is probably here the Yoruba form of Edo, an alternative name for the Bini. Egharevba, the Benin historian, refers to an attack by the Bini on 'rebellious Akure' during the reign at Benin of Oba Ewuare. During this war the town was surrounded and all resistance eventually crushed. The ruler, whom Egharevba calls the Alakure Orito – a name which does not occur in the list of forty-two rulers compiled by Arifalo – was allowed to remain as nominal head of the town, but Benin's authority was maintained by the posting there of a resident official, the Odionwere (equivalent to an Oyo ajele).[21] About a century later, in the reign at Benin of Oba Ehengbuda, Akure was again 'rebellious', and the Benin army under the Iyase, returning from a campaign in Yorubaland, passed through it in order to make a show of strength.[22] By the early nineteenth century Akure seems to have regained its independence, but the murder there of an ambassador announcing the accession of a new Oba at Benin was followed in or about 1818 by a reconquest in which the Deji was taken captive and executed.[23] It is nearly superfluous to add that none of these events have been admitted to Akure tradition as it is related today.

One of the smallest of the independent towns in Ekiti is Ire, some fourteen miles to the north-east of Ado. It is of interest as the centre of the worship of Ogun, god of both war and iron in the Yoruba pantheon. According to the ruler, the Onire, the town was founded by Ogundahunsi, son of Ogun, who himself was a son of Oduduwa – or so they say at Ire, though not at Ife. On return from a long campaign, Ogun lost his temper with his son and killed him. Overwhelmed by remorse, he sank into the earth at the place in Ire where his shrine now stands. The Onire claims descent from Ogun and recites a list of rulers, ending with himself as twenty-ninth.[24]

Another small kingdom deserving mention is Idanre, south of Akure and east of Ondo. Its old town lies under the peak of Mount Orosun – the highest point in Western Nigeria at 3,098 feet – and until a few years ago could only be reached by rope ladder up a vertical rock face. The ruler here, the Owa, claims the usual Ife ancestry, but his kingship and government are on the Benin pattern.[25]

Smaller even than these last two states are the independent villages of the Akoko to the east of Ekiti. In this area, writes Forde, 'No right or authority beyond that of the village is recognized and each village or quarter of a village has its own particular tract of land, the boundaries of which are jealously guarded.'[26] This form of social organization is in marked contrast to the system of kingship obtaining generally among the Yoruba and probably results from the uncertainty of life in a marcher country and from the intermingling here of Yoruba, Afenmai, and Bini customs.

Igbomina, Igbolo, Ila, and the north-eastern Yoruba

To the north of the Ijesha and the Ekiti and east from Oyo live the Igbomina (alternatively, Igbona).[27] Their somewhat fragmentary political organization resembles that of their Ekiti neighbours, like whom they are divided among a number of different rulers.[28] As with the Ekiti again, and other Yoruba groups too, their environment straddles the forest and the savannah. Their paramount ruler is held to be the Olumu of Omu Aran, but he is somewhat overshadowed today by the more powerful Olupo of Ajashe. The latter's ancestor, Igwana, is said to have come originally from Ife and to have been given a daughter in marriage by the Alafin of Oyo. Elphinstone lists the names of seventeen Olupo, of whom the tenth was the first to settle at Ajashe, but avers that many names have been forgotten. The Olupo paid tribute to the Alafin and in turn exercised some authority over the other Igbomina rulers. A feature of the Olupo's pre-eminence was his possession of a sacred oil with which other Igbomina kings, and allegedly even the Alafin, were required to be anointed during their coronation ceremonies.

Although the Igbomina form a distinct group with their own states, the payment of tribute to Oyo by the Olupo and their other rulers seems to be of long standing and may even date from the founding of the kingships. Moreover, the worship of Ogun is prominent among the Igbomina as among the Oyo (as is also membership of the Ogboni society, but this was probably not introduced into Oyo or Igbomina until the nineteenth century). By the end of the sixteenth century Igbomina had apparently become part of the Oyo empire, a development perhaps brought about by raids of the neighbouring Ijesha and Nupe which are recollected in Igbomina tradition. Thus, the association between Igbomina and Oyo has long been a close one, and Johnson indeed describes the Igbomina as 'Oyos with Ekiti sympathies'.[29]

An important town in this area is Offa, whose people are usually called Ibolo or Igbolo, said to mean 'oil palm gatherers'. For much of their history they have been an integral part of the Alafin's kingdom and are, therefore, sometimes considered as Oyo.[30] The names of nine previous settlements, of which two were abandoned

Plate 7   Seated figure from Esie. Soapstone. Date undetermined. Photograph by Dirk Bakker from Ekpo Eyo and Frank Willett, *Treasures of Ancient Nigeria*, London, 1982.

under pressure from Nupe raiders, and a list (to 1929) of sixteen rulers, the Oloffa, have been preserved. The founder of the town and first Oloffa, Oluwole, came from Oyo and his first six successors were all accounted Oyo men, but after the marriage of the eighth Oloffa, Olumorin, with a daughter of the Olupo of Ajashe, a close relationship was maintained with the Olupo, who anointed subsequent Oloffa on their coronations.[31]

Notice must be taken too of the large village of Esie, with its adjacent township of Oro. Here an annual ceremony centres on a collection of some 1,000 carved soapstone figures of men, women, children, and animals. The existence of these remarkable sculptures, which are stored in a local museum, became known outside the area only in the early 1930s, though the cult may date from the arrival at the site of the Esie people, said to have been migrants from Old Oyo, an event which local historians place in the eighteenth century. The provenance and history of the figures are the subjects of debate; the suggestion that they were brought here from Old Oyo, perhaps after its fall in the early nineteenth century, has little to support it. Dating of the sculptures presents the usual problems, though two recent thermoluminescent determinations on terracottas from Esie give a possible date in the twelfth century. Meanwhile much smaller caches of soapstone carvings in the Esie style have come to light in two other Igbomina villages, Ofaro and Ijara.[32]

The people of Ila, the most southerly town of this area, sometimes claim to be distinct from the Igbomina, though their dialect is almost the same. Their ruler, the Orangun, who ranks as one of the leading Yoruba oba, claims descent from Ife rather than from Oyo,[33] some substance being given to this by the naming after him of the last of the sixteen *Odu* (prophetic poems) of the Ifa oracle. The impression of separateness may be in part due to the re-founding of Ila town after the fall of Old Oyo on a new, and probably more southerly, site[34] and to its subsequent inclusion in the Ibadan empire.[35] Furthermore, Ila came to be included during the colonial period in the Oyo Division of Western Nigeria rather than in the Ilorin Province of Northern Nigeria, and thus from 1967 was in the Western State of Nigeria rather than in Kwara State to which most of this area belongs.

Still further to the east, beyond the country of the Igbomina and the Ekiti, are the hills of the 'Kabba people', a name commonly misapplied in recent times to the small groups of Yoruba-speakers properly known as Abunu, Ikiri, Ijumu, Owe, Iyagba, and Oworo. Like the neighbouring Akoko of Ekitiland, these north-eastern Yoruba lack both the distinctive system of sacred kingship and the pantheon of gods common to most other Yoruba. Their chiefs rule only over villages and seem to derive their authority from their original roles as priests of the hill deities (*ebora*) rather than from their political positions. The Obaro of Owe (or Kabba) alone exercise a wider jurisdiction, but this seems to date only from the nineteenth century when the Nupe were attempting to dominate the area. Though most of the north-easterners claim to have migrated originally from Ife (or in one case from Oyo Ile), it has been suggested that they should rather be regarded as 'proto-Yoruba', indigenous to the land and adhering to a political organization which characterized the whole language group before it became 'the heritage of Oduduwa'. Lloyd dismisses this, arguing that their isolation has been insufficient 'to warrant the assertion that their social and political structures have remained unchanged',[36] but support for the view is provided by linguistic evidence (for which see Appendix II).

Owo

The kingdom of Owo lay athwart the approaches of Benin to southern Yorubaland. Its role could appropriately be described as that of a palatinate were it not that the Yoruba, despite their common language and claims to a common ancestry and culture, neither acted nor regarded themselves as a nation before the present century. The major units were the kingdoms, and among these Owo, although lying in an exposed position between the more powerful Oyo and Benin states, was one of the largest, its territory stretching from the Kabba country in the north (bordering the Nupe) and Akoko in the north-east to Okeluse, some 100 miles to the south. The importance of the kingdom is reflected in its *afin* which, containing over one hundred courtyards, is among the largest in Yorubaland. Every town and village in the kingdom was obliged to contribute to the maintenance of this vast building.[37]

Owo's historian, Chief Ashara,[38] has arranged his account under the reigns of twenty-nine rulers, the Olowo. The first was Ojugbelu, alternatively called Arere and Omolaghaiye, one of Ododuwa's sixteen sons; his pleasant manner earned him from his father yet another name, *Owo*, 'respectful', and this came to be applied to his followers and their descendants. According to Ashara, Ojugbelu was absent from Ife on a hunting trip when the dispersal of princes took place and was obliged to hasten after his brothers and force them by his sword to give up a share of their father's treasure – a story recalling that of the Owa of Ijesha. He then parted from them and, after a halt at Uji, settled with his followers at Upafa in the south of the present kingdom. Thence, under his son, the Owo removed first to Oke Imade and then, seeking a good supply of water, to Igbo Ogwata, now called Okiti Ashegbo, near the centre of the present Owo town. There was already dwelling here a group of people led by a ruler called the Elefene. For a time the Owo were content to live alongside them, but in a later reign they drove them out. Ashara, presumably working from tradition about the length of reign of each Olowo, has assigned a date at the beginning of the eleventh century to the foundation of the kingdom by Ojugbelu.

Ashara, whose history (like many local histories) has a strong 'authorized' flavour, maintains that 'from the first dynasty, Owo was never conquered nor defeated by any kingdom'. This does not accord with several references to Owo in Egharevba's history of Benin. The first occurs in the reign of Ewuare, whose army is said to have captured Owo after a severe battle, but Egharevba admits that the Benin general, Iken, was attacked and killed before he could leave the city, having sent on his soldiers in advance.[39] A few reigns later, under Oba Ozolua at Benin, Owo was again attacked by a Benin army, this time submitting without a fight.[40] Egharevba and Ashara agree, however, that Oshogboye, heir to Olowo Omaro, was sent as a young prince to Benin for his education at the Oba's court and enrolled as a page to the Oba (*emada*, literally 'sword-bearer').[41] When Omaro died, Oshogboye seems to have returned to Owo to claim the throne without first obtaining the Oba's permission to leave the palace, and when messengers were sent to him from Benin he feigned illness. As soon as his coronation had been performed, Oshogboye set about fortifying the town against an attack from Benin, causing a ditch to be dug (and presumably also erecting a wall). The *History of Owo* implies that an attack was made and repulsed, but Egharevba confines himself to saying that the Oba now 'confirmed' the Olowo's appointment and bade him continue the payment of tribute. What seems to emerge from these conflicting accounts is that the Owo were able to maintain virtual independence for their capital and surrounding district, but that from time to time tribute had to be paid to Benin and probably also that the southern parts of the Owo kingdom were subjected to control by the Bini in order to maintain access to the coast on the south-west (although, as will be seen in Chapter 6, a route by waterway leading to and across the lagoon was also used).

Like many Yoruba towns, Owo was a centre of brass-casting and of sculpture in wood, terracotta, and ivory. Here again the influence of Benin is evident, and Owo art has been described as 'intermediate between the Yoruba and Benin styles'.[42]

Ondo and the south-east, Ikale and Ilaje

South-west from Owo live the numerous people known as the Ondo, 'the settlers'. Ode Ondo, the capital and principal town, is situated in the north-west of their extensive but somewhat amorphous kingdom in a countryside much broken up by the same system of hills as that which covers Ekiti and much of Owo, and which has served as a protection against the Oyo and the Bini; from the latter Ondo must also have been shielded to some extent by Owo. But the eastern and southern parts of the kingdom were much affected by Benin influence and settlers, and the southern region, which stretches to the intricate system of creeks and lagoons on the western edge of the Niger Delta, has been peopled by other Yoruba and also non-Yoruba, especially the Ijo. The Yoruba themselves are essentially an inland race, and those now in the creeks and near the coast are almost certainly late settlers there. The Mahin, living by the lagoon and coastal beach of that name, and ruled by the Omopetu, seem to have no lengthy tradition of occupation of their area, while the community of the Holy Apostles of Aiyetoro was established as a sort of phalanstery or kibbutz on a desolate and remote part of the coast, unclaimed by any of the nearby peoples, only in 1947.[43]

There are three main accounts of the foundation of the Ondo kingship. Egharevba claims that it was founded by migrants from Benin in the time there of Oba Ozolua;[44] Johnson writes that it was founded from Oyo by a wife of Alafin Ajaka with her twin children, the king having sent them away from Oyo instead of complying with the custom of putting twins to death;[45] finally, there is a tradition preserved in Ondo itself which is similar to Johnson's account but substitutes Ife for Oyo and is in more specific terms and, moreover, is re-enacted annually at the oba's festival there.[46] According to the Ondo account, it was one of the wives of Oduduwa who gave birth to the twins, a circumstance which was regarded at Ife with such horror that the mother with the two babies was driven into the forest. One twin was a boy, and it was he who founded Epe, about ten miles to the north-west of Ondo. The other was a girl, Pupupu, who became founder of Ondo and whose son Airo was the second ruler there and the builder of the town walls. The present oba, entitled the Oshemawe, claims to be the forty-seventh to reign over the kingdom.[47] An unusual feature of the government of Ondo is the importance given to women. There is, for example, a council of women chiefs which has access to the council of males, and the Oshemawe's installation is carried out by the leading woman chief, the Lisa Labun. This may be held to derive from the origins of the kingship as related in the second and third of the accounts above, while the more sceptical may hold that the traditions were manufactured after the establishment of the kingship in order to explain and support an existing situation in which not only do women participate fully in government but the Ondo also, like the neighbouring Ijebu but unlike other Yoruba, trace their descent from the founders of their families through both male and female forebears.

Although Ondo, for reasons which are unrecorded, has far surpassed Epe, now a mere village within the kingdom, the seniority of the ruler of Epe, the Jegun, is acknowledged. As elsewhere, traces of settlers preceding the establishment of the present dynasty are found. Here they are the Idoko, a people who still form a separate group in Ondo with their own gods and who do not participate in the Ondo festivals.

To the south of the Ondo kingdom, among the creeks and lagoons behind the coastline, live the Ikale. Here, according to Forde, the towns were 'independent and self-governing', with their administration in the hands of the senior age-sets. The senior ruler, the Abodi of Ikoya, apparently exercised little power in pre-colonial times. Still nearer the coast is the homeland of the Ilaje, again speaking a distinctive dialect of Yoruba and with a common form of landholding but without large-scale political organization. Their settlements seem to be divided into two groups, one being the Mahin referred to above and the other coming under the authority of the Olugbo of Ugbo.[48]

NOTES

1. Forde, pp. 34–7.
2. S. Johnson (1921), pp. 20–2.
3. Kenyo, Ch. 5; S. Johnson (1921), pp. 23–4; Olajubu.
4. Kenyo, pp. 74–5; other accounts name Ibokun as the first settlement.
5. Kenyo, p. 74, lists thirty-seven previous Owa; an anonymous article in the *Daily Times* (Lagos) listed thirty-nine, but maintained that the present Owa was the forty-eighth to occupy the throne.
6. S. Johnson (1921), p. 21.
7. Kenyo, pp. 38, 65.
8. S. Johnson (1921), p. 156, places the founding both of Ede and Oshogbo in the reign of Alafin Kori, one of the pre-Igboho rulers. The present Timi of Ede is accounted the twenty-seventh on the throne, whereas only fifteen rulers are recollected as having reigned at Oshogbo, though six predecessors of Olarooye, the founder, are said to have reigned at Ipole. See Olugunna, pp. 12–21, and Beier (1960).
9. S. Johnson (1921), p. 25.
10. Ibid., p. 168.
11. Kenyo, pp. 77–82; Egharevba, p. 33; Abiola, pp. 44–5, 47–8.
12. P. 35.
13. S. Johnson (1921), p. 23; Ojo (1966a), pp. 125 (map), 126–9.
14. Oguntuyi, pp. 14, 180. The kingship of Ado is examined also by Lloyd (1960a).
15. Bradbury. Egharevba does not mention Ado under this reign, but writes that Ewuare 'fought against and captured 201 towns and villages in Ekiti, Ikare, Kukuruku, Eka and

the Ibo country on this side of the river Niger' (p. 14). See also Akintoye (1969b), *passim*.

16. In his article in *Odu* (n.d.) the Ogoga writes, 'Ikerre was the only town in Ekiti Division which conquered almost every town, village and hamlet in Ekiti, and itself was never conquered.' It sold its captives as slaves and did not trouble to make territorial annexations. Its successes were due to the weapons which were provided by Benin.

17. The following account of Akure is based on Arifalo, supplemented by Egharevba and Oguntuyi. The name 'Akure' has been said to signify 'the land of two rivers', although there is only one river which encircles the town. Another explanation is that it refers to the breaking (*re*) of the beads (*akum*) worn by the founding oba, Asodeboyede, as he made his way through the bush. This illustrates the difficulties which arise in the interpretation of Yoruba place-names. A reliable and systematic study of the subject is much needed.

18. Arifalo, Chs. III and IV.

19. Egharevba, p. 33, asserts that the Deji's title means 'the leopard killer'. S. Johnson (1921), p. 22, lists the Akure title as Ajanpanda.

20. Arifalo, p. 22.

21. Egharevba, p. 16.

22. Ibid., p. 32.

23. Ibid., pp. 45–7.

24. D. Williams (1967a), p. 15; Ibigbami (1977), *passim*.

25. For the history of Idanre, see Akindoju and Olagundoye, also Bridges and the anonymous article in *Nigeria Magazine*, 46.

26. Forde, p. 60.

27. This account is based on Elphinstone (1921), pp. 9–18, Temple (1919/1965), pp. 446–521, and Stevens (1978), Chapter II. Additional material was kindly given by Dr W. Abimbola, of the University of Ife, and Mr O. A. Ajolore, of the University of Lagos, in personal communications.

28. Elphinstone, p. 15, lists seventeen Igbomina 'headmen', but of these several are in fact Ekiti rulers. Kenyo includes a still greater number in his lists.

29. S. Johnson (1921), p. 109.

30. Forde, p. 74; Temple, p. 390, who treats Igbona (*sic*) and Igbolo as synonymous; S. Johnson (1921), p. 13, lists Offa with a query among the towns of Oyo's Ibolo province.

31. Hermon-Hodge, pp. 97–101.

32. Stevens (1978), *passim*. Also see Obayemi in Ajayi and Crowder, Vol. I, pp. 232–3, about possible connexions of the carvings with an Oba state.

33. Kenyo, p. 51.

34. Elphinstone, p. 16.

35. There is an account of Ila in 1859 by May, who describes it (p. 221) as the principal Igbomina town and reports the presence of an Ibadan resident (ajele) there.

36. Lloyd in Biobaku (ed.) (1973), pp. 208–9.

37. Ojo (1966b), pp. 23–4, 64–6.

38. In addition, see the article on the Igogo festival in *Nigeria Magazine*, 77 (1963); this is based on information from the Olowo and a manuscript by Chief J. D. Akeredolu.

39. Egharevba, p. 15.

40. Ibid., p. 24.

41. Egharevba, pp. 33–4; Ashara, p. 10.

42. Willett (1967), pp. 180–1; Willett in Biobaku (1973), p. 132; Eyo (1976). For 'Yoruba' in Willett's phrase, perhaps 'Ife' should be substituted.

43. See Barrett (1977).

44. Egharevba, p. 37.

45. S. Johnson (1921), p. 25.

46. Beier (1956a), *passim*.

47. Kenyo, p. 49.

48. Forde, pp. 63–4; Akintoye (1971), p. 126, fn. 67.

FIVE

KINGDOMS OF THE WEST
Ketu, Shabe, and Dassa

The western kingdoms of the Yoruba lie for the most part beyond the frontiers of Nigeria in the neighbouring state of Bénin (formerly Dahomey) – the latter a French creation in the same sense that Nigeria was created by the British, and taking its original name from the Fon kingdom in the south-east of the country which had Abomey as its capital. There are some 200,000 Yoruba speakers in Bénin, where they form about 9 per cent of the population, living in their towns and villages in the centre and south of the country, and they even extend into Togo still farther to the west. By the French administrators they were called Anago, Nago or Nagot, a word probably deriving from an opprobrious nickname given them by the Fon and which is also applied to a specific group of western Yoruba (see pages 70–1 below).[1]

Like other Yoruba, those of the west formed themselves into kingdoms. The two most important of these, Ketu and Shabe in central Bénin, trace their origins to the dispersal of princes from Ife, while a third, Dassa, seems to be of less antiquity. To the west of these former states, and spilling over the Togo frontier, are the groups of Yoruba speakers known as Itsha or Sha; it has been suggested that at a remote period they migrated westwards from the neighbourhood of Ilesha, but there seems little basis for this beyond a superficial resemblance in the names.[2] A separate small group, which extends to the vicinity of Atakpame in Togo, is known as the Ife and claims to have migrated direct from Ile Ife. To the south of Ketu lie the marshlands of the Ahori or Holli. Asiwaju has described Ohori Ije as 'a small but very vigorous Yoruba kingdom' with strong traditions of independence, but little is known of its pre-colonial history.[3] On the coastal lagoon the small Egun (Aja) kingdom of Porto Novo (also known as Ajashe, New Allada or Little Ardra) seems to have come under the 'protection' of Oyo in the 1770s, falling later under the influence of Dahomey. In the hinterland of Porto Novo and stretching north to Pobe a number of once-independent towns and districts preserve traditions of migration from various parts of Yorubaland.[4] Finally, the Fon themselves are usually held to descend from a fusion of Aja conquerors with indigenous Yoruba living on the Abomey plateau.

Apart from that of Ketu, the histories of all these Yoruba are exceptionally complex and confused. Their kingdoms and chieftancies, situated precariously among other peoples and separated from each other by alien territories, were neither sufficiently large nor well organized to contain the external dangers which beset them in the eighteenth and nineteenth centuries. In the south the Egun (like the Fon, a branch of the numerous Aja-speaking peoples) and the Fon attacked, infiltrated, and overran their homelands; farther inland their enemies included the Fon again, the Borgu, then the Fulani of Ilorin, and even their kinsmen from Oyo and Egba – the latter, indeed, were known to the Sha as 'the sons of war' (*omojagun*). The impression which emerges is that these were the advance guard of a migration which finally petered out, leaving them in an exposed position far from the centres of Yoruba life and sources of strength.

Ketu

An account of the westward migration from Ile Ife which resulted in the founda-tions of Ketu and Shabe was recorded by the Yoruba missionary, and later Bishop, S. A. Crowther, in Ketu in 1853 and was used by Parrinder in his *Story of Ketu*.[5] Under the leadership of Shopasan,[6] a grandson of Oduduwa, the migrants crossed the Ogun river and then split into three groups: the first, under Shopasan and his nephew Owe, moved westwards and eventually founded Ketu; the second travel-led first to the north-west and then was forced south again, founding the kingdom of Shabe, while the third, according to this account, turned north up the Ogun and eventually founded the kingdom of Oyo. The first party settled on the hill known as Oke Oyan, apparently in the vicinity of Shaki (the River Oyan is a tributary of the Ogun), and later moved to Aro, where Shopasan died and was succeeded as leader by Owe.[7]

In the reign of the seventh oba, Ede, another migration took place, and this, like the original one from Ife, also split into three parties: one founded a village called Idofa after the hunter who was its leader, the second settled in Ibarapa country at Igbo Ora, and the third, apparently the principal one, under Ede and guided by the hunter Alalumon, settled on the present site of Ketu, building their town around an iroko tree (whose alleged fragments can still be seen). Tradition recounts that Ede was accompanied from Aro by 120 families, the founders of the present wards of Ketu town. The history of the journey from Aro to Ketu is re-enacted during the installation ceremonies of the ruler, the Alaketu. One principal event which is recalled is the borrowing of fire by Alalumon on the first night at Ketu from Ya Panka, an old woman who was found living a few miles to the south. Apart from this episode, there are other indications that the Ketu encountered people already in occupation of parts of their new homeland; Parrinder considers that these cannot have been Yoruba,[8] but there is not sufficient evidence for an assertion either way.

The traditions of Ketu have been unusually well preserved and recorded. The list of Alaketu, which numbers forty-nine (including the oba who was installed in 1963), is one to which considerable weight can be attached, since it was the special duty of a herald, the Baba Elegun Oyede, to recite the names and parentages of all preceding Alaketu during the coronation ceremonies. Moreover, approximate dates of reasonable reliability can be assigned to reigns from the eighteenth century onwards, partly (as in the case of Oyo) by cross-reference to the history of Dahomey as recorded by European writers.

Today the most striking feature of Ketu, now a remote and neglected town, is its fortifications, comprising a circuit of massive earthern walls, still in some places over twelve feet in height and nearly as broad, outer ditches to a depth of some eight or nine feet and twenty feet wide, planted with thorns, and above all the great Idena ('Sentry') Gate, a fortress in itself with inner and outer covered gateways and a central courtyard, certainly the most impressive example of Yoruba military architecture in existence.[9] Ketu historians attribute the building of these fortifications to Sha, the fourteenth Alaketu, and add that the oba himself supervised the work, which was accomplished by the townspeople with the aid of two giants living nearby. The Idena Gate is said to stand upon the place where Ede first entered the site of his new capital and where later a hunchbacked weaver, one of those already living on the spot when the immigrants from Ife arrived, was killed as a propitiatory sacrifice – a circumstance from which the town and kingdom are said to derive their name (a proverb in the form of a riddle: *Ke 'tu ike? Ke fo ilu?*: 'Who can straighten a hunchback's hump? Who can break our town?'). Sha's successor, Alaketu Epo, completed the fortifications, and it is claimed that to give strength to the walls the clay was mixed with palm oil instead of water.

The extent of the kingdom can only be tentatively described. On the east it included Meko, some twenty miles distant from Ketu (and now within Nigeria). This had been founded as a farm from Ketu and gradually grew into a town whose wards retained the names of the different areas of Ketu whence the inhabitants had come. During the 1860s a dispute arose over the Bale of Meko's claim to wear a crown and to rank as an oba, and eventually Meko seceded and paid tribute to New Oyo. But even down to the present time the subordination of Meko to Ketu is recalled by its inclusion in the ceremonial itineration of his kingdom by a new Alaketu, though he now has to cross a modern international frontier in performing this. To the west the kingdom was probably bounded by the River Weme (Ouéme), while on the north the Okpara seems to have separated Ketu from Shabe territory.

For the first centuries of its existence – perhaps for some 400 years if the suggestions about chronology in Chapters 1 and 7 are near the truth – the history of Ketu seems to have been uneventful. It may be that the passage of time has simply erased all record of triumph and disaster. On the other hand, it is equally likely, and somewhat more probable, that in this early period, when the Guinea forest and its hinterland were much denser[10] and more lightly inhabited than in modern times, a city state or small kingdom would be able to protect itself and to expand without much fear of disturbance or even much contact with outsiders. But if this happy isolation lasted up to the seventeenth century, conditions changed considerably in the following century. Ketu found itself in the path of the encroaching Oyo, a related state but none the less an aggressive neighbour, and for a period, probably of a hundred years or more, it seems to have been subject or tributary to the Alafin, though doubtless regarded as a distant and unimportant vassal when shorn of those areas where Oyo had erected its satellites to guard the route to the coast. Two of Oyo's subordinate rulers, whose territories had apparently been previously a part of Ketu, the Elehin Odo of Ifonyin and the Oniko of Ikolaje, are remembered as having been accustomed to travel in company with the Alaketu to pay their annual tribute of thatching grass to the Alafin.

But Oyo was not the only, nor in latter days the most dangerous, menace to the peace of Ketu. On the west the kingdom found itself confronted by the powerful Fon state of Dahomey.[11] From the reign of Agaja in the early nineteenth century, the Dahomeans had been intent upon controlling territory along the coast. As has been seen in Chapter 3, they came into conflict in this region with the Oyo, a conflict which resulted in the imposition of tribute on Abomey by Oyo. But Dahomey showed great powers of recovery, and the peace settlements of 1730 were followed by a rebuilding and consolidation of strength which enabled the kingdom to retain its hold on the slave port of Whydah and the coast as far east as Badagry. It was also extending to the north-west, and after a war with the Asante agreed upon a new frontier with that state. In 1789 the Dahomeans invaded Ketu for the first time. According to Dalzel, they crushed all resistance and carried off many captives, but Ketu tradition claims that they confined themselves to pillaging the nearby village of Iwoye and abstained from an attack on Ketu itself. Whatever the truth about this first encounter, Ketu was destined, like much of western Yorubaland, to suffer dreadfully at the hands of the Dahomeans in the next century.

Shabe

Ketu tradition describes how the westward migration of the Yoruba from Ife split into three groups after crossing the River Ogun. The second of these, under the 'youngest prince' in the Ketu version, moved north-west and settled at Kilibo, 'the forest of lions', whence they were forced southwards again to the hills of Shabe, where they established their capital.[12] A rather different version of what is nevertheless recognizably the same legend was gathered at Shabe by Fr Moulero, who relates that Saloube, the leader of the Shabe migration, was the senior of the princes, and that his group, after separating from the others at Oke Oyan, moved north into Borgu, where Saloube died. Here his followers founded the town of Parakou. Only under their third leader, Adjongou, and after an intermediate settlement at Tchaourou, did they come to Kilibo, where they remained for the duration of nine reigns. Finally, under pressure from their Borgu neighbours they retreated southwards into the Shabe hills. Here they encountered a people called the Ojodou, whom they defeated after a series of battles, some of whose sites are still remembered and one of which lasted five days.[13]

Fr Moulero has recorded the names of twenty-one rulers of the Shabe, from the exodus from Ife until 1848. These include only five rulers at Shabe itself, and the list seems, therefore, to be incomplete, especially when it is compared with that for Ketu, which at forty-two for what professes to be the same period is twice the length of that of Shabe. A recent study of the history of Shabe by Asiwaju shows that the Ife rulers there were ousted, probably 'somewhere in the middle of the eighteenth century', by a new dynasty from Boko in Borgu. Thereafter the kingship and the leading chieftaincies were held by Boko families, while subordinate chieftaincies continued to be filled by the Amushu, or Ife, group.[14]

As regards its physical boundaries, the kingdom of Shabe can be described as occupying the confluence of the rivers Weme and Okpara and as extending north to Tchaourou. Today, however, this area is by no means inhabited solely or continuously by the Shabe, and in recent years groups of Mahi and Dassa have been settling there. This may imply that the kingdom was never populous, or it may reflect the external troubles which beset it, especially in the last century, when after absorbing for several hundred years the menace of powerful neighbours to the north, Borgu and Oyo, it was attacked by newer powers, the Fulani of Ilorin, the Fon of Abomey, and even their distant Yoruba neighbours from Abeokuta and Ijaye.

Dassa

About thirty miles south-west of Shabe and forty miles north-west from Ketu is the town known in French-speaking Bénin as Dassa-Zoumé, capital of the former kingdom of the Dassa, or perhaps more accurately, Idassa. A list of twenty-six rulers has been compiled for this kingdom,[15] beginning with Jagou Olofin, the founder of the dynasty, who according to tradition came from Egbaland. A peculiar feature of the kingship is that it passes from a ruler to all his children in turn, including apparently women, and then to the eldest son of the first king of the preceding generation (excluding the children of the female rulers). The twenty-six rulers in the list – which includes two women – are arranged in nine generations, and from this it has been calculated, on the basis of allowing thirty years to each generation, that the kingdom was founded about 1700.

Little is known about the history of the Dassa. There is some recollection among them of pressure from Oyo, under a leader called in their tradition Adjinakou, a name which does not occur in the list of Alafin but may refer to an Oyo general (and is probably more correctly 'Ajanaku' or 'Elephant'). During the first part of the nineteenth century the Dassa found themselves harassed, like the Ketu and the Shabe, by the Dahomeans under their powerful warrior-king Ghezo, and they withdrew for greater safety to their hill-tops. Here they founded the present town of Dassa-Zoumé as a strong place.

John Duncan, a Scot who had been a member of the Niger Expedition of 1841, passed over the Dassa mountains on his return from Abomey in 1846. He describes the towns there as 'large and well-peopled, and their positions judiciously selected for defence'. The Dassa, whom he calls 'Anagoos', were skilful in manufacturing iron and possessed a particularly virulent poison into which they dipped their arrows. Thus they had so far succeeded in repelling the assaults of their numerous enemies.[16]

NOTES

1. Parrinder (1947), p. 122; Forde, pp. 42–7 and map.
2. Parrinder (1947), pp. 125–6; Forde, pp. 42–4; Cornevin, p. 56. In addition to the town of the Ijesha, there is at least one other Ilesha in Yorubaland, that lying on the Dahomean frontier north of Shaki.
3. Asiwaju (1974), pp. 258–9.
4. Law (1971), p. 26, n. 8; Parrinder (1947), p. 124; Cornevin, pp. 48–9, 89.
5. Parrinder (1956), p. 12 and *passim*. Parrinder also makes use of the work of Dunglas

and Moulero. For an account of the government of Ketu, see Asiwaju in Crowder and Ikime (1970), pp. 137–8.
6. Parrinder (1956) spells this name 'Sho-ipashan' (see his discussion on p. 11).
7. Parrinder (1956) writes that Shopasan was buried at Oke Oyan (which he spells 'Oke-Awyan') and Owe at Aro in the Ogun shrine there.
8. Parrinder (1956), pp. 16–17.
9. See Parrinder (1956), pp. 21–2, 76–7, and Ajayi and Smith, p. 27 and Plan 1.
10. Ojo (1966a), p. 53.
11. Argyle, Ch. II, especially p. 24; Parrinder (1956), pp. 31–5.
12. Parrinder (1956), p. 12.
13. Moulero, *passim*; Cornevin, pp. 51–6, based on Couchard, Dunglas, and Moulero; Asiwaju (1973), pp. 24–5, based on Palau-Marti; also see George, pp. 23–4.
14. Asiwaju (1973), p. 24.
15. Parrinder (1947), p. 126; Forde, p. 42 and map; Cornevin, pp. 156–8, based on Palau-Marti.
16. Duncan, II, Ch. VIII.

SIX

KINGDOMS OF THE SOUTH
Ijebu, Egba, Egbado, and Lagos

It has already been suggested that the Yoruba, as their traditions indicate, are in origin an inland people who had moved south from the savannah into the ever-deepening forest but had not until comparatively recent times settled near the coast. Among their major towns, only Lagos, founded apparently some centuries after the other kingdoms and not attaining importance until the eighteenth century, lies near the sea; Ile Ife is some eighty miles inland, and Oyo Ile, on the savannah edge, was 200 miles from the sea. Snelgrave was told of the Oyo that, 'For as their national *Fetiche* was the sea, they were prohibited by their Priests from ever seeing it, under no less a Penalty than Death.'[1] So far as is known, the Yoruba did not venture on the open sea until modern times, and it plays little part in their oral literature.

Nevertheless, the inhabitants of the southern kingdoms, Ijebu, Awori, and Egbado, must have been aware of the great and mysterious ocean which washed the boundaries of their land. The fishermen on the lagoon knew that these placid waters were separated by only a narrow strip of land from the tumultuous Atlantic waves. Among their gods, they numbered Olokun, owner of the sea, and Olokunsu his wife, goddess of the bar which runs eastward from the entrance to the Lagos lagoon to the Niger Delta. The health-giving properties of salt water were known, according to the Ijesha legend, at the far-off court of Ife. Then, towards the end of the fifteenth century, outsiders began to appear, coming from the sea. With their arrival, at first few in number, new developments in religion, trade, and government began, very gradually, to disclose themselves.

Ijebu

Twelve or thirteen leagues upstream from Lagos [wrote the Portuguese Duarte Pacheco Pereira in the first years of the sixteenth century] there is a large town called Geebuu, surrounded by a very large ditch. The river of this country is called in our days Agusale, and the trade which one can conduct here is the trade in slaves, who are sold for brass bracelets, at a rate of twelve to fifteen bracelets for a slave, and in elephants' tusks.[2]

61

Plate 8   Crossing a river in Yorubaland. From the *Church Missionary Gleaner*, 1856.

This seems to be the first clear mention in writing of any of the Yoruba kingdoms – 'Geebu' must be Ijebu Ode, while the 'river . . . Agusale' could be the Oshun or the Ogun but is more likely a miscopying of the Portuguese word for 'king' (*rey*) followed by the usual title, 'Awujale', borne by the rulers of Ijebu Ode. It is significant that this early account should refer to the commerce of the kingdom for the Ijebu, though hard-working farmers, are still better-known today as traders and middlemen, energetic and enterprising. Although the Portuguese never took the interest in Ijebu which they showed in Benin – probably because their reports of the trade in the Lagos lagoon were less encouraging than for other parts of West Africa and also because of the difficulty of access – *Ciudad do Jubu* continued to be marked on their maps in the sixteenth and seventeenth centuries, and there is a belief in Ijebu Ode that Portuguese traders once lived in the town. Two Portuguese ships are recorded as having gone to Ijebu in 1553, while Portuguese and probably also Dutch were trading there in slaves and cloth in the 1620s.[3] Eventually Ijebu disappeared from the records, cut off (Law considers) from direct contact with Europeans by the increasing importance of Lagos at the sea entrance to the lagoon until, 300 years after Pacheco, Captain John Adams writes of the same trade in slaves being conducted there and also mentions the export of 'Jaboo cloth'.[4] In one sense, however, it was inappropriate that the Ijebu should have just come to the early attention of Europeans since their reputation has long been one of hostility to strangers – meaning not only foreigners but all non-Ijebu – as well as of intense local patriotism. *Ijebu-Ode ajeji ko wo: bi ajeji ba wo laro, won a fi sebo lale* – 'Ijebu-Ode, a town forbidden to strangers; if a stranger entered it in the morning, he was sure to be made a sacrifice in the evening.'

The Ijebu kingdom was a large one, probably next in size to Oyo. At its greatest extent it stretched south-westward to the confines of Lagos and eastward across the River Shasha to the Oni; on the west it bordered the country of the Egba, on the north the Oyo, on the north-east the Ife, and on the east the Ondo. Most of this area of some 2,000 or 3,000 square miles is covered by rain-forest, still dense in places, but nevertheless it is a fertile land (though the soil has often proved rather too light for the spread of the cocoa tree). The south of the kingdom encompassed the coastal lagoon whose waters were fished by the inhabitants of the villages on the shore, while the farther side of the lagoon was a remote and sparsely inhabited land of swamps, creeks, and sandy wastes, bordered by the empty beaches beaten by the Atlantic.

The capital of the kingdom and seat of the senior ruler, the Awujale, was the centrally placed town of Ijebu Ode. But although the culture of the Ijebu is homogeneous and all speak the same dialect, their political organization has always been fragmented. The Awujale was recognized as first among their numerous oba rather than as king of all Ijebu. After the Ode the next largest group was the Remo, their capital now being Shagamu, the seat not only of the Akarigbo (of Ofin), the leading Remo oba, but also of three other crowned oba (the Ewusi, the Elepe, and the Amunisan) and the heads of the other former towns (there were in all thirteen) which concentrated here for greater security in 1872. Other towns in the kingdom with crowned oba were Idowa, Ago Iwoye, Ijebu Igbo, Owu Ikija, and Ijebu Ife, ruled respectively by the Dagburewe, the Ebumawe, the Orimolusi, the Olowu, and the Ajalorun.

Plate 9   A rustic bridge in Ijebu. From a Church Missionary Society journal.

Accounts of the foundation of the Ijebu kingdom describe three separate migrations into the area. The first was led by Olu Iwa, who settled at Iwode, now a part of Ijebu Ode town. His two companions, Ajebu and Olode, marked out the boundaries of the new land and town respectively, and the name 'Ijebu Ode' is said to derive from the combination of their names (though an alternative explanation is that *ijebu* means 'food of the deep' and refers to the supposed descent of the people from victims sacrificed by an Oba of Benin to the sea, while *ode* is used both in Yorubaland and elsewhere, for example among the Itschekri, to mean 'town'). Then a second group arrived, led by Arisu, and settled in the district known as Ijasi. The third migration was the most important, since it was led from Ife by Ogborogan, afterwards called Obanta and recognized as founder of the kingdom and first Awujale.

The legend of Obanta relates that he was a son of Oduduwa by a daughter of Olu Iwa. After the dispersal of princes from Ile Ife he travelled first east to Imesi and then south through Ondo before turning towards Ijebu. During this journey he was involved in many adventures, some of which are recalled in the elaborate ceremonial journey undertaken by a new Awujale before his installation,[5] and gained numerous adherents to his party. At Igbo he defeated the local ruler in a wrestling match, and from this derived his title, 'one who understands the art of wrestling on land'. (Johnson gives a different explanation, saying that an ilari was sent from Oyo during the reign of Alafin Jayin to adjudicate in a land dispute between Iseyin and Owu Ipole; this ilari later became ruler of Ijebu, and the title of Awujale derived from his name Agbeja-ile, 'an arbiter in a quarrel over land'.[6]) On entering Ijebu Ode Ogborogan was at once acclaimed by the inhabitants, who called out *oba wa nita*, 'the king is outside': hence the name 'Obanta' by which this founding hero is widely known. There now ensued a dispersal of princes rather like that from Itajero, Obanta sending his followers, among whom was Akarigbo, son of the Olu of Igbo, to rule over different parts of the land.

It will be noticed that, like most of the Yoruba legends of origin, the account of Obanta refers to a people already in occupation of the land before the arrival of the party from Ife. Here these included both Obanta's predecessors at Ijebu Ode in the first two migrations and also those whom Obanta met during his journey, especially the Olu Igbo, ancestor of the Akarigbo, and the Oloko of Idoko, who may have ruled a kingdom once more powerful than Ijebu. It has also been suggested that the cult of Agemo, the supreme deity of the Ijebu (to whom the other Yoruba gods seem to have been considered subordinate) and worshipped all over their country, originated not with Obanta, as is held by the orthodox, but in an earlier society.[7]

Obanta's descendants reigned after him on the Ijebu throne. As with most Yoruba monarchs, the Awujale's power was strictly circumscribed by his chiefs and councils: 'The Awujale did nothing for himself, though everything was done in his name.'[8] According to Ijebu custom, only a man born to a reigning oba – one of those called *abidagba* – might succeed to the throne, and the candidates were chosen in rotation from four branches of the royal house. But in 1960 these rules were set aside in favour of the present oba, the fifty-second (or, in another list, fifty-eighth) Awujale, a grandson but not a son of a previous ruler.

Tradition relates that during the reign of the thirteenth Awujale there was a split in the succession to the kingdom. This ruler fell ill, and after nominating his brother as regent left the capital to seek a cure in the small town of Idowa, a few miles to the south-west. When he recovered he found himself prevented by his brother from resuming his rule. Eventually the brothers agreed that the former Awujale should remain as an oba at Idowa and should take a share of the kingdom's regalia. The present ruler of Idowa, the Dagburewe, claims descent from this Awujale and is guardian of a fine collection of antique crowns and effigies (*okute*) of his royal ancestors.[9]

A testimony to the greatness of Ijebu's past, and probably also to the pre-eminence of Ijebu Ode among the other divisions of the kingdom, is the survival of much of the course of the vast earthwork known as the Eredo. This mud-built rampart (which may justifiably be identified with Pacheco's 'very large ditch')[10] has a circuit of some eighty miles and appears to enclose an area of some 400 square miles around the town of Ijebu Ode. It is still in places twenty feet high, with an outer ditch of twenty to twenty-five feet in depth. Legend describes it as the creation of Sungbo, a wealthy but childless woman who caused it to be built as a memorial to herself. But it has been suggested more prosaically that it may have been constructed in two phases, the eastern section being intended for the defence of the Idoko kingdom, which possibly preceded Ijebu as the power in this area, and the western section being a later fortification for Obanta's capital. There does not seem as yet much evidence to support this hypothesis, nor can the intention of the builders be confidently determined. The function of the Eredo in marking the limits of the Awujale's immediate area of authority – his *Hausmacht*, so to speak – was probably as significant as its use as a fortification, though doubtless these two roles were, as so often elsewhere, complementary. Meanwhile the Eredo awaits archaeological investigation, and especially a detailed survey of its course.

Tradition in Ijebu throws little light on the external relations of the kingdom. There are tenuous reports of contact with the Portuguese, but nothing to support or contest the claims of first the Oyo and then the Bini to have subjected Ijebu by arms. In the case of Oyo there is a tradition there[11] that Alafin Ajagbo (probably reigning in the seventeenth century) entered Ijebu Ode with his army and installed his candidate Fesojoye as Awujale. That there was a war about this time with Oyo is confirmed at Ijebu Ode, and Fesojoye appears on Olushola's king-list as thirty-sixth Awujale (out of a total of 57 to 1959). Johnson, describing the circuit of Yorubaland by the army of Alafin Ojigi in the early eighteenth century, implies that the expedition passed through Ijebu territory on its return to Oyo via the Popo country, and in his account of the extent of the Oyo kingdom under Agbolaje later in the century he includes Ijebu within the boundaries.[12] But an Oyo cavalry force would have encountered tremendous difficulty in penetrating the rain-forest, and for the Oyo to have retained political or military control here for any length of time seems almost impossible. With regard to Egharevba's assertion that Ijebu was conquered by the Bini in the reign of Oba Ozolua and ruled by them 'for some years',[13] Ijebu tradition is similarly silent. Yet Dapper, in his *Description de l'Afrique* of 1686, writes that the King of 'Jaboe', by which Ijebu must be meant, was one of the Oba of Benin's vassals.[14] There is no doubt that at some time before 1700 Benin had extended its influence along the coast to the west of Ijebu and had erected a tributary state at Lagos. This suggests that the Bini controlled at least the southern parts of Ijebu territory linking them to Lagos and the coast beyond. But it seems probable that they depended for their communications mainly on the waterways, passing through the creeks around Mahin and across the lagoon, quicker and more convenient than the land route and less provocative to the Ijebu. Finally, from the early eighteenth century onwards, the Dahomeans to the west were a growing menace to Yoruba security, despite the checks administered to them by the Oyo. Snelgrave mentions what may have been an attack on Ijebu by a Dahomean army in or about 1731.[15] But nothing else is known of this war, and even if it took place it seems unlikely that the Dahomeans obtained any major results from an ambitious push so far to the east of their kingdom.

Meanwhile the Ijebu continued both to keep away strangers from their towns and to play their profitable role of traders and middlemen, principally supplying slaves to the Atlantic trade in competition with the Oyo and importing European cloth and miscellanous goods. According to Clapperton, Ijebu merchants used to travel into Nupe before the outbreak of the civil wars there, and in 1826 their cloth was still being sold as far north as 'Koolfu' (Kolfo).[16] Apart from their ports of Ejinrin and Epe at the north-east corner of the lagoon, the Remo town of Ikorodu at the north-west corner developed a famous market, and in the nineteenth century the Ijebu were able to control the important trade in firearms between Lagos and the interior through this market. Their commercial ability has never deserted them, and today their country still looks more prosperous than other parts of Yorubaland, with its many 'storey houses' and the Brazilian-style mansions which were built at the end of the last century.

Egba and Owu

Since about 1830 the Egba have been concentrated in their great metropolis of Abeokuta, the town 'under the rock', and in the surrounding district on both sides of the River Ogun. Until the collapse of the Oyo and the outbreak of the civil wars in the early part of the last century, however, the Egba state – or the 'Egba forest' as it is more distinctively called – extended considerably farther to the north-east than the present area of Egbaland, and included the sites of Ibadan, Ijaye, and other towns which were subsequently occupied by refugees from the Oyo kingdom. Ajisafe[17] describes old Egbaland as stretching 'from the river Oba on the north to Ebute-Metta on the south, and from Oshun River on the east to Ipokia with Yewa River on the west'. This, as regards the southern and western boundaries at least, is probably too extensive, but in any case the Egba frontiers marched with the Ife and Ijesha kingdoms on the east, Ijebu to the south and south-east, Egbado on the south-west, Ketu on the west, and Oyo to the north. Much of this area is covered by the rain-forest; the name 'Egba' is itself said to be a contraction from *egbalugbo*, 'the wanderers towards the forest'.

Like the Ijebu, the Egba were ruled as a federation rather than centrally, and Egba towns, said by Ajisafe to be 'not less than three hundred in number', were grouped into three provinces.[18] The largest and most northerly province was that of Egba Agura (or Gbagura), said to consist of 144 towns of which seventy-two owed allegiance to the Agura in his capital at Iddo and seventy-two to the Onigun of Ilugun; later the Agura became predominant over most of the area except Ilugun, which then adhered to the province of Oke Ona. This second province, Egba Oke Ona, was so called from its situation to the south-west of the River Ona in the vicinity of the Ijebu Remo. The principal oba was the Oshile (or Oloko) of

Oko. The third province, which occupied the south-west of the Egba forest, was that of Egba Alake. This was originally called Egba Agbeyin and subject to the Ojoko of Kesi, who was later displaced as leading oba by the Alake, whose capital was at Ake, but who was chosen by king-makers from the five sister towns (*omo iya*) of Ijeun, Kemta, Iporo, Itoku, and Ake. Among the provincial heads the Alake came to be accepted as senior, followed by the Oshile, the Agura, and the Onigun. The different towns within the provinces also had their oba, but in the whole kingdom only the Alake, the Oshile, and the Agura wore beaded crowns. All the major rulers now live with their peoples in their several sections of the town of Abeokuta, where they were joined by a fourth crowned oba, the Olowu, and his followers from the ruined town of Owu, and later still by Oyo refugees from Ijaye. The sites of many of the original towns have long been abandoned, their ruins being now barely discernible in the bush or in other cases obliterated and forgotten, but a few, such as Ilugun and Iddo, are again prosperous villages, and some, such as Ikereku, have been refounded on new sites.

The organization of the Egba suggests that their entry into the forest took place in three or four migrations, each associated with one of the provinces. Biobaku considers that the first to arrive were the Gbagura, settling in the north, then the Oke-Ona, followed by the Agbeyin, who went farthest to the south; the arrival of the Alake with his followers represented 'probably a fourth and certainly the last major wave of migration into the Egba Forest'.[19] Johnson maintains that the Egba rulers mostly descend from the Esho, the warriors of Oyo, and cites in connection with this the absence of a distinct royal family and the consequent eligibility of any Egba, whatever his birth, to be chosen as oba.[20] Although some towns, for example, Ilugun, are indeed said to have been founded from Oyo, Egba traditions for the most part look to Ife for the origins of their towns. It is in particular maintained that Ajalake, the first Alake, was a son (or grandson) of Oduduwa who after the dispersal of the Ife princes travelled and for a time settled with the Alaketu – a tradition which receives some support at Ketu.[21] The tradition continues that Omonide ('child of brass' – the most precious metal then known), mother (or grandmother) of the founding princes, had a special love for the Alake which led her to settle with him in the Egba forest. After her death every new Alafin sent presents to the Alake because of Omonide's burial in his town. The prestige accruing to the Alake from his legendary membership of the house of Oduduwa may account for his success in replacing the Ojoko of Kesi as the leading southern oba of the Egba, though it seems equally possible that the tradition was the result rather than the cause of his ascendancy. The Egba account explains his rise in more material terms since, according to this, the Alake overcame the Ojoko by first breaking his monopoly in the supply to the other Egba of corn, which only the Kesi knew how to grow; his capital at Ijoko was then destroyed and its ruler killed.

There seems no doubt that the Egba were subjected to the empire of Oyo at some period since, in addition to both Egba and Oyo traditions about this, a considerable assimilation of culture and governmental practice seems to have taken place; this can be observed especially in the case of the northern Egba, the Gbagura. How and when the Egba came to accept Oyo domination is not known, but it seems likely that this occurred during the century following the return of the Alafin from Igboho to Oyo Ile; Biobaku suggests that the situation evolved peaceably, the Egba having (he asserts) no military organization capable of defending their land

and so being prepared to pay tribute to Oyo in return for protection.[22] But this Oyo overlordship came to be increasingly resented. The Alafin placed his ajele in the Egba towns to represent him and to collect annual tribute, and the presence and exactions of these officials, who had become 'the lords of even the kings',[23] eventually provoked a national rising.

The liberator and hero of the Egba was Lishabi, born at Itoku and living in Igbein, both in the Alake's province. He is remembered as a man of gigantic stature, and his career shows that he was a great organizer and leader. At first he worked in secret, grouping his followers into the Egbe Aro, a society of farmers pledged to help each other in their work. This society gradually extended over the whole of Egbaland and at the same time changed its character, becoming an underground army, the Egbe Olorogun. When the time was ripe, Lishabi gave the signal for a general rising by killing the ajele in his own town of Igbein, and from here the movement spread through the Egbe to all the other towns of the land. Tradition claims that over 600 of the Oyo ajele were massacred in this rising. The Alafin replied by sending a large army, make up of Oyo, Ibarapa, and Egbado troops, against the rebels. This army crossed the Ogun at Mokoloki and advanced towards Igbein. Lishabi now showed his qualities as a general. Having ordered the town to be evacuated, he concealed his followers in the nearby Melego ravine and then, as the Oyo searched the deserted town, fell upon them, routing them and gaining at one stroke independence for his people.

It is uncertain at what point in the decline of Oyo this revolt of the Egba occurred. Circumstances suggest that it may have been at some time during the long reign of Alafin Abiodun; Biobaku places it during the disturbance at Oyo which resulted in the downfall of Bashorun Gaha, and Akinjogbin considers that it was in those latter years of Abiodun which also saw the unsuccessful Oyo campaigns against the Borgu (1783) and Nupe (1791).[24] But tradition in the Oyo kingdom, as recorded by the Bada of Shaki, places the revolt during the short regency of Bashorun Ashamu at Oyo after the suicide of Alafin Awole, and therefore in or about 1796 or 1797.[25] This would accord with what is known of the general military and political decline which had set in at Oyo by the end of the eighteenth century and also with developments among the Egba under Lishabi and up to the opening of the long wars of the nineteenth century in Yorubaland.

Lishabi's role was not confined to winning independence for the Egba. Biobaku describes him as the Egba Lycurgus who gave his people laws. He was yet more than that. He taught them the art of defending themselves by arms and fortifications, so that they were able to throw back the raids of their fierce neighbours, the Dahomeans. He also encouraged the Egba to take advantage of the changed political conditions of the country by engaging in trade on a wider scale than before, especially in sending kola from their forests to the markets in the north. He boasted that he had fought for the Egba so that they should wear the best kinds of cloth, *alari* and *sekini*, and his countrymen still look on him as father of their nation and on themselves as his children, *omo Lishabi*.

The circumstances of Lishabi's end are mysterious. He is said to have died in the forest, perhaps murdered by a group of jealous chiefs, though another account is that he was killed during a Dahomean raid. It seems that towards the end of his life he lost his popularity with the Egba, despite the benefits which he had brought them. Biobaku suggests that they did not understand his anxiety about the defence of their land and resented the conscription into his militia of men whose labour was needed on the farms.[26]

After the removal of Lishabi's influence and example, political conditions among the Egba deteriorated and local differences re-emerged. Tradition recollects four outbreaks of civil war preceding the wider conflagration of the Owu war.[27] The first arose from a quarrel between the people of Igbein and Itoku, both towns subject to the Alake, over the petty offences of a former slave, now a wealthy trader, Ogedepagbo. The second grew out of a competition for office between rival chiefs in Ilugun, which drew in other towns as mediators and then participants. The third came about when Alake Okikilu raised an army in Egbado under the warrior Agbaje (who gave his name to this war) in order to attack a group of towns in his province whose court was depriving him of the revenue which he expected from his own jurisdiction. The last was a bitterly fought contest between the Ijeun and Itoku against the Oba people; this again concerned towns within Ake, apparently the most disturbed and unruly of the Egba provinces.

Thus the stage was set for the Owu war of the early nineteenth century, which was to bring in its wake the direst and most far-reaching consequences for all the Yoruba. Among these consequences was the destruction of the town and kingdom of Owu and the eventual removal of its ruler and people to Abeokuta, the new metropolis of all the Egba, where they have since then occupied the south-west part of the town.

The Owu did not orginally belong to the Egba. Their kingdom lay to the east of the Egba forest across the River Oshun, with Ife to the north-east and Ijebu on the south. Little is remembered about the early history of Owu, except for a couple of wars fought against Ondo, but the impressive remains of fortifications at Owu Ipole, consisting of massive earthen walls still some twenty feet high, suggest that here was a formidable power. Johnson describes the Owu as a martial race and adds: 'Hardihood, stubbornness, immorality and haughtiness are marked traits in their character'; to illustrate the equal fierceness of their women he quotes a proverb: 'a child is born at Owu and you ask (whether) male or female: which will be a proper child?' (*abi omo l'Owu, o ni ako tabi abo ni, ewo ni yio se omo nibe?*) Nevertheless, like their Egba neighbours, the Owu were subject to the Oyo, and indeed were proud to act as the Alafin's warriors in the south. 'From the days of Shango,' claims Johnson, 'they (had) been very loyal to the Alafin of Oyo.' This loyalty in latter days was to lead to their downfall.[28]

Egbado, Anago, and Awori

To the west of Egbaland across the River Ogun lived the Egbado, their name contracted from *egbaluwe*, 'the wanderers towards the river' – probably an allusion to the River Yewa, which runs through their land to the lagoon at Badagry. They seem never to have constituted a state or federation as did the other major Yoruba peoples. The traditions of origin of their towns are disparate, referring to Ife, Oyo, Ketu, and Benin, and the population includes communities of Awori, Egun, Anago, and Ohori, the last three being outposts of peoples, already described in Chapter 5, whose homes lie mainly to the west of the modern Nigeria–Bénin frontier (and all, except the Egun, being Yoruba).

The oldest of the Egbado communities are probably the Ilobi and Erinja, who have traditions of migration from Ife via Ketu;[29] the Ilobi, indeed, claim that their ancestor, Onidokun Leke, was a member of Oduduwa's house. Later arrivals in the area were the Ado and the Ipokia, of Awori and Anago descent respectively, though the people of Ipokia have been joined by emigrants from Oyo. Other Egbado towns, such as Igan, Egua, and Aiyetoro, seem to have been founded by Anago groups moving – or possibly, returning – eastward from Dahomey. But the most important of the Egbado towns are those founded directly or indirectly by Oyo. There are two main groups of these, and in each case the settlements were apparently made by the Oyo in order to protect their communications with the coast.[30] The first group consists of the former Anago kingdom of Ifonyin, ruled by the Elehin (or Elewi) Odo ('the king behind the river'), and its daughter kingdoms of Ihumbo and Ikolaje, to whose rulers the Elehin Odo, with the Alafin's permission, granted crowns. (Ifonyin lies across the present frontier in Bénin.) They seem to have been founded about 1700, at the time when Oyo became aware of the threat to her route to the coast from the westward expansion of Benin and the growing power and ambition of the Fon of Dahomey. A later offshoot from Ifonyin was Ilashe. The second group was founded (or, in some cases, given a new role and importance) probably late in the eighteenth century by Alafin Abiodun when the Oyo trade route was moved farther to the east; it includes the two leading towns of Ilaro and Ijanna, established in an area which, perhaps as a result of slave-raiding, was only lightly populated. Ilaro (whose origins, according to Folayan, ante-date Abiodun's reign by some two centuries) was ruled by its oba, the Olu, who was crowned by the Alafin; according to Johnson, each Olu ruled for a period of only three years and then retired to Oyo Ile with ten of his wives. Ijanna was subject to an official known as the Onishare ('he who acts as envoy'), who was chosen from among the Alafin's ilari, the titled slaves; he had the alarming honour of being one of the Oyo *abobaku* – those required to take their own lives on learning of the Alafin's death. Johnson writes that he was always a Nupe, but the Onishare whom Lander met in 1830 was described as a Hausa.[31] Ilaro became the principal town of Egabadoland, while nearby Ijanna took second place. Formerly their rulers held a ceremonial meeting once a year, sitting back-to-back on a hilltop boundary between their kingdoms – since kings should never see each other.

These satellite kingdoms of Oyo in Egbado country seem to have fulfilled well their purpose of protecting the road to the coast up to and even some years beyond the outbreak of the general wars of the nineteenth century. They had their own troops and remained, as Johnson writes, 'very loyal subjects of the Alafin'.[32] Many travellers passed through the towns between Oyo and the coast, and though the tolls which they were required to pay (in cowries) on entering and leaving had to be transmitted to the Alafin, their patronage of the local markets was profitable and the Egbado grew wealthy. When Clapperton and Lander, the first Europeans to give a first-hand account of Yorubaland, travelled up this route at the end of 1825 they were impressed by the order, peace, and prosperity which they saw around them. But four years later, as the Landers noted, conditions had deteriorated.

Two towns lying in the mainly Awori area to the south of the Egba and Egbado countries (and sometimes included in one or the other) must be mentioned. The first is Otta, ruled by a crowned oba, the Olota, who claims to derive his title from Ife, and now a wealthy centre of cocoa production and trade. The second is the former port and slaving centre of Badagry, which is situated, like other West African ports, not directly on the coast but on the coastal lagoon; from the west it is protected by the Yewa estuary and on other sides by swamp and forest. The town seems to have been founded in about 1736 by a Dutch trader and populated mainly by Egun refugees driven eastwards by the Fon. As it became important as an outlet for the trade of Oyo and for the commerce of the Egbado, its population grew, other Popo refugees and Awori from the surrounding district being attracted there, as well as Spanish, Portuguese, French, Dutch, and English slave traders who established their barracoons along the shore. All the eight main chieftaincies in the town were held by the Aja and there was a preponderance of Whydah influence. The leading chief, the Akran, was normally a member of the Jegba ward of the town which traced its descent from Whydah (Ouidah, Huéda), the Popo port some fifty miles to the west, but he had little authority over the other wards. The town seems to have constituted a semi-independent city state; in the eighteenth century it was apparently tributary to Oyo, which controlled the hinterland down to Ipokia in the south, while in 1830, according to the Landers, it was tributary to Lagos.[33]

Lagos

The interaction of geography and history, of trade and politics, of the outside world and of local affairs: all this is illustrated in the past of Lagos. This is the first of Nigeria's ports and also the terminus of the railway which, far more than the River Niger, has linked together the disparate regions. Today Lagos is still (though perhaps for not much longer) the Federal capital, a crowded, cosmopolitan city of several million inhabitants. Its names reflect its past; to the Yoruba it is Eko, deriving probably from the farm (*oko*) of the earliest settlers, though alternatively – or additionally – it may be the Bini word (*eko*) for a war-camp; to other Nigerians and to the rest of the world it is Lagos, contracted from the Portuguese Lago de Curamo (the name Kuramo survives for an inlet of the great lagoon nearby), while there are traces of yet another, probably later but now almost forgotten name, Onim or Aunis, apparently also used by the Portuguese.[34]

Here at Lagos occurs the first permanent break in the miles of beach and dune of the outer coast-line to the east of the Volta estuary. The bar which had to be crossed in order to gain access to the harbour was one of notorious difficulty and danger, and so shallow and of so narrow a tidal range that until the completion of the breakwaters in 1916 entrance was denied to ships of over twelve-feet draught. But once across the bar and in the calm waters of the lagoon, there opened up a vast system of inland waterways connecting Lagos by canoe (and today by motor-launch) with Porto Novo and beyond on the west and with the creeks 100 miles to the east. This Rio de Laguo, or entrance into the lagoon, was noted by the earliest Portuguese visitors to the West African coast, and appears on a Portuguese map as early as *c.* 1485.[35] Pacheco writes of it in his *Esmeraldo de Situ Orbis:*

> There is no trade in this country nor anything from which one can make a profit. All this region of the river Lagua, of which we spoke above, as far as the river Primeiro, and beyond for a distance of a 100 leagues, is all broken up inland by numerous other rivers in such a way that the whole consists of numerous islands. It is very unhealthy and is very hot throughout the year, on account of the proximity of the sun. The middle of the winter occurs here during the months of August and September when it rains heavily.

The Blacks of this country are idolaters and circumcised, without having any law, and without knowing the reason for their circumcision.[36]

But even if Pacheco's rather superficial account of Lagos is correct in its estimate of trade at the end of the fifteenth century, three centuries later the position had entirely changed. Captain John Adams, describing conditions at the end of the eighteenth century, wrote that an 'active traffic in slaves' was carried on at Lagos, a town 'built on a bank or island, which appears to have been raised from Cradoo lake, by the eddies, after the sea and periodical rains had broken down the boundary which separated it from the ocean'. He continues:

It has always been the policy of the Lagos people, like those of Bonny, to be themselves the traders and not brokers. They therefore go in their canoes to Ardrah and Badagry, and to the towns situated at the NE extremity of Cradoo lake, where they purchase slaves, Jaboo cloth, and such articles as are required for domestic consumption.[37]

The early traditions of Lagos[38] ascribe the peopling of this sandy waste near the edge of the ocean to a small-scale migration of Awori Yoruba, who had first settled under the leadership of a hunter named Ogunfunminire about twelve miles up the River Ogun at Isheri, a village which though still mainly inhabited by Awori is now at the southern limit of Egbaland. Ogunfunminire is said to have been a member of the royal house of Ife, but his settlement of hunters and fishermen seems to represent the farthest and latest extension of one of those movements which people the Awori region. From Isheri the settlers spread to Ebute Meta (the name means 'three landing places') on the lagoon, but the uncertainties of life on the mainland (perhaps due already to the ambitions of Benin in this area) led them to seek greater safety across the channel on the small island now called Iddo, whence they spread farther to the adjacent larger island – some five by one and a half miles – which is Lagos and which lies by the entrance into the lagoon from the sea. According to legend, the islanders were at first subject to a ruler known as the Olofin, on whose death the land was divided among the ten eldest of his thirty-two sons, these ten chiefs being the ancestors of the Idejo, 'owners of the land', better known today as the White Cap Chiefs of Lagos. The senior of these, Aromire ('friend of the water'), had his farm at Isale Eko (meaning 'under' or, in modern use, 'downtown' Lagos). The present afin of Lagos is situated on this site and is called Iga Idunganran, 'the pepper palace', a recollection in the Lagos Awori dialect of the pepper bushes on Aromire's farm.

A series of attacks had now been launched against Lagos by the armies of Benin. At first these were repulsed under the leadership of the Olofin. After the Olofin's death, however, the Bini succeeded in establishing themselves on Iddo island under Asheru, one of their warriors. The impression given by Lagos tradition is that this was achieved by peaceful infiltration rather than by conquest; perhaps the Lagosians, seeing themselves outflanked by the advance of the Bini along the coast to their west, lost hope of being able to prolong their resistance. According to the traditional history of Benin as related by Egharevba, Oba Orhogba of Benin, campaigning in person, made a war-camp on Lagos island which he used as a base for extending his control over the area. An early corroborative account is provided by the German, Josua Ulsheimer, who visited Lagos in 1603 and who described the island as a military camp occupied by the soldiers of the King of Benin and governed by four of his generals.[39] Some time later, it seems, the Oba appointed a ruler for Lagos to represent the interest of Benin and to forward tribute there. The man chosen is named in both Lagos and Benin tradition as Ashipa. The Lagos account is that the Bini warrior Asheru died while campaigning on the mainland near by and that Ashipa, an Isheri chief and (like Ogunfunminire and the Olofin before him) of the Ife royalty, carried his body home to Benin, thereby gaining such favour with the Oba that he was sent back to Lagos as its king. Egharevba describes Ashipa ('Esikpa' in his spelling, but the name is clearly the same) as a grandson of the Oba of Benin, and adds that after his death his remains and those of his successors were taken for burial to Benin, a claim which is confirmed in Lagos tradition. Ashipa founded a new dynasty which continued to rule Lagos, using the title either of Ologun (contracted from Oloriogun, 'warrior') or of Eleko, and the present Oba of Lagos – the modern use of the general word for king as the title is reminiscent of Benin – is his twentieth successor and descendant on the throne. The dynasty's dependence on Benin was emphasized by the appointment of another chief, the Eletu Odibo – still one of the Akarigbere, or kingmakers, of Lagos – who alone had the right to crown the oba and who in early times probably maintained close connection with Benin. Meanwhile, the senior descendant of the Olofin, the Oloto, maintained a nominal independence as ruler of the northern corner of Iddo island and as first among the Idejo.

The extension of the rule of Benin to Lagos and its neighbourhood has been gradually assigned to the sixteenth century, possibly associated with the use of firearms obtained by the Bini from their European trade. Ulsheimer's account, referred to above, shows that Benin was in military control of the island at the very beginning of the seventeenth century, but suggests that the appointment of a single vice-regal representative had not yet been made. On the other hand tradition in Benin asserts that Ashipa took up his office, thus founding the present ruling dynasty of Lagos, during the reign at Benin of Oba Orhogba, which Bradbury agrees with Egharevba in placing in the latter part of the sixteenth century. Here, however, the king list at Lagos presents a difficulty. Adele, who died in or about 1836 (after being deposed and later restored), appears as only the sixth oba. Thus, if Egharevba and Bradbury were right, and if the list were complete, the average length of reign would be between thirty-three and forty years, which is too long to be credible. But it is possible, even likely, that the names of some oba have been forgotten, particularly of those early ones whose bodies were taken to Benin for burial.[40] The problem remains, but for the present it seems reasonable to conclude that, while Benin established its ascendancy in and around Lagos during the sixteenth century, the kingship there came into being some time during the seventeenth century.

From its physical situation Lagos can be assumed to have long been a centre of the indigenous lagoon trade. For the Europeans who began to operate intermittently along this coast from the end of the fifteenth century the Lagos river and lagoon were of some importance as giving access (despite the hazards of the bar) to Ijebu, a source of locally produced cloth. Thus there began, at first very slowly, what Law describes as 'a fascinating interaction between the two waterborne systems', that of the Yoruba and their neighbours around the lagoons and that of the Europeans sailing across the Atlantic. In 1603 Ulsheimer noted that Lagos was the resort of traders coming 'by water and land', and like Adams two hundred years later he makes specific mention of the buying of cotton cloth. Communication between Lagos and Benin, the centre of power, was probably also maintained mostly by water. Mahin, giving access to the lagoon at its eastern end, had been conquered by Benin at about the same time that Lagos was brought under control, and tradition records that Oba Ehengbuda met his death while on his way by canoe to visit Lagos.[41] It was not until the 1760s that direct European trade with Lagos can be described as regular or continuous. This development was almost certainly due to the rise of Lagos as a slave port, which in turn stemmed from the gradual eastward drift of European trade from Whydah where local conditions were increasingly unfavourable. It is said to have been Oba Akinshemoyin, fourth ruler of Lagos after Ashipa, who invited Portuguese slave-dealers to the town, and that his Portuguese friends presented him with tiles for roofing his palace, the Iga. A Portuguese report of 1807 ascribes the growth of the slave trade at Lagos to warfare between Dahomey and Porto Novo which interrupted supplies to ports further west, so that Lagos, beyond the reach of Dahomean raiders, now became the principal slave mart of the western lagoon, some 7,000 to 10,000 slaves being sold there annually. After the fall of Owu in c. 1820 these numbers probably rose even further as the devastating wars of the Yoruba provided an abundant supply of enslaved captives from the hinterland.[42] Thus until the British occupation in 1851 Lagos remained the main centre of the slave trade on this part of the West African coast.

As Lagos grew richer, the annual tribute rendered to Benin presumably increased and became an important source of revenue for the latter kingdom. This tribute was paid until about 1830, and Egharevba writes that an official was sent to claim it as late as 1845 during the civil war at Lagos between Akitoye and Kosoko, the two rival claimants to the throne.[43] Their wealth may well have encouraged the rulers to assert their independence, and according to Dalzel, the 'powerful King of Lagos' took part with the Dahomeans in an attack on Badagry in 1784, an operation from which Benin could hardly have derived benefit.

A few years before the establishment of British influence in Lagos in 1851 it was estimated that the population of the town was some 25,000 to 30,000.[44] Apart from descendants of the early Awori settlers, and presumably some of remotely Bini origin too, and newcomers, there were now many domestic slaves, both Yoruba and non-Yoruba; Mahi from the hinterland were particularly numerous. Indeed, Campbell, the British consul, thought the majority of Lagosians around the middle of the nineteenth century to be of slave orgin. Most of these people were occupying the western half of the island, Isale Leko. In addition to Eko and Iddo, however, the small kingdom also embraced scattered villages on the mainland, stretching some 20–30 miles to the west and (if claims advanced in the nineteenth century are accepted) as far along the coast to the east as Lekki, though here the population remains Ijebu.[45]

NOTES

1. Snelgrave, p. 59.
2. *Esmeraldo de Situ Orbis*, quoted by Hodgkin, p. 92.
3. Law (1983), p. 325; Law (1986), pp. 246–7.
4. Quoted by Hodgkin, p. 173.
5. Described by Lloyd (1961).
6. S. Johnson (1921), pp. 171–2.
7. Lloyd (1959), p. 20, and Lloyd (1961), p. 7; Ogunba (1965). The name Idoko is said to survive at Imushin near Ijebu Ode.
8. Ogunkoya, p. 54.
9. Ogunba (1964). For lists of Awujale, see Odutola (1946) and Olusola (1968).
10. See Lloyd (1959).
11. Recorded by Chief Ojo, Bada of Shaki, in an account of Oyo history in the files of the Yoruba Historical Research Scheme.
12. S. Johnson (1921), pp. 174, 179.
13. Egharevba, p. 24.
14. Dapper, p. 311.
15. Lloyd (1960b), p. 60. This is presumably based on Snelgrave's reference (pp. 148–9) to an attack by the Dahomeans on the 'Yahoo', who lived 'far inland' and retreated 'among their mountains and woods'. It is conceivable that the 'Yahoo' were Ijebu, but Dalzel (pp. xvii, 59) thought that they were the people of Mahin.
16. Clapperton, p. 136. Kulfo is forty miles south-west of Kontagora.
17. Ajisafe, pp. 18–19.
18. Ajisafe, Ch. 6: Biobaku (1957), Ch. 1 and map, p. 129.
19. Biobaku (1957), p. 3.
20. S. Johnson (1921), pp. 17–18.
21. Parrinder (1956), p. 12.
22. Biobaku (1957), p. 8.
23. Ajisafe, p. 14.
24. Biobaku (1957), p. 9; Akinjogbin (1966b), p. 458–9.
25. Ojo (n.d., a), p. 13. For the evidence on which 1796 is preferred to the Bada's dating of Lishabi's revolt to 1810, see Ch. 10.
26. Biobaku (1957), p. 10.
27. Ajisafe, pp. 45–9.
28. S. Johnson (1921), p. 206. See also Mabogunje and Omer-Cooper, *passim*. The inhabitants of Owu Ipole now call their settlement Orile Owu ('home' or 'old' Owu), and it is so marked on the Ordnance map. But there is another, probably older, site also known as Orile Owu near New Oyo. See note 30 to Ch. 10 below.
29. Egbeola, *passim*; Folayan (1967b), pp. 15–16.
30. Morton-Williams (1964a), pp. 30–1, 40–2; Folayan (1967b), pp. 15–25.
31. S. Johnson (1921), pp. 226–7; R. L. and J. Lander (1832), p. 62.
32. S. Johnson (1921), p. 226.
33. Avoseh (1938), *passim*; Newbury, pp. 30–2 and Figure 2; Hodder (1962–3), *passim*; Law (1977), p. 175; Asiwaju (1979), p. 19.
34. See Verger (1959) for examples of the use of this name. 'Awani', also found, is presumably Awori.
35. Law (1983), p. 324.
36. Hodgkin, p. 93.
37. Ibid., p. 173.
38. Burns, pp. 33–4, mainly based on Wood; Losi.
39. Egharevba, p. 30; Law (1983), p. 329; Jones (1983), p. 24.
40. Hodgkin, pp. 25–6; Egharevba, pp. 30–1; Bradbury, p. 285.

41. Law (1983), pp. 321-4; Jones (1983), pp. 40-1; Egharevba, p. 34. The river Aghan where the Oba met his death does not seem to appear on any map.
42. Law (1983), pp. 343-8.
43. Egharevba, pp. 47-8; Burns, pp. 35, 38. Talbot, Vol. I, p. 68, claims that tribute was paid to Benin until Lagos became a British colony in 1861.
44. The estimate was made by Freeman, the Wesleyan missionary, about 1844 and is quoted by Newbury, p. 56, n. 1.
45. Smith (1978), pp. 40-2; Public Record Office, Kew, FO 84/950, Campbell to Clarendon, 1 May 1854; Robertson, p. 287; Payne, p. 1.

PART II

SEVEN

THE TRADITIONS REVIEWED

The acceptance of oral tradition as a form of evidence commits the historian to an attempt to answer questions which neither concern nor would greatly interest the guardians of tradition itself – the rulers and their officials, the drummers, the praise singers, the local patriots. These questions arise from the historian's need to establish a coherent narrative which, however isolated the people concerned, must at some point link up with events elsewhere, and then to interpret that narrative according to his usual criteria. In a reconstruction of the past of the Yoruba, which up to about the middle of the nineteenth century must be largely from their traditions, and before 1700 almost wholly so, many such questions present themselves, and for every question a host of difficulties. A prospect of detailed work, kingdom by kingdom, opens up, but at this stage the questions may be resolved into two broad groups, each of fundamental importance. The first concerns the interpretation of the traditional accounts of the origins of the Yoruba polity, and the second the fixing of the main developments and events in early Yoruba history into, first, a chronological sequence and then into a temporal framework which can be related to, or at least put alongside, the history of other peoples.

In the traditions of origin which are summarized in the preceding chapters of this book, discrepancies and contradictions abound, and even when supernatural elements are left out of account, credibility is constantly strained. In this the guardians of tradition find no difficulty; their duty, and often their passion, is to maintain orthodoxy. Historians must approach tradition otherwise, treating it always with respect but never with credulity. A generation ago, in the absence to an important extent of conventional sources, they gave an enthusiastic (perhaps an over-enthusiastic) welcome to the notion that oral tradition – much of which had already been gathered in the field by local non-academic historians, colonial officers, missionaries, and anthropologists, but of which much still remained to be gathered – offered a promising means for the recovery of the African past. The last few years have seen a growing sophistication and selectivity in the use of oral tradition by historians, and also a growing scepticism about the extent to which it can be accepted as evidence. In this edition, this scepticism has especially influenced the treatment in preceding chapters of Ife and Oyo, but it affects too the pre-colonial, and above all the pre-nineteenth century, histories of all the Yoruba kingdoms and peoples whose traditions are all equally open to question and re-interpretation.

In any event, the historian is confronted here by a body of myth and legend which suggests, perhaps as strongly as such evidence can, that there came to Ile Ife a leader and a group of people who established there a political authority of an enduring kind, that there was a subsequent emigration from Ife of the founders, with their followers, of a number of kingdoms, and that there continued to be reference back to Ife as the centre of authority and legitimacy by the scattered 'children of Oduduwa', including both those who had formed and those in process of forming new states and towns. The first two questions which arise from these assumptions ask whence came this dominant group, the house and followers of Oduduwa as they may be called, and then who were the people whom they found already living in the land.

Numerous answers have been proposed to both these,[1] and the subject is still an open and a controversial one. But two points are relevant, equally to each question, and may point to a single answer. The first is that, as noted in Chapter 1, linguistic evidence seems to show that by the time they began to form the states with which this book is concerned, the Yoruba had occupied more or less their present habitat for several hundred or even thousands of years. Secondly, the traditions relate that as the emigrants from Ife spread over the land they almost everywhere encountered earlier settlers ('the aborigines', as they are sometimes termed)[2] who were often hostile (not unreasonably, since they had a prior claim to the land) but who apparently neither were unfamiliar nor spoke an unknown tongue. It appears likely, therefore, that the Oduduwa cycle describes not a conquest from outside but a process of state-formation from within a people in which the leaders belonged to a dominant but probably not alien lineage.

If this much is accepted, that Ife was an early centre of Yoruba political and cultural development (as archaeological evidence indicates), it must still be asked how far the legends of origin of the individual kingdoms can be accepted as recalling for each case an actual migration from Ife, and a migration (or series of migrations) which took place more or less within the lifetime of a leader who had established his throne at Ife. Here, again, the persistence over a wide area of a narrative in which the essential elements remain recognizably the same argues that an actual event is represented and its memory preserved, and that indeed there was a concerted movement of the younger generation of a vigorous line, a movement which continued a process begun a generation (or perhaps two generations) before at Ife. There is nothing inherently unlikely in this – other than a complete lack of objective evidence in support. But in any case there seems no ground for preferring the suggestion of a recent writer that the legend of Oduduwa represents a migration to Ife by a people coming from the Benue valley, while that of Oranyan refers to a conquest of Ife and its dependencies by a different people, arriving apparently centuries later, from the Middle Niger.[3] Hardly more convincing is the theory, alluded to above (pages 30, 34), that the Oranyan story camouflages a conquest of northern Yorubaland by Borgu invaders. It is difficult to find anything in tradition or any substantial evidence from secondary sources (such as differences in dialect or social organization) to support any part of such speculation – that there were two migrations, that they were widely separated in time, that they were made up of differing peoples, that they came from different directions and from a great distance. Nor does there seem any justification for regarding the names of Oduduwa, Oranyan, and other heroes as representing not individuals but groups of persons, nor for regarding them as 'humanized deities' rather than as 'deified mortals'.[4] Every movement has its leaders, and it is their names which are usually recollected.

Yet if the broad outline of the legend of a dispersal of princes from Ife is accepted as a possible explanation of the foundation of a number of the Yoruba states, this cannot explain the origin of all the kingdoms, even though most of them claim to derive their crowns from Ife. The criteria necessary to satisfy a claim to have originated from the early setting forth of the founders – from Itajero, as the Ife account has it – seem to be, first, a specific tradition to that effect, especially if the kingdom's own tradition is supported by a similar tradition at Ife or in other kingdoms; secondly, a king-list of sufficient length, that is, with about thirty-five names or more, and last, a recognized position of seniority among the other kingdoms of Ife origin. Such criteria would seem to be satisfied most nearly in the cases of Ijebu Ode, Ketu, Ondo, and Ijesha, and also for the second dynasty of the Edo kingdom of Benin, while the claims of Shabe, Ake, Akure, Ado Ekiti, and Owo, though less strongly supported by tradition, cannot be set aside. The criteria would seem also, and at first even pre-eminently, to be satisfied by the case of Oyo, yet, as has been seen in Chapter 3, the connection between Ife and the foundation of Oyo has been authoritatively questioned and there is more than a possibility that the dynasty of Alafin was in origin not Yoruba but Bariba. On the other hand, the argument above does not deny that other rulers may have obtained their crowns from Ife since, whatever the origin of the Oni's own kingship – and the Oyo legend about Adimu seems somewhat suspect – Ife remained the source of legitimacy to which aspiring rulers would look for the sanctioning of their kingship. Biobaku suggests how this might have happened: 'The Yoruba dotted the tropical forest belt with towns and hamlets. A bold hunter usually led the way and when a suitable site was struck, he founded a town. He might go back to Ile-Ife for the symbol of authority, which was a beaded crown.'[5]

As to what gave these founders of the first states their power to attain leadership and to accomplish a political revolution of enduring importance among the Yoruba, tradition is silent. They may have been associated with some technical innovation, for example, yam cultivation or iron-working or a new weapon – perhaps the bow – or they may have learnt through external contact and unusual receptivity those ideas of strong government and divine kingship which have been termed the 'Sudanic state'. Less plausible is the suggestion which links the formation of these states (like some other African states) with the introduction of horses and the arrival of leaders on horseback. More prosaically, the founders may have been successful traders, men of wealth and initiative, who came to dominate a race of poor farmers. The possibilities are many, and there are no clear pointers. The simplest explanation seems still a possibility in at least some kingdoms: that a family arose (like that of Cunedda and his sons[6] or the house of Hauteville) in which at least two or three generations were exceptionally gifted by nature as warriors and as politicians, and whose ambition made them leaders of their fellow men and founders of states.

Turning to the problem of chronology, the difficulties are at first sight somewhat less, since much has been asserted about the dating of reigns. A closer examination proves disconcerting. The early written references to the Yoruba by European travellers are meagre, and with regard to dating are particularly unhelpful; this is the position up to the end of the seventeenth century, and it is not until the nineteenth century that satisfactory accounts begin to appear. The traditions are related in an almost timeless vacuum. Occasionally indications are given about the lapse of time, usually concerning the length of a reign, but these are inherently unreliable. For the most part events are said to have taken place in 'olden times' (*igba lailai*) or 'before the Europeans came' (*ki oyinbo too goke*). There are no dates and no recognizable references to datable events elsewhere.

As has been seen in Chapter 2, archaeologists and their colleagues have established by the radiocarbon method that the site of Ile Ife, the city which is at the centre of Yoruba traditions of origin and of religion, was occupied on quite a substantial scale between the ninth and twelfth centuries of our era, and may have been founded even earlier. Meanwhile, a combination of radiocarbon and thermoluminescent datings places the bronzes (more properly, brasses) of Ife in the fourteenth century (possibly thirteenth to fifteenth centuries). This implies that the art both originated and flourished before the arrival of Europeans on this part of the West African coast. Although some slight resemblances to the terracottas of Nok have been noted (see pages 23–5 above), this is far from providing sufficient grounds to claim cultural continuity between Nok and Ife. Nor has any connexion been detected between the art of Ife and the traditions preserved by the Yoruba about early times. On the other hand, as Law points out, the existence of this range of sculptures adds confirmation to the view of Ife as a centre of early monarchy.[7]

At Oyo Ile archaeological investigations have been carried out intermittently since 1956. As mentioned in Chapter 3, microliths discovered in a cave on the site point to Neolithic occupation, but no positive evidence as to the date of the foundation of the Yoruba city has yet been obtained, although the dating of pottery at Oyo Ile has suggested the fourteenth century as the beginning of the Yoruba–Borgu settlement there (see page 34 above).

Meanwhile, resort must be had again to tradition, bearing in mind that from this source no more can be hoped than a tentative approximation to a time-scale. In this situation it is the king-lists which promise the best means of establishing a chronology. Unfortunately only about a dozen among the many lists which tradition must still preserve have been recorded – and time runs short as tradition is submerged by modern preoccupations. But in a few kingdoms it seems that the lists have been comprehensively and conscientiously kept and may be treated with some confidence. In other towns, however, the information available is confined to the statement that the reigning oba follows a known number of predecessors.

In some cases where king-lists were available, historians have drawn on traditional accounts of the lengths of the different reigns and then worked backwards to provide a chronology, including a date of origin. This was done by Chief Ojo, the Bada of Shaki, in his histories of Oyo (in which, for example, he assigns 829 as the year of Oranyan's death) and Shaki, by Fr Oguntuyi in his history of Ado Ekiti (he claims that the second Ewi reigned precisely from 1444 to 1471), and by Chief Ashara for Owo (where the first Olowo is described as having reigned 'c. 1019'). These writers may have been influenced in this respect by Chief Egharevba's famous *Short History of Benin*, first published in 1934, in which dates are given for all the oba of the kingdom from Oranyan, whose coming is said to have been 'about A.D. 1170'; this list was compiled with the help of the Esekhurhe, or priest of the royal ancestors.[8] The method seems likely to be reasonably accurate for reigns within about the last hundred years, but for earlier periods it cannot be accepted as providing more than a rough indication of the time-scale, and for the earliest times even this can hardly be claimed. At Oyo, for example, it is said that Alafin Abipa was born twenty years after the fall of Oyo Ile, that Orompoto ruled for twenty years, and that the return to Oyo from Igboho was accomplished in the twentieth year of Abipa's reign; each case can be taken as signifying no more than 'rather a long time' or 'towards the end of the reign'. But in any event the whole account of the sojourn of the Oyo at Igboho seems now to be open to question.

Another approach consists in establishing an average length of reign for a kingship over as long a period as possible and then multiplying the number of known oba by the average to obtain an approximation to the date of origin of the dynasty and other events.[9] For Oyo, an average of 11.8 years reign can be calculated, taking 1754, established as the probable date of the accession of Alafin Labisi,[10] as the starting-point and ignoring the two interregnums which are recollected in order to compensate for the series of extremely short reigns during Gaha's tyranny. Then, basing the calculation on the list of Alafin given by Johnson, to which the name of Oluodo has been added, making a total of 41 reigns between Oranyan, the putative founder, and Adeniran inclusive, and working backwards from the deposition of Adeniran in 1946, it would seem that Oyo was founded in *c.* 1462.[11] If, however, the foundation is assumed to be have occurred on Abipa's arrival at Oyo Ile from Igboho, then this would be *c.* 1604. Yet it must now be observed that in any event the Oyo king-list is of doubtful accuracy. Law considers that the list published by Johnson was his own compilation rather than a recording of tradition. It is likely to be too long rather than the reverse, and the order may be confused.[12] In Oyo it is said that the names of many early Alafin who died away from the capital and were not buried in the Bara, or royal mausoleum, were deliberately omitted from any enumeration – as apparently happened with Oluodo who, according to some accounts, succeeded Obalokun and was drowned in the Niger while being pursued by the Nupe. Indeed, it is claimed at Oyo that there have been in all some seventy Alafin, which is twenty-three more than those usually enumerated and would give by averaging a founding date of about 1170. A similar statement about unrecorded oba is made in connexion with the king-lists at Ilesha and Ado Ekiti, and doubtless elsewhere (since a long list implies antiquity and thus prestige among Yoruba as with others). But at Ketu the list of Alaketu seems to have been kept with unusual care and commands more confidence. As recorded by Parrinder, it contains forty-nine names; the average length of reign, calculated from that of Oje (*c.* 1748–60) is 21.5 years and from Adegbede (1853–8) is 18.5 years. The first average would give approximate dates of A.D. 931 for the putative emigration from Ile Ife and 974 for the foundation of Ketu on its present site under Ede, while the second yields 1085 and 1101 respectively. Both averages, incidentally, are long in comparison with some other African king-lists.[13]

Clearly, the averaging method cannot be accepted as giving more than the broadest approximation, to be cited only in the absence of more reliable information. Experiments carried out with lists of rulers whose completeness is unquestioned, for example, the sovereigns of England, illustrate the range of possible inaccuracy.[14] In the case of Oyo, moreover, there seems to have been a change in the method of succession from primogeniture in early times, which would tend to produce long reigns, to a combination of the hereditary and elective systems, which would produce greater stability but shorter reigns. But before attempting to reach any conclusion, even provisionally, it will be useful to examine the king-list of a related kingdom, that of the Oba of Benin.

The Benin list is relevant to a discussion of Yoruba chronology, since not only is the dynasty held, in both Benin and Yoruba tradition, to stem from Oduduwa, but there has also been considerable contact between Benin and its Yoruba neighbours and, as has been seen, a number of events in the history of the latter are assigned in Benin to the reigns of particular Oba. Fortunately, the list of Oba of Benin appears to have been preserved with singular care. Unfortunately, on the other hand, the fifteenth-century Portuguese visitors to the capital did not include in their accounts the names of the Oba with whom they dealt, so that the first identifiable name from written record is that of Osifo, the personal name of Obanosa, mentioned by Landolphe, who came to the throne only about 1804.

The list of Oba of Benin, in the versions collected by Roupell (in 1898), Talbot, and Egharevba, has provided the basis for a study of Benin chronology by R. E. Bradbury[15] who, working backwards and adducing local traditions and some information from non-Benin sources, establishes approximate dating for the Oba back to the late fifteenth century. His conclusion about the earlier period is that if the strong tradition in Benin that Ozolua was ruler at the time of the Portuguese visit in 1485 is correct, and if he is correctly enumerated as the fifteenth Oba, then 'it appears likely that the dynasty began not later than about 1300'; Egharevba's claim that it began about 1200 must on his own evidence 'be regarded as too early. But for this period nothing is certain.'[16] This conclusion is reached without reference to the averaging method, but it is worth noting that taking 1735, the probable date of accession of Oba Eresoyan, as the starting-point, a high average length of reign of 24.7 years is reached; this would give a date of *c.* 1050 for the beginning of the dynasty and of about 1390 for the accession of Ozolua, both of which seem, in the light of the other evidence, much too early. This discrepancy may be due to the change from brother-to-brother succession to primogeniture in the Benin kingship, which took place possibly as late as 1700. As explained above, primogeniture tends to produce a longer average reign, so that extropolation backwards can be expected to produce a result which is too early.[17] But Bradbury has also shown that Egharevba's assignment of the Oba from Ewuare to Orhogba to part of the fifteenth and most of the sixteenth centuries is probably accurate, and this in turn enables approximate dates to be affixed to a number of events in Yoruba history. In particular, it seems that at the turn of the fifteenth century Benin was engaged in wars with the eastern Yoruba kingdoms, and also with Ijebu, and that from the mid- or late sixteenth century Benin was extending her authority in a south-westerly direction along the coast and founded the politically subservient dynasty at Lagos soon after this period. For this Ulsheimer's account (see pages 73–4 above) provides support.

The indications from the traditions examined above are contradictory and confusing, and it seems rash to attempt even the most tentative conclusion about the circumstances under which the Yoruba kingdoms originated and the times at which this took place. Yet since it is unlikely that further evidence of importance on this point will come to light, the attempt must be made, and made on the basis of what has been adduced here. On the one hand, it is still possible to maintain what amounts to a maximizing position in accepting the traditions as an historical account of events and to postulate an early state at Ife which was a centre of high art and ruled by a vigorous king who sent forth some six or seven of his princely sons to found independent kingdoms, an event which (by averaging the averages, by reference to the king-list of Benin, and from datings of terracottas and bronzes at Ife and pottery fragments at Oyo Ile) may be placed between *c.* 1100 and *c.* 1400, which may be expressed as *c.* 1250. (Yet parenthetically it should be noted that some Yoruba historians would date the dispersal of princes from Ife much earlier, at the end of the eighth or beginning of the ninth centuries A.D.[18]) On the other hand, a minimizing position, while accepting the early foundation and prestige of Ife, coming to its full status in the eleventh or twelfth century, and its role in the recognition (and even legitimizing) of sister kingdoms by the bestowal down the years of beaded crowns, would claim no more than separate and independent origins at different periods and under different circumstances for the main kingdoms, with a terminal date for their foundations of *c.* 1500. It is this minimizing position which in the present state of knowledge seems to give the more credible picture, albeit a shadowy one, of the emergence of the kingdoms. Finally, each of these kingdoms had its pronounced individuality and history, many were parent to other, usually smaller kingdoms, and yet all were linked by a transcending language, tradition, and culture which enabled them to absorb the mysterious earlier inhabitants of the land and the imposition in some cases of alien dynasties and which led them to look back to Ife – Ile Ife, 'home Ife' – as their mother.

NOTES

1. For examples, see Biobaku (1956a); Law (1973a).
2. References to settlers who had preceded the emigrants from Ife may be found in the legends of foundation at Ado, Ekiti, Akure, Ijebu, Ilesha, Ketu, Ondo, Owo, Oyo, and Shabe; there is also the account at Ife of the Igbo whom Oduduwa found living there. See also the account of the 'Kabba people' as possible 'proto-Yoruba'. For speculation about the aborigines, see Beier (n.d.).
3. Lloyd (1960a).
4. For example, Willett (1967), p. 125.
5. Biobaku (1957), p. 2.
6. There is useful comparative material in D. N. Dumville, 'Sub-Roman Britain: History and Legend', *History* 62, 1977.
7. Law (1973a), p. 211; Shaw (1978), pp. 125–67.
8. The Esekhurhe had the tasks of memorizing the dynastic list and of performing sacrifices to every previous Oba during the annual Ugigun rites; see Bradbury (1959), pp. 267–8.
9. For general observations on the use of king-lists for the measurement of time, see McCall, Ch. 8.
10. Akinjogbin (1966b), p. 454.
11. See Appendix D in Crowder (1966) for a version of the Oyo king-list.
12. Law (1984), pp. 205–13, which includes Johnson's list of Alafin.
13. Average lengths of reign for the Nupe, Zamfara, and Bakuba work out at 13, 12.3, and 15.6 respectively.

14. Taking the accessions of James I (1603), George III (1760), and William IV (1830) as starting-points and the accession of H. M. Queen Elizabeth II (1952) as terminal point, average lengths of reign of 21.8, 24, and 20.3 years are obtained, giving dates for the establishment for the Norman kings in England (1066) of 1102, 1016, and 1161.
15. Bradbury (1959) also obtained his own version of the list from the current holder of the office Esekhurhe.
16. Bradbury, p. 285.
17. These difficulties in the averaging method were pointed out by R. C. C. Law in a private communication.
18. Akinjogbin and Ayandele in Ikime (ed.) (1980), pp. 123–4.

EIGHT
AN OBA AND HIS PEOPLE[1]

Two closely associated institutions dominated the political life of the Yoruba in pre-colonial times: the king and the town. Nearly all Yoruba were (and are) townspeople in the sense that they belonged to a town, even though they might spend most of the year on farms up to 20 miles distant (and perhaps nearer to another town than to the parent one).[2] This was a feature which, apparently for centuries, distinguished them from most other African peoples. Their towns are many and populous, and at the centre of each (with one or two relatively recent exceptions) dwelt an oba in his afin or palace, a building of some pretensions with its gabled entrance and external veranda, usually facing on the main market-place.

The settlement of the oba provides the most probable explanation of this Yoruba propensity for town-dwelling and the willingness of many of them to live at a distance from their farms. The oba's office and person were sacred; he was the priest and protector of his people, and they naturally wished to live in his shadow. Considerations of defence supplied another motive, for though most Yoruba towns do not seem specifically sited for defensive purposes, all settlements of any importance were walled and surrounded by a protective zone of thick bush. The town was also the centre of commerce, where markets were regularly held, usually every four days,[3] and tolls paid to the oba. Finally may be cited that intangible but real factor, national character: the Yoruba are a social and gregarious people, and these qualities can best be satisfied in an urban life.

But transcending the town and its oba was the kingdom or state, and it could be maintained that the most imposing political achievement of the Yoruba in pre-colonial times was in organizing themselves into substantial units of government well adapted in size to their resources. Among these states Ife enjoyed seniority and prestige. Its ruler, the Oni, commanded respect not so much as the ruler of one of the Yoruba group of kingdoms, since Ife is not remembered as having attained political or military importance, but as the king of a town which was regarded as the cradle of the race whence the rulers and leading elements in the populations of most of the other kingdoms traced their origins. According to Akinjogbin, the traditions of relationship between the kingdoms and of the seniority of Ife amounted to a system of government to which he gives the Yoruba word for family, *ebi*. He claims that under this *ebi* system the Oni exercised a constitutional

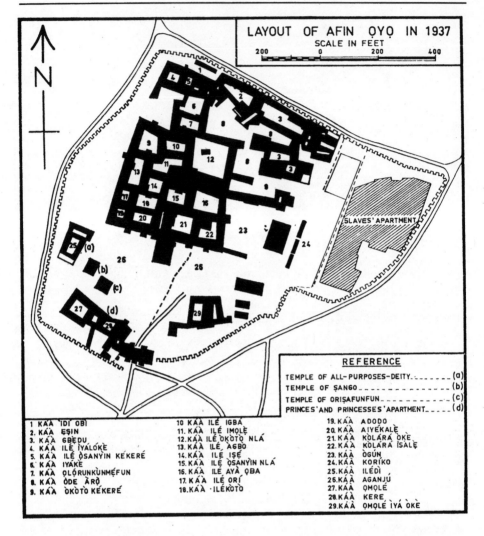

Plate 10 Ground plan, Afin Oyo, in 1937. The palace of the Alafin of Oyo. From G.J.A. Ojo, *Yoruba Palaces*, London, 1966.

and divinely sanctioned control over the other kingdoms, expressed especially in his influence over the consecration of their rulers. The custom of sending a sword of state and divination calabashes (*igba iwa*) from Ife to a new Alafin provides some support for this in the case of Oyo. Nevertheless, the individual traditions and histories of all the kingdoms, and of Oyo in particular, refute this theory, and indeed it seems that the Oni's own state was politically subordinate to its stronger neighbours in at least two periods of its history – to the Oyo empire and later to the short-lived Ibadan empire. Under the stable conditions of the colonial regime the Oni of Ife did attempt to assert a superiority over the other oba, and on one recent occasion he was rebuffed, when he told the chiefs of Ekiti on his visit to Ado in 1936, 'I am on the throne as the father and you are on thrones as sons'; to this the

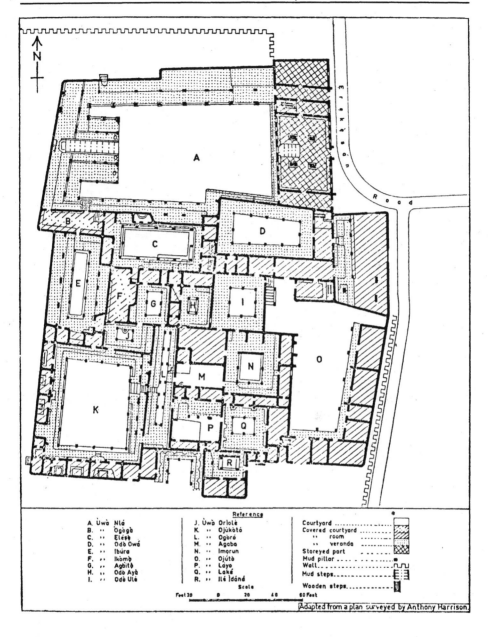

Plate 11 ˈGround plan, Afin Akure. The palace of the Deji of Akure. From Frank Willett, *African Art*, London, 1971.

Deji of Akure, in the names of his brother oba, replied that as the Oni was on the throne of his father, so also were all the Ekiti oba on the thrones of their own fathers.[4] In like manner the pretensions of the Alafin to seniority were resisted by the other Yoruba kings whenever their political power allowed this independence, and it is remarkable that even where Oyo extended military and economic control over adjacent states, this was exercised indirectly through resident officials accredited to the rulers of the respective towns. No case seems to be recollected where an oba, much less a royal family, was dispossessed by either an Alafin or an Oni (though on one occasion, as related on p. 66 above, an Alafin seems to have intervened to impose a new Awujale at Ijebu Ode).[5]

Each of the Yoruba states was thus a sovereign entity, though related by tradition and sentiment to Ife and the other states of the Ife family (much like the ties between the seven Hausa Bakwai of northern Nigeria). The kingdom had a recognized centre in its capital town where the leading oba resided, surrounded by his chiefs, officials, and priests. This leading oba was the wearer of a beaded crown, bestowed on his ancestor, according to legend, from Ife, and his town was defined as *ilu alade*, 'crowned town' or capital. Subordinate towns were classified as *ilu ereko* (literally, 'towns on the fringe of the farmland'), which in turn ranged from the *ilu oloja* (a market town with an oba not entitled to a beaded crown) to the *ileto* (village), *abule* (hamlet), and *ago* or *aba* (camp, settlement); village heads were known in Oyo as Bale, a title which has now spread to most kingdoms. In some cases a kingdom contained more than one crowned oba and *ilu alade*; as a result of regrouping during the nineteenth-century wars at least two towns, Abeokuta and Shagamu, each had a number of crowned oba reigning in their different quarters. The titles of the oba usually derived from their towns, as in the case of the Olowo ('the lord of Owo') and many others. There are some notable exceptions to this, such as the Alafin and the Awujale, where other circumstances explain the title. The practice of forming titles from the name of a town or village has spread in recent years, and former Bale, such as the Olubadan of Ibadan and many lesser rulers, have assumed territorial designations.[6]

In addition to its recognized centre, there were also recognized boundaries to the Yoruba kingdom. These were apparently sometimes demarcated by earthworks, of which the Eredo of Ijebu Ode is the most conspicuous, but in any case the allegiance of every town was known, though liable to change with the fortunes of the kingdom, and there were clear, and strongly held, opinions about the extent of its farmland and forest. Certain obligations were laid on the subordinate towns by the government of a kingdom, for example, G. J. A. Ojo has identified the towns within the Owo kingdoms from which service was required in maintaining and repairing the ruler's palace, the Afin Olowo.[7]

In size the kingdoms varied considerably, from Oyo, covering over 10,000 square miles, to the miniature states of Ekiti where, for example, the Ewi of Ado ruled over only some seventeen small towns or villages. The larger kingdoms were subdivided into provinces. In addition, there were city states, such as Badagry and the Egbado towns. In Oyo, which seems to have been the most centralized in government as well as the greatest in extent, there were six provinces or *ekun*: three, the ekun Osi, or left-hand provinces, to the east of the Ogun and three, the ekun Otun, or right-hand provinces, to the west of the river. In each there were a dozen or more lesser oba ruling over the more important towns with their internally autonomous sub-kingdoms; in the Ekun Osi, for example, the leading oba was the Onikoyi of Ikoyi. These rulers were required to visit the Alafin during the annual Bere festival, when they presented him with thatching grass (*bere*) for his palace.[8] The large Ijebu and Egba kingdoms consisted of distinct but associated sub-kingdoms, among which two of the crowned oba, the Awujale and the Alake, were respectively pre-eminent. This quasi-federalism seems to reflect the historical development of these two kingdoms, each of which has traditions of several separate migrations into their areas.

The Yoruba oba is usually described as a sacred or divine king.[9] His coronation and installation were performed with solemn and lengthy rites which set him apart. He lived a life thereafter of ordered ceremonial, secluded in his palace, subject to many ritual restraints and approached only with infinite respect and by designated persons of the court. He rarely appeared in public, and then always robed and, in the case of the great oba, wearing a beaded crown whose fringe hid his face. He was not only the head of the town and kingdom but their personification, reincarnating also all his ancestors back to the origin of the dynasty, and he was titular head of all religious cults in the kingdom. This sacred aspect of Yoruba kingship did not lead to the oba's becoming an autocrat but rather the reverse. Not only was he bound by rules and precedents in his personal life but these also required him to submit all business to councils of chiefs and officers, and only after consultation and deliberation by these bodies could a policy be decided upon and proclaimed in the oba's name. Every oba had at least one council of chiefs who formed a powerful, usually hereditary, cabinet, and in most kingdoms there were lesser councils for the regulation of the different aspects of government. Moreover, the chieftaincies were hereditary within the 'descent groups' or extended families which made up the population of the town. Thus the chiefs were representatives of their family groups as well as being officials of the king and kingdom. Although the oba's authority expanded and contracted according to his personality and to the political, economic, and other conditions obtaining during his reign, he still seems normally to have been subject to many restraints.[10] It was these restraints which most sharply distinguished the Yoruba kingdom from the authoritarian monarchies of, for example, Benin and Dahomey, and from those based on conquest, like the Fulani emirates of northern Nigeria.

There is a tradition that the kingship at Oyo originally descended by primogeniture in the male line, and this may have been the case in other kingdoms of the Yoruba. But at some period, probably in the seventeenth century, the patrilineal hereditary system was modified at Oyo so that the choice of Alafin was exercised by the Oyo Mesi among a number of candidates from the royal house. This system was followed in most of the kingdoms and towns, with the notable exceptions of Egba Alake and Oke Ona, where all freemen were theoretically qualified to be chosen as oba by divination.[11] The royal family in most cases divided into two or more branches occupying different compounds in the town (and the usual practice in the present day is for the branches to take turns in presenting candidates to the leading chiefs as kingmakers on each vacancy). With a few exceptions (for example, the reputedly Borgu dynasties of Shaki and Kishi and the Bini dynasty at Lagos), the royal lines claim descent from the founders of the town who were of the same Yoruba stock as their followers.[12] There is thus no trace of a ruling caste in these kingships, such as obtains in the Hausa and Nupe states since the establishment of the Fulani dynasties in the nineteenth century. The royal wives were usually chosen from local women, and at Oyo new members of the Oyo Mesi were required to present a daughter in marriage to the Alafin. Oyo tradition, however, records an occasional marriage alliance with a neighbouring dynasty; Shango's mother is said to have been given in marriage to Oranyan by her father, the King of Nupe; Ofinran was the offspring of a Borgu woman, and in 1729 the King of Dahomey bestowed 'one of his Handsomest Daughters' on the Alafin.[13]

Many considerations determined the kingmakers' choice of an oba, but a guiding principle was to select a ruler who would respect and conform to the constitutional conventions of the kingdom. This would usually be a man neither youthful nor elderly, and in certain circumstances the kingmakers deliberately avoided a candidate whose presence or personality seemed too commanding; at Ketu an Alaketu designate had to be physically perfect and show no tendency towards autocracy, while at Ado Ekiti in 1910 a prince was rejected because he was so tall he would have looked down on his subjects.[14] The rules governing the succession varied from kingdom to kingdom. At Oyo there was a custom, broken on the death of Atiba in 1859, that the Alafin's eldest son, the Aremo, who was associated with his father in the government, should take his life on his father's death. In Ijebu and Owo it was held that no prince was eligible for the throne unless he had been born to a reigning oba. In early times it was not necessarily a male who was chosen as ruler, and the traditions of Ife, Oyo, Dassa, Ondo, and Ilesha record the reigns of female oba.

Despite the limitations on his power, the oba was no cipher or fainéant. In the first place, the sacredness of his office was neither empty nor nominal; he was really regarded by his people as a divinity with whose well-being their own condition was bound up. Then he was almost always the richest man in the town, since all tolls at gates and markets were paid to him, as well as various other forms of tribute. He was also the source of honour, able to bestow (usually within certain families), and in some cases to withdraw, titles and chieftaincies. With the chiefs he controlled the use of all land belonging to the town. Though legislative and judicial matters were discussed and decided by his councils, all laws were promulgated in his name, and he was the supreme arbiter in appeals. Military power was not in his hands, since the army was controlled by the war chiefs, but he alone could authorize a campaign; he also had at his disposal a personal bodyguard of household officers and slaves. Thus, if relations with other parties in the town or kingdom were strained the oba had many means of exerting his influence, though intrigue rather than a display of force was his usual weapon. For their part the chiefs could assert themselves against the oba by boycotting the palace, but an attempt to govern for long without his participation would be considered detrimental to the welfare of the town. In extreme cases of disagreement or the collapse of a policy the chiefs could contrive the deposition of an oba or even require his suicide. In general, however, 'a delicate balance of power' (in Lloyd's words) was achieved, and all parties in the state were usually at pains to maintain this.

The organization of the Alafin's household as re-created at New Oyo by Atiba is described in detail by Johnson.[15] It is clear that the life led by the inhabitants of the palace at Oyo was as elaborately ceremonious as that at Versailles or Schönbrunn, and based similarly on a hierarchy of office and honour; it has been stigmatized by

Morton-Williams as 'over-elaborate and anachronistic', and certainly it no longer reflected the true power of the king and his ministers at New Oyo. After the long rites of his coronation and installation, the Alafin disappeared into the seclusion of the palace and thereafter appeared in public only on the annual Ifa, Orun, and Bere festivals when, crowned and robed, he took his place in the throne room (*aganju*) or on its gabled veranda (*kobi aganju*). Apart from this, he rarely left the palace officially, although on moonlit nights he was permitted by custom to take an evening stroll incognito. Within the palace he was attended by numerous, carefully graded officials: his master of the horse, chaplains, musicians, drummers, and others, amounting to several hundreds. In addition, there were two bodies of officials of particular importance. The first were the eunuchs, called *iwefa* or 'lordlings of the palace' in Johnson's agreeable translation. The three principal iwefa bore high titles and represented the Alafin in various ways: the first, the Ona Efa ('eunuch of the centre') personated the Alafin in judicial processes, the second, the Otun Efa ('eunuch of the right'), in religious ceremonies, especially the Shango rites, and the third, the Osi Efa ('eunuch of the left'), in administrative and military functions. Secondly, a grade lower than the iwefa were the sixty-eight tonsured *ilari* ('scar heads'), royal slaves, each of whom bore a title alluding to some attribute or intention of the oba (for example, the *oba ko she tan*, 'the king is not ready'). Members of this corps provided the royal bodyguard, while others journeyed round the kingdom supervising the government or acted as the Alafin's diplomatists. Almost equally powerful were the ladies of the palace, led by the *iya oba* or official mother of the Alafin (his real mother having been invited to 'go to sleep' and 'decently buried' on her son's accession) and including numerous wives (*ayaba*, 'the queens'), officials, priestesses, and a group of female *ilari*. Apart from all these palace residents, certain members of the royal family held official positions at court. These included the Aremo, the three relatives designated as the 'fathers of the king', and his six 'brothers'.

Though the court of Oyo, the most powerful and highly organized kingdom, was probably the most elaborate, descriptions of the households of other oba suggest that it was repeated on a smaller scale, and with local differences in titles and duties, in the capitals of the other kingdoms and, on a still diminishing scale, in the subordinate towns everywhere. A visitor to any Yoruba ruler today, even in a small town or village, is at once aware of the courtly and privileged atmosphere which surrounds these kings.

The court and palace were complemented at Oyo by the council known as the Oyo Mesi (a title said to imply that 'Oyo knows the answers').[16] This consisted of seven chiefs or councillors, all holding titles hereditary in their families. Of these the leader was the Bashorun, whose power and influence, according to Johnson, were 'commonly greater than those of the others put together'. His position derived from his roles as principal kingmaker and as interpreter through annual divinations of the Alafin's personal *orun*, or spirit, as well as from his command of the army of the capital. Johnson writes that, 'There were times in the history of the nation when the Bashoruns were more powerful than the Alafin himself', and the example of Gaha at once comes to mind. A third element in the government, the Ogboni society, seems to have been introduced only in the nineteenth century at New Oyo, probably by Alafin Atiba (*c.* 1837–59).[17] This was a semi-secret cult devoted to the worship of the earth, which wielded both religious and political sanctions. At New Oyo it played a mediatory role between the palace officials and the Oyo Mesi, and is described by Morton-Williams as second to that council in its 'capacity to sanction the king's rule'. Members of the Oyo Mesi attended its meetings, held within the palace, though they had no priestly office. Its transactions were reported to the Alafin, who took no part in its deliberations or decisions, by a woman member. Its priests played an important role in the installation ceremonies of a new Alafin, ensuring the transmission to him of the powers of his ancestors.[18] The society was of greater antiquity and even greater importance in the Egba kingdoms where (as later at Abeokuta) it constituted the leading civil authority.[19] It was prominent also at Ife and in Ijebu, being known in the former kingdom as Imole and in the latter as Oshugbo. In addition to the Ogboni, other cult organizations, usually of lesser importance, existed in all towns and kingdoms; at Oyo the Egungun, a masked association led by the Alapini, a member of the Oyo Mesi, had a share in government by virtue of its function of recalling the ancestors.

Overlapping and parallel with all these bodies were associations of chiefs concerned with particular aspects of government and daily life, especially the conduct of war, of trade, and of hunting. Among the Egba the leading chiefs were members of the Ogboni; the Parakoyi were the trade chiefs, while the hunters, who in war acted as scouts for the main army, were grouped together as the Ode. Under Lishabi a fourth order was created in the towns, the Olorogun, leaders of the militia or war chiefs. Biobaku writes that the first three organizations 'corresponded very much to the division of life into youth, middle age and old age'.[20] In the Ijebu kingdom there were three main councils, occasionally overlapping in membership. The highest, the Ilamuren, consisting of the great magnates and officials under the presidency of the Olisa, discharged legislative, executive, and judicial functions relating to the whole kingdom. Next came the Oshugbo under the Oliwo, mainly concerned with the maintenance of order and the dispensing of justice, and then the Ipampa, composed of the younger men and overseeing administration and warfare. Whereas there was only one Ilamuren, that of the Awujale's capital, Oshugbo and Ipampa councils on the lines of those in Ijebu Ode existed in all the other major towns.

The government of a Yoruba kingdom and its capital thus presents a complex and somewhat confusing picture, mainly because of the fusion of political, judicial, and religious concepts and the division of responsibilities. Even in so small a kingdom as Ikere (in Ekiti), for example, the government exhibited this Byzantine quality; there were two groups of leading chiefs, each divided into three grades, and four main councils: the Iyare Mefa, or inner council, meeting daily; the Ajo Iyare, meeting every eight days to discuss town affairs; the Ajagun, or war council, and the Ajo Ilu, or general council of the town, held four times yearly.[21] Yet in practice all seems to have worked smoothly enough in these delicately balanced governments, except when some external pressure or crisis intervened to overthrow the slow and deliberate processes of the constitution. Naturally each kingdom developed different mechanisms for dealing with its individual problems, so that it would be futile to postulate any 'model' constitution for a Yoruba kingdom. On the other hand, with the notable exceptions of the new states of the nineteenth century, the main features of government – the town, the sacred oba at its centre, the hierarchy of hereditary chiefs and priests with their jealously guarded responsibilities – remained constant.

This form of government was not confined to the capital, but was repeated throughout the kingdom, every town forming a microcosm of the central government. The place of the crowned oba was taken by a lesser ruler, generally entitled to wear only a simple crown or coronet (called *akoro* in Oyo) or a cap of office. Usually these rulers were chosen like the greater oba by kingmakers from royal or chiefly houses and presented for approval to the oba of the kingdom, while in some cases the latter nominated the provincial rulers. In the Ijesha kingdom the majority of the provincial rulers were cadets of the royal family of the capital, and an Owa of Ilesha was required to have served as a Loja in the provinces before becoming eligible for his throne. Another centralizing feature of the Ijesha kingdom was the council known as Agbanla, consisting of three provincial rulers and three chiefs of Ilesha, who met to advise the Owa on matters concerning the kingdom as a whole. In most kingdoms the leading oba exercised the right to promote his uncrowned subordinates by conferring simple crowns and other insignia on them and their descendants. Like the office of oba, that of village head or *Bale* was hereditary, as indeed were most chieftaincies in town or country (military chieftaincies being among the common exceptions). Another device linking the capital with its provincial population was the system of clientship by which chiefs in the capital were recognized as patrons of one or more vassal small towns or villages. These chiefs represented the interests of their clients, to whom they were known as 'little fathers' (*babakekere*), at the ruler's court and transmitted tribute from the clients to the ruler, receiving a part back as their own dues. The system has been studied in Oyo and in Ibadan,[22] was also practised in Lagos, and probably obtained in most of the Yoruba kingdoms.

Although Yoruba society was nearly everywhere patrilineally based, so that a woman could not head a lineage, in most towns the women were represented by a female chief who co-ordinated their activities and participated in the political direction of the state. This chief, known by various titles of which Iyalode was the most common, was generally chosen by the oba and his chiefs and sat in their council. In Ilesha and Ondo, which both have traditions of female rulers and other traces of bilateral descent, the female chiefs (respectively, the Arishe and the Lobun) enjoyed unusual influence, while in Ibadan during the time of Are Latosa the powerful Iyalode Efunshetan was the focus of opposition to his rule.[23]

Turning from the oba and his court and nobles, the oba's people[24] must be considered. From the sociologist's point of view, the most important feature of Yoruba society was its organization into patrilineal 'descent groups' or 'extended families' of which the royal lineage was one. These consisted of persons who claimed descent from a common ancestor, usually living together in one ward (*adugbo*) of a town and often numbering over a thousand. Exceptionally, in Ijebu and Ondo descent is traced through both male and female ancestors. The living quarters or compound (*agbole*) of the extended family was subject to its senior (usually the eldest) member, the *bale* (who is not to be confused with the *Bale*, a village head in the Oyo and other kingdoms).

Despite its hierarchical character, Yoruba society was in practice surprisingly democratic. Distinctions of rank and wealth were offset by the obligations and benefits of the family and by common ownership of the land; opportunities to acquire high office and wealth were many, and no freeman was without a protector among the chiefs of his town. Then, just as all Yoruba were townspeople in the sense of either living in or having close ties with some parent town, so all were farmers, having a share in the family land and taking a part in its cultivation. But for many, farming was only a part-time or seasonal occupation, and a variety of crafts and trades were practised in the towns and countryside. Among the most prominent crafts were weaving and the working of iron, while some important crafts, such as pottery making and cloth dyeing, were reserved for women. The followers of these occupations often came from one family or group of families and compounds, and were bound together in guilds under the protection of their own deities and chiefs. In addition to these guilds, the population was grouped into associations (*egbe*) of different kinds; in some places, notably Ekiti, these were 'age-sets', associations of those born within a certain period to whom appropriate duties and public works were assigned by the town authorities, but elsewhere, for example at Oyo, the age-set system either never existed or was long ago replaced by associations of a social or professional kind.[25] In this society women played an important role, engaging in trade and crafts and admitted to a share in the conduct of government and religion.

Apart from the free subjects of the oba, every kingdom contained an unfree population.[26] A distinction must first be made between slavery and the system known as *iwofa*, which was practised among the Yoruba. In the latter a person could voluntarily pawn either himself or a relative (usually a child) as security for debt or to raise capital for trading or other purposes. This was a temporary measure which was discharged after the agreed services had been rendered to the creditor by the debtor. True slavery also existed, apparently on a large scale. The slaves were usually employed as farm labourers or servants in households, as bodyguards to the chiefs and as long-distance traders (*alajapa*). Just as only freemen were eligible to perform certain functions in society, so other roles were reserved for slaves; a proverb states, for example, that a 'a freeborn man is never made a gatekeeper' (*a ki ifi omoluwabi je onibode*). Royal slaves (called in different courts, for example, *emese, odi, eru oba*) fulfilled important functions inside and outside the palace, including that of ambassador. Though they were liable to be used as sacrifices by their masters, all slaves, even the humblest, seem otherwise to have been well treated. They were allowed to own property and to cultivate their own plots of land, and, as Oroge puts it, were slaves only to their own masters. The children of slaves remained the property of their parents' master, but the child of a freeman and a slave was free. It was possible for a slave to emancipate himself if he succeeded in accumulating enough property to satisfy his master. The ranks of the slaves were recruited from debtors, criminals, and (probably the major source) prisoners of war. Thus they were of mixed origin, some being native to the kingdom, others Yoruba from elsewhere, and others non-Yoruba. Unfortunately there is little evidence to determine either the proportion of the population which was unfree or the proportion of slaves who were of foreign origin. Oroge considers, however, that until about 1790 the majority of the slaves were taken from outside the respective kingdoms and that after that time recruitment was extended on a large scale to the native-born in order to meet the growing demands of the war chiefs for followers and of the coastal export trade. To Clapperton and the Landers the establishment of the regimes of Afonja and the Fulani at Ilorin was repeatedly described as a revolt of the Alafin's Hausa slaves,[27] which suggests that in the Oyo kingdom the alien slave population had increased to a dangerous extent.

Finally, an historical account of the Yoruba must include some description of the religious beliefs which played so large a part in their lives. Something of these has already appeared in passages in the first two chapters concerning the traditions of origin. These traditions refer to a creator or 'high god', called Olorun, 'owner of the sky', or Olodumare, 'all-highest', according to context. However remote such a god may be from man's daily activities, the concept has enabled scholars such as Idowu to claim that Yoruba religion was (and is) essentially monotheistic. But far nearer to the Yoruba were the numerous cult groups (such as the Ogboni) and their associated pantheon of greater and lesser gods (*orisha*), some common to the majority of the people and some associated with or even immanent in particular localities. Then, as has been seen above, the oba was himself a representative on earth of his divine ancestor and was thus a sacred being, a feature which emphasizes both the immediacy of Yoruba religion to daily life and the theocratic nature of Yoruba forms of government.[28]

The theological content of this religion proved insufficient to enable it to resist the advance of two world religions, Christianity and Islam. The first, as will be seen in subsequent chapters, was introduced in the 1840s, and by the end of the century congregations had been built up in most of the major towns. The latter penetrated Yorubaland much earlier, possibly in or even before the seventeenth century,[29] and there were groups of Muslims in the Oyo towns in the eighteenth century.[30] Travellers in the first half of the nineteenth century met numerous Muslims all or most of whom, however, were visitors like themselves. It was not until the second half of the century that conversions took place on a large scale, partly as a result of the dispersion over Yorubaland of many Oyo who were already Muslims.

NOTES

1. The institutions of the Yoruba kingdoms are described in this chapter in the past tense, since this is an historical work, and the traditional system of government has in any case been largely superseded. Nevertheless, much survives, though in attenuated form.
2. Goddard, *passim*.
3. Hill, p. 302.
4. Oguntuyi, p. 118.
5. The term *ebi* refers to the living family, excluding ancestors. For the 'system', see Akinjogbin (1966b), p. 451. Akinjogbin (1965) describes the sending of the sword from Ife as 'The most important ceremony at the coronation of any Alafin', a view which is not held at Oyo. Other oba, for example the Awujale of Ijebu, have state 'swords of justice', but none of these swords seems to have any connection with Ife. For a detailed refutation of the ebi theory, see Law (1968b) and (1969). Akinjogbin and Ayandele re-state the ebi theory in Ikime (ed.) (1980), p. 125.
6. See Ojo (1966a), pp. 126–9. The word 'Bale' (*oba ile*, 'head of the land') must be distinguished from 'bale' (*oba ile*, 'head of the house').
7. Ojo (1966b), pp. 63–6.
8. S. Johnson (1921), pp. 68, 75–7; Morton-Williams (1967), p. 40.
9. Much of this section derives from Lloyd (1960a).

10. Law (1977), pp. 96–7, considers it 'misleading' to try to identify the specific rights enjoyed by an Alafin.
11. Ajisafe, pp. 103–4. There is a royal family of Egba Gbagura.
12. Agiri (1975), p. 10, believes that Alafin Abipa on re-occupying Old Oyo rewarded his Borgu followers by giving them towns to rule. In this way dynasties still reputed to be of Borgu origin were established at Kishi, Igboho, and Igbetti, and at certain new settlements, in particular Ogbomosho. See also the lists in Kenyo, Chapters 1–3, which identify Benin as the 'centre of origin' of several kingships, and in one case, that of the Oloje of Oje, give Nupe as the origin.
13. S. Johnson (1921), pp. 149, 159; Snelgrave, p. 135.
14. Asiwaju in Crowder and Ikime, p. 137; Oguntuyi, p. 91.
15. S. Johnson (1921), pp. 40–69; Morton-Williams (1967), *passim*.
16. S. Johnson (1921), pp. 70–2.
17. Atanda (1973): Agiri (1972). Agiri (1966), p. 47, first concluded that the society was 'not traditional to the system of government in Oyo Ile but was an innovation of the nineteenth century'.
18. Morton-Williams (1964b), p. 253; (1967), pp. 42, 53. He concludes from field-work in New Oyo that Ogboni existed also in Oyo Ile, though in his article in 1960, p. 364, fn. 1, he noticed that 'Johnson, curiously, does not mention the Ogboni in Oyo, but only among the Egba'.
19. Ajisafe, pp. 27–8; Biobaku (1956b), *passim*. Ogboni was probably a late-comer in Egbado too.
20. Biobaku (1957), p. 6.
21. Adegoriola, *passim*.
22. Awe (1964a,b), pp. 53–4; Law (1971), p. 30.
23. Awe (1974), *passim*.
24. The word 'people' in Yoruba presents some difficulty. In the sense of 'all men' it is *omo araiye*, 'children of the world'. The word 'Yoruba' for the whole linguistic group has been in use for only about a century and is still not always understood in that sense; historically it only applies to the inhabitants of the Oyo kingdom. In the case of the people of a kingdom and sub-kingdom (for example, Egba, Remo), the names connote the inhabitants as well as the political and physical division. The name of a town is also applied to its people, though they are more usually described as its 'children' or 'relatives'; for example, *omo Oyo*, a man belonging to and born in Oyo, and *ara Oyo*, a man of Oyo though not necessarily born there – the distinction between these is not, however, strictly observed. Other distinctions are made between a town-dweller (*omo ile*), a countryman (*ara oko*), and (sometimes pejoratively) a 'highlander' or rustic (*ara oke*).
25. Forde, pp. 10–27.
26. Forde, pp. 26–7; Oroge, *passim*.
27. Clapperton, pp. 25, 28, 39; R. L. and J. Lander (1832), pp. 91–2.
28. Dr Harold Turner kindly read and criticized this passage.
29. Bivar and Hiskett, p. 115. See also El-Masri in Lloyd, Mabogunje and Awe, p. 249, on the basis of a statement by Ahmed Baba of Timbuktu.
30. Gbadamosi (1978), Chapter 1. There were a few 'nominal' Muslims in Ibadan from its foundation: El-Masri, loc. cit., p. 250.

NINE

WAR

The reviewer of a recent history of Dahomey complained that *l'histoire-bataille* played too large a part in the work.[1] This suggests that the critic had not thought enough about the nature either of man or of his history. War is the most decisive act of policy undertaken by any nation. Moreover, among the Yoruba kingdoms, and most West African states, campaigns were so frequent as to be a normal, though seasonal, activity. Political and military history are so closely connected in the area and period covered by this book as to be almost synonymous. Wars, campaigns, and battles are of first importance, both in themselves and in their consequences. It is therefore pertinent to consider how they were fought, though until the latter part of the nineteenth century the evidence is fragmentary.[2]

In most of the Yoruba kingdoms and towns, leadership in war was exercised by chiefs whose roles and titles were specifically military. The Oyo system[3] seems to have been the most highly developed, and as well as being reproduced in the provincial towns of that kingdom, it became the pattern for Ibadan and other states in the nineteenth century. The Alafin, like other oba, rarely took the field himself, and on Atiba's accession it was decided that in future he should never do so. The commander of the army of the capital, and so the senior general, was the Bashorun, who was also the Alafin's first minister and head of the Oyo Mesi. The field command was exercised by a series of war chiefs of whom the leader was the Balogun ('war lord'). Separate ranks or titles were conferred on the leaders of the vanguard (made up of youthful warriors), the cavalry, and the older chiefs, the last of whom accompanied the army as advisers and looked after the camp and baggage. Apart from these officers, and perhaps overshadowing them on the field, was the *corps d'élite* known as the Esho, consisting of 70 principal war chiefs of the capital, each bringing his retainers with him. The Alafin had his own bodyguard, recruited from the palace officials. In war these metropolitan forces were substantially reinforced by contingents raised in the provinces. These, led by their own rulers or war chiefs, were under the command of the Are Ona Kakamfo (a title usually abbreviated to Kakamfo or Are) or generalissimo, whose office apparently dated from the latter half of the seventeenth century and who was usually chosen from the minor provincial rulers.[4] The Kakamfo was given wide powers to carry out specific military operations, and presumably gave orders in battle to the metropolitan as well as to his provincial forces. He established an independent base near the frontiers of the kingdom and was not usually allowed to visit the capital.

Military service in all the Yoruba states was theoretically obligatory on all able-bodied freemen. The households of the chiefs, with their numerous slaves and bodyguards, formed the nucleus of the army but, apart from these, troops were raised on a short-term basis from those who responded to the call to arms for each campaign and enrolled with their weapons in the ranks of the chief to whom each owed allegiance; most of these recruits would already have had training of a sort as hunters in the bush. The army of the capital provided the main army of the kingdom, but every town could raise some sort of force, and contingents from the towns were absorbed into the army of the kingdom where conditions allowed; in the Ibadan empire of the mid-nineteenth century, and probably in other states too, quotas of troops, food, and ammunition were required from the provincial towns.

Important changes were taking place in Yorubaland during the nineteenth century, as will be seen from Part III of this book. Although many traditional war chieftaincies were non-hereditary, and therefore could be conferred on suitable candidates, these changes, in particular the introduction on a growing scale of firearms and the tendency towards larger armies which also remained much longer in the field, led to the emergence of a class of professional military leaders. Such men, of whom Ogedengbe of Ilesha and the chiefs of Ibadan are examples, owed their positions to their soldierly qualities rather than to birth, and their restless ambitions contributed to the prolongation of the wars. Their swarming followers, the 'war boys' (*omo ogun*), who were mostly slaves, constituted an element which grew in importance, especially in Ibadan, until it resembled a standing army.

The size of the Yoruba armies must have varied considerably according to the resources of the kingdom and the situation. Snelgrave writes of an Oyo army sent against Dahomey in the early eighteenth century as consisting of 'many Thousands' of horsemen,[5] and Norris writes:

> The *Dahomans*, to give an idea of the strength of an *Eyoe* army, assert, that when they go to war, the general spreads the hide of a buffaloe before the door of his tent, and pitches a spear in the ground, on each side of it: between which the soldiers march, until the multitude, which pass over the hide, have worn a hole through it; as soon as this happens, he presumes that his forces are numerous enough to take the field.[6]

According to Clapperton, in 1826:

> The military force of Oyo consists of the caboceers [chiefs] and their own immediate retainers, which, allowing one hundred and fifty to each, will not give such immense armies as we have sometimes heard stated: that of Yoruba is perhaps as numerous as any of the kingdoms of Africa.[7]

On the other hand, Jones, a British officer who wrote a report on the Egba army in 1861, emphasized that the chiefs' warrior retainers formed only a small proportion of the Egba forces when that state engaged in full-scale war; the majority were 'farmers or engaged in peaceful occupation' who either enlisted voluntarily or, in time of crisis, were conscripted. He estimated that in the battle which he witnessed at Ijaye on 23 May 1861 '17,000 men engaged in mortal combat' – of whom 'the killed on both sides, as ascertained by spies were five and the wounded under fifty!'[8]

Bosman writes that the (presumably) Oyo army which attacked Allada in 1698 was a wholly cavalry force.[9] Snelgrave and Dalzel[10] confirm that the Oyo armies sent to the south-west in the first part of the eighteenth century were cavalry, though the passage quoted above from Norris suggests the occasional inclusion of infantry. It seems reasonable to conclude that the predominance of Oyo over its neighbours, and also the exceptional extent of the kingdom, were based upon the possession of a skilled cavalry mounted on the larger type of horses bred in the savannah and deriving from imports across the Sahara (rather than on the Yoruba ponies). The capital and most of the kingdom lay within the savannah, where cavalry could move with ease and speed. Horses could be better maintained here than in the tsetse-ridden forests of the south, and though breeding was unprofitable because of the combination of the long gestation period of the horse with some danger even in the savannah from tsetse, remounts of good quality could be readily obtained from the north and north-east, a position which was to change in the troubles of the late eighteenth century.

In the other Yoruba kingdoms, situated mainly or wholly within the forest belt, it is doubtful whether a cavalry arm was developed to any extent, despite the adoption of cavalry ranks and titles by the Ibadan and Abeokutans in the nineteenth century. These armies must therefore have been almost wholly composed of infantry, though, as nineteenth century observers noted, chiefs and their immediate followers (the latter acting as scouts and messengers) were mounted. The majority of the horses in the south were small and usually of poor quality, though Jones observed of the Egba horses that they were 'numerous and hardy'.[11]

Before the general introduction of firearms into Yoruba warfare the primary armament of the soldiers consisted of swords, thrusting and throwing spears, and bows and arrows, including cross-bows, all of which continued to be used as supplementary to firearms up to the end of the nineteenth-century wars.[12] Infantry and cavalry weapons do not seem to have been differentiated; the spear and the lance were apparently the same weapon, and in the eighteenth century the Oyo horsemen were sometimes armed with bows as well as the more usual swords and lances.[13] Swords were of two main types: the heavier, single-bladed and eccentrically curved *agedengbe*, and the *ida*, usually double-bladed and either with an elongated leaf-shaped blade or approximating to European or Near Eastern types. Other varieties of swords and knives were also used, such as the short *jomo*, the *tanmogayi* (sabre), *ada*, *ogbo* or *ele* (cutlass), and *obe* (dagger). With the exception of the *obe*, all these were designed primarily for cutting rather than for thrusting or stabbing. Spears and arrows all carried iron heads, often barbed. In addition to these primary weapons, clubs of different types, in both iron and wood, throwing knives, fighting bracelets, and slings were used as secondary armament, though probably only by foot-soldiers. Apart from that small proportion of the swords and knives which had steel blades, all these weapons were of local manufacture.

Firearms were not brought into general use in the Yoruba armies until around the 1840s, considerably later than in some other Guinea states.[14] Yet the Ekiti had encountered firearms probably as early as the sixteenth century, when Benin soldiers, armed with guns, supported the Ikere in a war against the Ado.[15] Again, in the early eighteenth century an Oyo cavalry force lost an engagement to Dahomean infantry armed with guns, the noise of the firing so alarming the Oyo horses that their riders could not bring them to charge the enemy.[16] Unlike the older weapons, firearms could not be manufactured locally, but it is surprising that the Oyo did not earlier obtain supplies from their non-African partners in the Atlantic slave trade. It is significant that the first use of firearms on any considerable scale by a Yoruba army was in the 1820s, when the Ijebu, noted for their trading contacts on the lagoon, equipped their soldiers with guns in the Owu war, while about this time the Oyo, according to Lander, were procuring 'quantities of muskets' from the east, though they were of little use as 'the people . . . do not know how to handle them with effect' and sometimes carried them into battle without powder or ball.[17] As late as the battle of Oshogbo, about 1840, firearms played little part, but by the time of the Ijaye war, opening in 1860, the musket had become the primary weapon of the Yoruba infantry. These muskets were primitive flintlocks firing shot.[18] They were known as Dane guns, though probably more came from Holland and England than from Denmark. Breech-loading rifles, firing cartridges, were introduced by the Egba during this war, and these modern precision weapons assumed great importance during the Sixteen Years' War.[19]

The dress and accoutrement of the Yoruba warrior can be reconstructed in some detail, at least so far as nineteenth-century use is concerned. Though Jones refers to the Egba foot-soldiers at Ijaye as wearing distinctive striped war jackets,[20] there does not seem to have been any concept of uniform; friend could usually be distinguished from foe at close quarters by his facial marks. Most soldiers doubtless wore the padded jackets, sewn over with cowries and charms, such as are still used by hunters, and their leaders would have worn more elaborate versions of these with such additions as the *wabi*, or war-apron. Except for the tradition that Alafin Ofinran's Bashorun wore a coat of iron (*ewa irin*), and the preservation of two (probably imported) coats of chain mail in the palace at Owo, there seems no trace of any use of metal armour by the Yoruba. Horse trappings and equipment probably varied according to the status of the rider. Both 'English' and Oriental saddles were in use, the latter with high pommel and cantle. Bits and stirrups were often cast in brass and handsomely decorated with geometrical patterns; surviving metal stirrups are all of the curved Arab type.[21]

Most towns were encircled by walls. These were usually mounds or ramparts of banked-up earth, though in places free-standing mud walls were built; exceptionally, low dry-stone walls were constructed in hill country, where this material was abundant.[22] Elsewhere, fences of stakes were constructed, as around Oshogun in the Oyo kingdom or along the lagoons in the south. Though these all served to mark the boundaries between the town and its outer farmland, they seem to have been primarily designed as fixed defences, and there are several accounts of their construction or repair in time of danger and of fighting along them. Often there was a double circuit of walls, enabling an army to be drawn up in the intervening space of one or two hundred yards, and sometimes – as at Oyo Ile and Igboho – there were even three walls. The walls were of two main types: a mound up to about twenty feet in height and correspondingly broad, and a low breastwork only about four feet high. Both were provided with outer ditches planted with thorns and converted into a partial moat by the rains, beyond which there was usually a zone of dense bush for further protection. Gates and gatehouses were inserted at intervals; in some cases these were elaborate structures with angled entries and free-standing walls with slits for bowmen. Presumably the tops of the higher walls were flattened to allow movement along them; occasionally the lower walls were protected against erosion by a sloping roof of thatch, and elsewhere were increased in height by the addition of a bamboo palisade. In the nineteenth-century wars the Egba and Egbado erected wooden watchtowers along their walls, though more often sentries were posted in high trees at the edge of the town or camp. At Ijaye, Jones noted that most of the chiefs used 'reconnoitring glasses or telescopes' for observation of the enemy.[23]

Plate 12 Gateway of Ipara, Ijebu Remo. Engraved from a sketch by Dr E.G. Irving, R.N. From the *Church Missionary Gleaner*, 1855.

Several European observers of the 'interior wars' of the Yoruba in the nineteenth century have dismissed them as mere slave raids and as conducted in a desultory and haphazard way, without strategy and with little attempt at tactics. But as has been demonstrated elsewhere,[24] the issues of these wars were primarily political, concerning, as in most wars in the world's history, questions of power, and this seems equally to apply to the earlier wars described in the first part of this book. This is not to deny the connexion between power and wealth, and in West Africa between wealth and the holding of slaves. Certainly war had considerable economic importance for the Yoruba and their neighbours as a source of captives.

Nor were strategic concepts lacking. The encirclement of the Oyo empire by Ojigi's army, for example, was an enterprise on a grand scale (if the tradition is accepted) while the nineteenth century withdrawal into the forests and Alafin Atiba's subsequent redisposition of responsibilities to Ibadan and Ijaye suggest an appreciation of the military and political situation at the level of strategy. Yet it is also true that war was often undertaken, at least before the nineteenth century, mainly as an annual or bi-annual exercise. Johnson writes: 'In early times expeditions were sent out every other year by the Alafin of Oyo to distant countries chiefly among the Popos. War was then for spoils and to keep their hands in . . .'[25] The dry season was chosen for such campaigns, and Snelgrave was told by the Dahomeans that the Oyo were obliged to retire at the beginning of the rains for want of forage.[26]

Warfare was undertaken by the Yoruba with deliberation. Only after lengthy discussion in the councils of the kingdom, exhortatory speeches to the troops, and sacrifices to the war standard did the army move out to the vicinity of the enemy. The next step was the formation of a camp. In the nineteenth-century wars, which were often prolonged from year to year, these camps were of such extent and elaboration as to resemble small towns. Walls (of the breastwork type) and an outer ditch were built, and within these the living-quarters of the troops were constructed of mud or branches and thatched with grass, and farms were planted with maize, cassava, and other crops.[27] A large part of the military operations in the nineteenth century consisted in skirmishes around these comfortable camps and in the maintenance of sieges, with only occasional clashes in the open and assaults along the walls of a town or camp.

The character of the fighting in the field was largely determined by the contrasting nature of the country. In the open savannah cavalry was predominant,[28] while in the forests of the south – as the Fulani learnt – horses were hindered in their movement and decimated by disease.[29] When battle was joined it usually took the form of isolated skirmishes, tactics being confined after the initial deployment to the use of reserve troops. Commanders were, however, able to exercise some control over their men by beating out orders and information on their war-drums, which could also be used for deceiving the enemy. The introduction of firearms led to a decrease in close fighting, though it did not otherwise greatly affect methods of warfare. Descriptions of the fighting at Ijaye agree that the respective armies engaged in a series of short advances and retreats, each line of infantry discharging its weapons and then retiring to the rear to reload.[30] No concepts of covering fire or of fire and movement by even the smallest formation seem to have developed. This is understandable when the only firearms in use were the inaccurate and short-range flintlock muskets, but these tactics – if they can be so called – persisted even after rifles had become available from the 1860s onwards. Despite the high price of the rifles, there were considerable numbers in use by both sides in the later stages of the Kiriji war, though they continued to be used by individual marksmen rather than as a mass weapon, and were accordingly less effective than would be expected. In the fighting between the Ibadan and the Ilorin farther north, firearms played little part, even down to the final skirmishes on the Otin in the 1890s. This last phase of the wars, indeed, resembled the sometimes unreal warfare of Rennaissance Italy, and at Ile Aro near Ilobu in one of the last actions a battle was opened in Ariosto-style by single combat between two mounted champion lancers from the respective armies.[31]

Almost all reports about Yoruba warfare concern fighting on land. But naval battles also occurred on the lagoon, where the Ijebu and Awori peoples maintained fleets of war canoes. There is a glimpse of this form of warfare in the eighteenth century when Dalzel, describing operations against Badagry by the Dahomean army, assisted by Oyo and Lagos, writes that the Oba of Lagos sent thirty-two large canoes up the western lagoon in order to cut Badagry's communications, and took many prisoners in the course of this action.[32]

Finally, though West African warfare apparently followed its conservative pattern for many centuries, human ingenuity could always play a part. On one occasion in the early eighteenth century, according to Snelgrave, an Oyo cavalry force invading Dahomey was baited with brandy and then attacked while they slept off their drunkenness.[33] Again, in 1825 the Fulani, Clapperton was told, mounted an aerial incendiary attack against a group of Yoruba villages near Oyo Ile. Clapperton writes:

> Algi consists of three walled villages, and before it was burnt down had been of considerable size: they pointed out a rock close to the south side of the town, from whence the Fellatas [Fulani] flew the pigeons to set fire to it. The mode of doing it was, by making combustibles fast to the tails of the birds, which, on being left loose from the hand, immediately flew to the tops of the thatched houses, while the Fellatas kept up a sharp fire of arrows, to prevent the inhabitants extinguishing the flames.[34]

But it seems more likely that what was being described was an attack by incendiary arrows, a method well-known to the Fulani.

Evidence about the casualties inflicted in Yoruba warfare is contradictory.[35] It seems likely that the scornful references by Burton and Jones to casualties almost derisorily low in comparison with the numbers involved in the nineteenth-century battles cannot be considered as applying to all the major engagements. The reports of missionary observers at Ijaye and Abeokuta show that on occasion the numbers of killed and wounded were high; this applied particularly to engagements with the fierce Dahomeans. The fate of captives varied according to circumstances; the most unfortunate were executed on the battlefield, the most fortunate were released or redeemed, while the majority were sold into slavery.

As to the general effects of the wars, it is likely that both in the nineteenth century and earlier economic and social dislocation was confined to the towns which were the main protagonists, and that the lives of the country people continued to follow the old patterns. By the nineteenth century it seems that warriors were coming increasingly to prefer taking captives in battle, as slave material, rather than to kill or maim their enemies. Paradoxically, this both aggravated the incidence of war and also mitigated its effects. Nevertheless, these wars cannot be dismissed as mere slave raids nor as, in Trevor-Roper's picturesque phrase, 'the unrewarding gyrations of barbarous tribes'. They concerned real issues of politics and power, and in their consequences for the men and women of the Yoruba kingdoms they were momentous.

NOTES

1. Review by Béatrice Olympio of Cornevin's *Histoire de Dahomey* in *Etudes Dahoméenes*, No. 2, June 1964.

2. S. Johnson (1921) deals with warfare on pp. 131–7; his account seems to derive mainly from the Ibadan army in the nineteenth century rather than from Oyo in its heyday. See also Ajayi and Smith, *passim*, for the nineteenth-century evidence.
3. See Law (1977), Chapter 9.
4. The Onokoyi, or king of Ikoyi, as the most important subordinate ruler of the Ekun Osi, or home province of the Oyo kingdom, was sometimes appointed to command the forces of the province or provinces. This seems to date from a time before the first appointment of a Kakamfo.
5. Snelgrave, p. 56.
6. Norris (1789), pp. 11–16 (Hodgkin, p. 167).
7. Clapperton, p. 57.
8. Ajayi and Smith, pp. 133, 139.
9. Bosman, pp. 397–8.
10. Snelgrave, p. 56; Dalzel, pp. 12ff.
11. Clapperton, p. 34; Ajayi and Smith, pp. 15–16, 134–5; Law (1980a), *passim*.
12. See Smith (1967), *passim*.
13. Snelgrave, p. 56; Lander (1830), p. 80.
14. For example, the Asante and the Dahomeans were using guns probably before the end of the seventeenth century, and the latter even acquired a few cannon in the eighteenth century.
15. Oguntuyi, pp. 27–8; Bradbury (1959), p. 279.
16. Snelgrave, p. 56.
17. Lander (1830), ii, p. 222; S. Johnson (1921), p. 208.
18. Ajayi and Smith, pp. 17–21.
19. S. Johnson (1921), pp. 357, 415.
20. Ajayi and Smith, p. 134.
21. Clapperton, p. 2; Lander (1830), p. 69; S. Johnson (1921), p. 160; Smith (1967), pp. 110–13; Smith (1971b), *passim*.
22. For example, at Erin, near Iseyin (see Smith (1964), p. 25), Oke Amo (see Ojo (1966a), pp. 149–50), and Gbagba (see Church Missionary Society (CMS) Archives, CA 2/085, Townsend's Journal, January 12 1855). As regards the building of these walls, Clapperton's description of the work which he saw going foward on the walls of Bussa in Borgu would probably apply to Yoruba practice. He writes (p. 98): 'Bands of male and female slaves, accompanied by drums and flutes and singing in chorus, were passing to and from the river with water, to mix the clay they were building with. Each great man has his part of the wall to build, like the Jews when they built the walls of Jerusalem, everyone opposite his own house.'
23. Ajayi and Smith, pp. 23–8.
24. Ajayi and Smith, *passim*.
25. S. Johnson (1921), p. 131.
26. Snelgrave, pp. 121–2.
27. Ajayi and Smith, pp. 27–8, 136–7. At the conclusion of the Kiriji war, S. Johnson (1921), who was acting as an interpreter to the peace commissioners appointed by the Governor of Lagos, contrasted the quarters in the Ekitiparapo camp, which were constructed of bamboo walls under roofs of leaves, with those in the Ibadan camp, which had mud walls and thatch roofs: p. 552. Possibly the Ibadan built more solid quarters for protection against the greater number of breech-loading rifles used by their adversaries, and their huts certainly withstood the firing of the camps after the peace treaty longer than those of the Ekiti and their allies. For the Dahomean camps with thatched quarters 'resembling bee-hives', see Snelgrave, pp. 28–9.
28. Snelgrave, pp. 56, 121–2; S. Johnson (1921), p. 263.
29. S. Johnson (1921), p. 222; Ajayi and Smith, pp. 33–6.
30. Ajayi and Smith, pp. 138–9; Stone, Ch. XVIII.
31. S. Johnson (1921), p. 604.
32. Dalzel, pp. 183–4. For the Ijebu war canoes, see Osifekunde in Curtin (1967), p. 287.

Clapperton (p. 2) notes that the Badagri mounted cannon in the prows of their canoes, as did the warriors of the creeks farther east (thus taking advantage of an excellent natural means of absorbing the recoil).

33. Snelgrave, p. 57–8.
34. Clapperton, p. 62.
35. This paragraph is based on Ajayi and Smith, pp. 50–3, 127–8.

PART III

TEN

THE DECLINE AND FALL OF OLD OYO

On 23 January 1826 Captain Hugh Clapperton, R. N., accompanied by his servant Richard Lander, an English merchant from the Benin River, Mr Houtson, and a small party of Africans, reached Oyo Ile after travelling for forty-seven days, at first by canoe and then by horse and on foot, from Badagry up the road which was the main artery of the trade of the Oyo kingdom.[1] Lander was destined to return down the road to Badagry at the end of 1827 after Clapperton's death, taking only thirty days on this occasion,[2] and then travelled up it again with his brother John in 1830 on the journey from which he returned by sailing down the Niger to the sea, settling the long controversy about the course of the river. Although Clapperton and his companions may not have been the first Europeans to visit Oyo, having been preceded, according to Adams,[3] by a French officer from a slave ship, their accounts[4] provided the first known descriptions of the interior of Yorubaland.

Perhaps the most striking aspect of these journeys is the comparative ease and security with which they were accomplished. The diseases prevalent in West Africa took their toll, and before Oyo was reached Clapperton's colleagues, Captain Pearce and Dr Morrison, as well as the sailor Dawson, had died, but this was no reflection on political conditions along the road. Everywhere peace and order seemed to prevail. Escorts, carriers, and horses were available throughout without great difficulty, and the travellers and their goods went forward in safety. At 'Jannah' (Ijanna in Egbado) Clapperton writes:

> I cannot omit bearing testimony to the singular and perhaps unprecedented fact, that we have already travelled sixty miles in eight days, with a numerous and heavy baggage, and about ten different relays of carriers, without losing so much as the value of a shilling public or private; a circumstance evincing not only somewhat more than common honesty in the inhabitants, but a degree of subordination and regular government which could not have been supposed to exist amongst a people hitherto considered barbarians.[5]

When the forest with its tortuous paths had been left behind, the going was easier, and Lander described the road near 'Chaadoo' (about a day's journey south-west of Shaki) as 'not at all inferior to a drive round a gentleman's park in England'.[6] The towns were busy, populous, and prosperous; in Ijanna, for example, cloth and earthenware were manufactured and the market was supplied with many commodities, while the number of inhabitants of the 'large, double-walled town' of Kushu was reckoned to be at least twenty thousand.[7] The farms were planted with many different crops, and the people owned horses, asses, and mules and 'a great abundance of sheep and goats'.[8] From Oyo down to the coast the country still seemed firmly under the control of the Alafin. The kingdom, according to Clapperton, extended in the south to 'Puka' (Ipokia, a few miles inland from Badagry across the River Yewa), Lagos, and Whydah, and was bounded in other directions by Ketu, Borgu, 'Accoura, a province of Benin' (presumably Akure), and Ijebu. But the Alafin's claim that 'Badagry, Alladah, and Dahomey' belonged to him was a nostalgic recollection of the past tributary relationships rather than a description of the contemporary situation, since all three had by this time escaped from their allegiance to Oyo.[9]

The capital of this still large state was built 'on the sloping side and round the base of a small range of granite hills which, as it were, forms the citadel of the town', and was of imposing size.

> A belt of thick wood runs round the walls, which are built of clay and about twenty feet high, and surrounded by a dry ditch. There are ten gates in the walls, which are about fifteen miles in circumference, of an oval shape, about four miles in diameter one way, and six miles the other, the south end leaning against the rocky hills, and forming an inaccessible barrier in that quarter.

From the north gate to the palace was an hour's ride, or about five miles, much of the intervening ground being 'open and cultivated'. Within the town seven different markets were held every morning, selling a great variety of foodstuffs, animals, cloth, and apparently also slaves. Of the palace, Clapperton writes that it occupied about a square mile and was built of clay with thatched roofs, 'similar to those nearer the coast', and presumably the other compounds in the town were built in this way. He admired the decoration which he saw applied to the houses: 'The people of Katunga are fond of ornamenting their doors, and the posts which support their verandahs, with carvings; and they also have statues or figures of men and women, standing in their court yards.'[10] Lander was deeply impressed by the principal 'fetish hut' with its many carved figures, and noted that there were fifty other such shrines in the capital.[11] Most of these statues were presumably carved in wood, but these and other passages, together with a small number of objects associated with the town, suggest that there may also have been a tradition at Oyo of sculpture in bronze, stone, and terracotta, and there was evidently an Oyo art as distinct in style as the arts of Ife and other towns of Yorubaland.[12]

But despite all the evidence afforded to Clapperton and the Landers, both on their journey from the coast and in the capital, that the people of Oyo enjoyed good 'mild' government and a prosperous economy, there were disquieting reports and signs that all was far from well in the kingdom. In the first place there had occurred the serious 'rebellion of the Hausa slaves against the king of Yarriba', as it was described to Clapperton at Shaki,[13] which led to the establishment at Ilorin, only some twenty miles to the south-east of Oyo, of a base for the advance of the Fulani-led jihad of the recently founded empire of Sokoto and Gwandu. But the Fulani did not comprise the only danger with which the Oyo – and indeed, the Yoruba as a whole – were now faced. In addition, a number of the rulers of other large towns within the kingdom followed the example of Ilorin in asserting their independence, and then, after successfully defying the Alafin, fell to quarrelling among themselves. Even more serious, a general state of war involving almost the whole of Yorubaland was approaching, usually referred to, rather misleadingly, as the 'civil' or 'inter-tribal' wars. This was precipitated by a war which broke out in the south between the Owu and a coalition of the Ife and Ijebu, but fundamentally it was a consequence of the decline in the power of Oyo which, as has been seen, set in towards the end of the reign of Alafin Abiodun in the late eighteenth century. The security and economy of the kingdom were breaking down; already Borgu bandits and slave-raiders infested the roads of northern Oyo,[14] and soon armies were marching and counter-marching about the country, leaving in their wake desolation and confusion.

The collapse of this ancient kingdom, once the most powerful of the Guinea states, presents a problem which has already received considerable attention from historians.[15] The problem is twofold: to explain in general terms why the kingdom collapsed – to isolate the 'dispositional factors', if jargon is resorted to – and then to explain why the collapse took place as and when it did, for the abandonment of the capital and of much of northern Yorubaland was a discrete event. Again, as in most problems of this kind, internal factors have to be balanced against external ones, and the historian must be on his guard against confusing cause with effect.

As has already appeared in Chapter 3, the mid-eighteenth century was a time of political instability at Oyo. This has been explained on various grounds. Undoubtedly, the personalities of those concerned, especially of the ambitious Bashorun Gaha, played a part in this situation. Beyond this, Lloyd has speculated that competition for control of the new resources which derived from the territorial expansion of the kingdom and its share in the lucrative Atlantic slave trade upset the balance of power between the Alafin and the Oyo Mesi.[16] On the one hand, the king used his new wealth to increase the staff of palace slaves, mainly non-Yoruba, through whom much of his administration was conducted, while on the other the great chiefs, enriched by war booty and by their part in the slave trade (there being at Oyo no royal monopoly of this), retained the allegiance of their kin and built up their own power in dangerous rivalry. As Morton-Williams suggests, the chiefs may well have resented the administration by palace slaves of the new territories acquired for the protection of the south-western trade route. It is this factor, speculative as it remains, which Law accepts as the most plausible explanation for the *coups d'état* of 1774, by which Alafin Abiodun overthrew Gaha, and of *c.* 1796 when, as will be seen, Alafin Awole was faced by a mutiny in his army and forced to take his life.

Another factor which seems to have contributed to the decline of the kingdom was the decreased effectiveness of the army. Expansionist wars were no longer undertaken and important provinces and tributaries escaped from control. Akinjogbin's suggestion that Abiodun deliberately contrived the weakening of the army in an attempt to undermine the power of the military chiefs seems inherently unlikely and there is no evidence for it, but it remains difficult to adduce specific causes. One development which does seem to have been of importance in either causing or accelerating the military decline was the difficulty which the Oyo must have encountered in obtaining suitable mounts for their famous cavalry, especially after the Nupe had asserted their independence; the best horses came from the north, and breeding was rarely possible south of the Niger bend. Significantly, it was the cavalry element within the army over which the Alafin could most effectively exercise control.

As Law puts it, by calling in the provincial rulers to resolve the struggle inside the capital between himself and Gaha in 1774, Alafin Abiodun 'let out the "secret of empire", that the balance of military power lay with the provinces against the capital'. According to this view, the empire 'collapsed from the centre outwards', and after the revolt of Afonja at Ilorin the process quickened and became irreversible.

In his most recent analysis of the disintegration of the Oyo kingdom, Law seeks to attain 'A fuller understanding of political developments in 18th-century Oyo . . . by relating the traditional narrative to some general model of how the political system of the kingdom worked'.[17] Intent now on identifying 'fundamental causes' of the decline of Oyo and reacting against interpretations which 'personalize' the internal disputes, he emphasizes the two 'crucial institutional changes' which took place in the kingdom, apparently at the end of the seventeenth or early in the eighteenth century: first, the emergence of the theory according to which the Basorun with other leading chiefs of the capital were entitled to reject an Alafin by demanding his suicide, and secondly the alteration to the principles of succession to the royal office by requiring the king's eldest son, the Aremo, to commit suicide on his father's death, thus opening the succession to competition among rival princes. These changes, Law writes, suggest that 'the tensions within the Oyo polity had structural rather than personal causes'. Thus, in the competition for wealth (expressed mainly in the form of slaves and other household followers) in order to attain power, 'The political structure has to be seen as determining, as much as reflecting, the distribution of resources.'

But in addition to the operation of these internal factors, grave, and more specific, dangers from without were also threatening the Oyo. In the latter part of the eighteenth century the successful wars waged by the Borgu, Nupe, and Egba against the Alafin had undermined the empire. Then in the first years of the nineteenth century the reforming movement of the Fulani preacher, Usman dan Fodio, swept through Hausaland, transforming the peaceful Muslim farmers there into a holy army bent on carrying the Koran to the sea. Islam had already penetrated among the Yoruba, and thus the Fulani found co-religionists and sympathizers as they rode south. The subversion and capture of Ilorin by the jihad threatened to cut off Oyo Ile, already exposed to attack by the nearby Borgu and Nupe, from the major part of the kingdom, and when the Landers reached the city in 1830 its situation must have resembled that of Byzantium in the first half of the fifteenth century. Finally, under Ghezo their warrior king, the Dahomeans not only threw off their allegiance to Oyo but also began a determined drive eastwards across southern Yorubaland.

It is impossible, in view especially of the limited evidence available, to assess the relative weights of the internal and external factors outlined above. Moreover, to seek to impose a 'model' on this (as on any other) historical situation is a dangerous device which suggests an inevitability inconsistent with human experience. The decline of the Old Oyo kingdom was not, or not yet, 'irreversible'. To take but one hypothetical case, the emergence of a strong personality as Alafin might at this point have saved it. This was not to be. Decline continued, and its pace accelerated.

The complex events in the half-century which elapsed between the death of Abiodun and the abandonment of Oyo Ile, covering the reigns of six Alafin and one interregnum in the kingship, are described in detail by Johnson.[18] Yet even for this relatively recent period, much of the history of which has been preserved, there is great difficulty in establishing a clear narrative. Not only are the dates of the main events unknown but even their sequence cannot always be determined with confidence.

Abiodun's successor was Awole Arogangan, a man whom Johnson describes as 'too weak and mild for the times'. One of his first acts was to order out his army against the town of Apomu in Ife territory in order to satisfy a personal quarrel which he had had with its ruler in the days when, before ascending the throne, he was trading up and down the country. Fearful of the consequences, the Bale of Apomu fled to the court of the Oni at Ife, where he later took his own life. Awole now abandoned the chastisement of Apomu and ordered his army to march instead against the strong town of Iwere.[19] But now he was faced by a revolt of his leading chiefs. Akinjogbin's explanation of this revolt is that in threatening war on an Ife town, the Alafin had flouted the constitution of the land and rendered illegitimate not only his own authority but that of his successors.[20] Whether this is so or not – and in the absence of support in tradition it remains no more than a suggestion based on a theory of the relationship between Ife and the other Yoruba states which is not generally accepted – the army leaders, who included the Bashorun and the Owota (a leading Esho) from the capital and the Onikoyi and the Kakamfo with the troops from the provinces, during the course of a half-hearted siege of Iwere conceived and carried out a plot against their king. After murdering the palace officials who had accompanied them, the mutineers marched back to Oyo. For some weeks they camped irresolutely outside the walls, until at length they sent to the Alafin an empty, covered calabash as an indication of his rejection. Awole pronounced a solemn curse on the traitors, shooting arrows to the north, south, and west to signify the directions in which they would be carried into slavery, and then obeyed custom by taking poison.

The decline of the kingdom now became precipitate. An Oyo song reflects the times:

Laiye Abiodun l'afi igba won 'wo	In Abiodun's day we weighed our money in calabashes,
Laiye Awole l'adi adikale	In Awole's reign we packed up and fled.

As was the practice at Oyo the Bashorun took charge of the affairs of the kingdom on the Alafin's death, and the tradition has already been cited above (p. 69) that it was during this short regency of Bashorun Ashamu that the revolt of the Egba under Lishabi took place. When Adebo was eventually chosen as successor to Awole the new Alafin proved to have little authority, and now even towns within the metropolitan area of Oyo were falling away from their allegiance. The assertion of independence by Afonja the Kakamfo at Ilorin was especially menacing. In the midst of these troubles Adebo died after a reign of only a few months, to be followed as Alafin by Maku. A deputation was sent from the capital to inform the Kakamfo that 'the New Moon has appeared', meaning that a new king had ascended the throne; Afonja replied arrogantly, 'Let that New Moon speedily set.' After leading a disastrous military expedition against the town of Iworo in the south-east of the kingdom,[21] the unhappy Maku was required within three months of his accession to take his own life. (An alternative tradition in Ilorin maintains that he was killed in battle and buried in that town.) There followed an interregnum of unknown length until Majotu, who is usually identified with the elderly Alafin who entertained Clapperton at Oyo in 1826 and Lander in 1827 and 1830, was chosen as king.[22]

Afonja, whose actions contributed so largely to the Yoruba catastrophe, was a nephew of Alafin Awole and ruler of Ilorin, which his great-grandfather Laderin had built up into one of the most important towns in the Oyo kingdom;[23] his praise-name, *l'aiya l'oko*, describes him as 'the brave warrior with the spear'. From Awole he obtained the office of Kakamfo, generalissimo of the kingdom and foremost of the Esho. Even before Awole's death he seems to have aspired to the throne itself,[24] despite the fact that he was only connected to the royal house through his mother, and he was a leading member of the conspiracy which led to Awole's enforced suicide. During the brief reign of Adebo, Afonja proclaimed his independence of Oyo, as did the Bale of Gbogun and the rulers of other towns in the north of the kingdom. But he now took steps which were to prove disastrous both to himself and to his country; he enlisted into his army the numerous Hausa slaves who were employed (as 'barbers, rope-makers and cowherds', Johnson says) in the surrounding towns, protecting them against their masters and, according to the account of a contemporary observer in Yorubaland, Ali Eisami of Borno, who had himself been brought to Oyo as a slave, giving them their freedom.[25] He also invited to Ilorin a Fulani preacher from Sokoto, Salih, usually called Alimi ('the learned'), whose sons were destined to be leaders in the southward drive of the jihad. With this alien help he succeeded in beating off determined attacks made on him by Ojo Agunbambaru, a son of Gaha, who was acting nominally in the cause of the Alafin. It is significant that Ojo, like Afonja, relied largely on soldiers from outside the kingdom, having recruited his army among the dreaded warriors of Borgu.

'Afonja was now the sole power in the kingdom; the King and the capital were left to manage their own affairs by themselves,' Johnson writes[26] – the king at this time being, presumably, Alafin Majotu. But the disloyal Kakamfo was encompassing his own doom. He had offended by his arrogance, and doubtless alarmed by his ambition, the rulers of the neigbouring towns, and even his friend and ally, Sholagberu, a leading Yoruba Muslim, whom he had established with his followers at Oke Suna on the outskirts of Ilorin. At last, realizing the precariousness of his position, isolated from his natural allies and dependent upon his Hausa troops, the Jama'a ('disciples'), he attempted to reconcile himself with the Onikoyi and other chiefs. Hearing this, the Jama'a rose against him; according to an Ilorin account their leader was Alimi's eldest son, and successor as Imam of the Muslims there, Abdussalami. He was besieged in his compound and deserted by some of his guards. Sholagberu refused his plea for help. But he fought on until 'He fell indeed like a hero. So covered was he with darts that his body was supported in an erect position upon the shafts of spears and arrows showered upon him.'[27]

Ilorin now passed under the control of the Fulani leaders, and Abdussalami was recognized by the Sultan of Sokoto as an Emir within the Fulani empire (and flattered by his Yoruba subjects as *oba digi aiye*, 'king, mirror of the world').[28] But the overthrow of Afonja had at last roused some of the Oyo to a sense of their peril. The new Kakamfo, Toyeje of Ogbomosho, made a first attempt to dislodge the Fulani from the base which they had acquired through his predecessor's treachery, but was defeated in a bloody engagement at Ogele, where the Fulani cavalry was aided by Sholagberu with his Yoruba Muslims. Again the Oyo rallied, this time obtaining help from the ruler of the Nupe at Rabba across the Niger, but again they were defeated in the 'locust fruit' (*mugba mugba*) war, when this was the only food to be found by the troops on the now desolate farms. Yet, despite the growing danger, the Oyo chiefs, no longer restrained by the power of the Alafin, began again to quarrel among themselves. A coalition was formed against the Onikoyi in which Sholagberu joined. The Onikoyi thereupon sent a message to Ilorin affirming his adherence to the Emir. Abdussalami, doubtless rejoicing that the Oyo were playing into his hands in this way, sent his army against the allies and routed them at Pamo. Sholagberu fled back to Oke Suna, but his turn soon came and, his religion notwithstanding, he met the same fate as Afonja.

Meanwhile a serious war had also broken out in the south of the Yoruba country.[29] It arose out of the kidnapping of Oyo subjects by the Ife for sale at their market in Apomu. The Onikoyi and Toyeje of Ogbomosho, hearing of this and acting probably during the interregnum in the kingship, asked the Olowu, always a loyal upholder of Oyo interests in the south, to take punitive measures against a number of towns in Ife territory. Johnson lists thirteen towns which were chastised by the Owu in obedience to this order, including Apomu, Ikire, and Gbangan. The Oni of Ife in retaliation sent an army against the Owu, but this was routed at Safirin, near the confluence of the Oshun and Oba rivers. Soon after this victory the Owu became involved with a more powerful enemy. The new quarrel grew out of a fracas between Owu and Ijebu traders in the market at Apomu, which led the Owu to destroy the town there. The Ijebu now made common cause with the Ife. In the ensuing war the Owu, with swords as their main armament, were unable to check the advance of the Ijebu, who had obtained firearms from the European traders on the coast with whom their kingdom had long been in contact. A lengthy siege of the town of Owu, with its strong walls,[30] now began, during which the allies were reinforced by some neighbouring Egba and also by refugees from Oyo towns already overrun by the Fulani. The superior arms and numbers of the allies, aided by famine inside the walls, could not prevail against the obstinate Owu until at length the Olowu himself opened one of the gates and made good his escape. His town was entered and completely destroyed by the enemy, who forbade that it should ever be rebuilt – an interdict which was obeyed until recent times.

The collapse of Owu and the ending of the war released into the south of Yorubaland many Oyo soldiers. Since their own towns and villages had been conquered or destroyed by the Fulani, these men could no longer return to their farms; thus they came to look on war as their profession and found their reward in captives who could be traded as slaves. A number of these 'war boys' (*omo ogun*) now moved under Ijebu patronage to Ipara, where they were employed in subjugating some of the Remo towns in the name of the Awujale and in raiding the adjacent Egba districts.[31] The situation grew more serious when this army of freebooters, reinforced by some Ife chiefs with their followers, were involved in a dispute between the Egba Oke Ona and the Egba Gbagura provinces. Taking sides with the former, they overran the northern parts of the Egba forest, burning and laying waste, until finally they settled on the abandoned site of Ibadan. This was one of the few Gbagura towns which had escaped destruction and, as its name implies (*eba oda*, 'near the grassland'), it lay just within the sheltering Egba forest.

Here a great military camp was formed in which the numerous Oyo refugees came together with contingents under Ife, Ijebu, and Egba leaders.

While the kingdoms of the south were being plunged by these events into a general state of warfare, Oyo was fast breaking up. The rulers of the subordinate towns, their obedience to the Alafin forgotten and the example of Afonja's fate ignored, quarrelled and leagued among themselves, while the Fulani cavalry scoured the country. One of many similar episodes which must have occurred at this lawless time, and which contrast with Clapperton's experience of peaceful conditions on the Badagry road, was the overrunning in March 1821 of the small town of Oshogun in Ibarapa (south-western Oyo) by a mixed band of Oyo and Fulani horsemen, among the former Kurunmi, later the ruler of Ijaye. A vivid account of this was given by Samuel Crowther who, as a boy of about 15, was taken captive there and sold into slavery.[32]

The end of Oyo Ile was approaching. Johnson describes Majotu's successor, Alafin Amodo, as 'virtually King of the capital only',[33] and relates that during his reign the Ilorin succeeded in entering the town after a siege; however, having plundered its treasures (including some 'Oyo beauties') and forced the citizens to profess Islam, they withdrew without taking captives: a rather mysterious episode. But even now the leaders of those Oyo towns which maintained their independence of the Fulani were unable to sink their differences and forget their ambitions in the common cause. When at length the Alafin succeeded in raising an army and leading it against Ilorin any chance of victory was ruined by the treachery of Edun, the ruler of Gbogun, and the Oyo were routed at Kanla. The Fulani followed up this success by intervening in the disputed succession to the kingship at Ikoyi, installing their own candidate and bringing the town under their control, and then by making war on the important town of Gbogun, which fell to them after a desperate resistance.

A number of the kingdom's war leaders had meanwhile withdrawn southwards towards the forests under the Kakamfo Ojo Amepo. The wisdom of this move was shown by the defeat of the expedition sent into Ijesha territory by the Fulani, whose cavalry found itself unable to operate in the close country there and suffered severe losses in the Pole war. For a time the Ilorin encamped at Ago Oja, the town later to be renamed Oyo, in order to keep up pressure against these remnants of the Alafin's forces, but eventually the Oyo succeeded in disengaging and securing a base at Ijaye, a deserted Gbagura town, where leadership was assumed by Kurunmi, the Balogun of the abandoned town of Esiele.

Oyo Ile was now isolated, and in the midst of these troubles Alafin Amodu died, worn out by anxiety. Oluewu, the new oba, was required by Shitta, who had succeeded his brother Abdussalami as Emir, to visit him in Ilorin. On this occasion the Alafin was treated with honour, but when he received an invitation to pay a second visit during which he would be asked to profess Islam by 'tapping the Koran', he declined and preferred to risk calling on the Borgu for help. Oyo Ile was now besieged by the Ilorin, who were joined by Lanloke, the renegade ruler of Ogodo, a Yoruba town on the Niger east of Oyo Ile, where in more prosperous times much trade had been done between the Oyo and the Nupe.[34] The highest of the kingdom's officers, the Bashorun and the Ashipa, had already entered into communication with the Fulani, but they were put to death, and the Alafin and his Borgu allies, aided by a providential storm, succeeded in repelling the enemy.

Realizing that the capture of Oyo, a city of formidable size and strength, still presented many difficulties, Shitta now turned upon Gbodo, probably the last of the towns in the north-east of the kingdom which had not acknowledged Fulani rule.

Once again the Alafin had to rely on his Borgu allies, but on this occasion the forces of the old kingdom secured a real victory in the field against their enemy. The Ilorin army outside Gbodo had been joined by a number of Oyo chiefs, including even Atiba, a son of Alafin Abiodun – though to his credit (Johnson thinks) his men were only firing blanks! Now the besiegers were attacked from the rear and put to so precipitate a flight that many were driven into the River Ogun and drowned. Though the victory had been achieved with outside help, and has been attributed to the skill in archery of the Borgu,[35] the battle of Gbodo demonstrated that the forces of the jihad were not invincible, even against a divided foe.

The Borgu leader is known in Yoruba accounts as the Eleduwe and seems likely to have been ruler of Nikki or possibly Kaiama.[36] This brave prince now encouraged the Alafin to follow up his success at Gbodo by an attack on Ilorin itself. Oluewu agreed, and determined to raise as large an army as possible from those parts of the kingdom not yet overrun by the Fulani. A number of leading chiefs, including Atiba from Ago Oja, Kurunmi of Ijaye, and the Okere of Shaki, rallied to the camp which Oluewu and the Eleduwe formed at Otefan[37], about thirty miles west of Ogbomosho. Numbers there grew so large that the Emir of Ilorin sent in alarm to Sokoto for help, and was reinforced by the Nupe of Raba (where the Fulani had by now established their ascendancy). The combined forces of Ilorin and the Nupe then attacked the Otefan camp, but the defenders, inspired by the example of the Eleduwe, drove them back. This victory was a costly one, but it nevertheless encouraged Oluyole of Ibadan and other Yoruba leaders to join the Alafin.[38] But as the army passed slowly on to Ogbomosho, and thence, after some indecision, towards Ilorin, the usual rivalries and disaffection broke out, complicated by jealousy of the Borgu, who were contributing so much towards the war, and by fear that if the campaign were successful the Alafin would turn next on his over-mighty subjects. Before Ilorin was reached a conspiracy had been made among the chiefs to desert the Alafin and his ally, and a message was sent to tell the enemy of this. Thus, when the army took the field only Oluyole, who had not been party to the plot, attacked vigorously, while Atiba and the Timi of Ede, firing no shot, retired before the enemy and opened a way for them to surround the two kings. The Eleduwe fought desperately, but at last was slain; his defeat was a disaster from which Nikki and Kaiama took many years to recover.[39] The fate of the Alafin Oluewu is less certain; by some he is believed to have fallen in the battle, but according to Johnson, he was taken captive to Ilorin and there put to death.[40]

The defeat at Ilorin sealed the fate of Oyo Ile. Already the city was being pressed by the rapacious Lanloke of Ogodo, and by this time it is probable that many of the citizens had left their homes to seek greater security in the south; from the time of Awole they had been 'packing up to flee', and on his visit there in 1830 Lander had remarked on the emptiness and desolation of the streets. Men still remained to hold the walls against Lanloke's attacks, but when news came of the disaster at Ilorin all those left in the city decided upon immediate flight. Some escaped to Kishi, others to Igboho, some even to Ilorin, and their descendants may be traced in these and other towns of Yorubaland.[41] But to the Fulani the city was now of little importance and, ironically, it was not they but Lanloke and his marauders who, learning of its abandonment, entered the undefended gates and pillaged what remained of its riches: an epitome of the treachery and tragic opportunism which marked and in large measure accounted for the swift decline and fall of Oyo Ile, 'Katunga, the great metropolis'. The visitor today to its remote and lonely site may lament with Jeremiah, 'How doth the city sit solitary, that was full of people!'

The narrative above is based on Johnson's *History*. The attempt to construct a chronology of the period which follows is based on indications about dating given by Johnson and on other sources, especially the chronologies drawn up by Akinjogbin and by Law.[42] The only absolute dates in this account are those of the situation as recorded by Clapperton and Lander in their journeys, though information collected by the Yoruba missionary Crowther at Egga on the Niger in 1841 and the evidence of two liberated slaves in Sierra Leone, Ali Eisami of Borno and Osifekunde of Ijebu, are also valuable.[43]

Clapperton refers several times to the troubles in the Oyo kingdom. At 'Assula', twenty-six days from Badagry, he found that the inhabitants had newly dug a ditch round the town 'on account of the existing war' – almost certainly meaning events at Ilorin – and three days later he wrote that, 'A war is now carrying on only a few hours' ride from us; not a national but a slaving war.'[44] At Shaki and 'Enkoosoo' he learnt that his journey was being interpreted as a mission to make peace between the Alafin and his Hausa slaves. The Hausa

> have been in rebellion these two years, and possess a large town only two days' journey from Katunga [Oyo], called Lori [Ilorin]. The Youribanis are evidently afraid of them; they say they have a great number of horses, and have been joined by many Fellatahs [Fulani].[45]

Both from the wording and the context, these remarks seem to describe the overthrow of Afonja and the establishment of Ilorin as an outpost of the jihad, and the information from 'Enkoosoo' enables this to be dated at about 1824. This evidence also accords with a statement by Ali Eisami describing what seems to be Afonja's revolt as taking place in *c.* 1817.[46] At Oyo the Alafin 'feelingly deplored the civil war occasioned by his father's death' and said that he had 'sent to his friend the King of Benin for troops to assist him'; he reminded Clapperton of the ruined towns on the Badagry road, all 'destroyed and burned by my rebellious Hausa slaves, and their friends, the Fellatahs'.[47] This is best explicable as a reference to the mutiny of Afonja and the other leaders at the end of Awole's reign, the interregnum, and Afonja's assertion of independence and its aftermath. Unfortunately, tradition has not recorded Majotu's parentage; it seems probable that he was a son of Awole, though in any case he might speak of his predecessor as his 'father'. When Lander was in Oyo in 1830 the signs of trouble had multiplied: '. . . the wandering and ambitious Falatah has penetrated into the very heart of this country . . . with little, if any, opposition'. Lander adds that the discontented slaves of the kingdom had been flocking to 'Alore [Ilorin] as far back as forty years'.[48] Presumably this again refers to Afonja's rebellion and subsequent defiance of Oyo, rather than to the more recent establishment of Ilorin as a Fulani base. Even so, this seems a considerable over-estimate, since according to Ali Eisami, the period can hardly have exceeded fourteen or fifteen years.[49] Early in the 1840s Crowther made inquiries about events in Oyo. His most important information, so far as a chronology is concerned, was that Awole reigned for seven years and Adebo and Maku for only about three months each, and that the interregnum at Oyo lasted for five years. He also implies that the battle of Gbodo was fought in 1834 and that at Oshogbo in 1838/9.[50]

Crowther's statement about the interregnum raises considerable difficulty. A date has been suggested for Abiodun's death of *c.* 1810, yielding a five-year interregnum between *c.* 1818 and *c.* 1823, which would be consistent with the tradition that Majotu ascended the throne as an elderly man and was the Alafin whom Lander names as Mansolah. But Akinjogbin has adduced evidence from a contemporary French source according to which it appears that Abiodun died as early as 1789.[51] This, taken in conjunction with traditions about the short reigns of his first three successors, leads to the conclusion either that Majotu's reign was of unexpected length or (though this is less likely) that the interregnum lasted for much longer than five years, perhaps even up to twenty-five years as Akinjogbin suggests.[52] Meanwhile, Crowther's information, combined with Johnson's narrative, places the battle of Ilorin and the subsequent abandonment of Oyo Ile in or about 1835.

As regards the chronology of the war in the south, the difficulties are even greater. The Owu war was fought in two stages: first, the Ife–Owu war, and secondly, after an interval of about five years (according to Johnson) during which the shattered Ife army took shelter at Adunbieye in Iwo territory, a combined Ijebu–Ife attack on Owu, which culminated in the fall of that town after a five-year siege, followed by an extension of the war to the Egba forest.[53] Osifekunde told his questioner in France of a 'six-year war' between Ijebu and Owu which ended in the annexation of the latter by the former at about the time he was taken prisoner;[54] this is good evidence for dating the fall of Owu at 1820. Next, there is evidence, again from liberated slaves, that Kesi, a town in Egba Alake, and Ikereku, a town in Egba Gbagura, were destroyed in about 1823 and about 1826 respectively, apparently in the last phase of this war.[55] It thus appears that the war must have opened about 1810. There are two minor obstacles to this dating. First, according to Johnson, it was Toyeje of Ogbomosho as Kakamfo of Oyo and in concert with the Onikoyi who ordered the Owu to chastise the Ife slave traders.[56] Toyeje was Afonja's successor in the office of Kakamfo, presumably appointed by Alafin Majotu – though a little later the Onikoyi was to usurp the Alafin's functions and appoint Edun of Gbogun as rival Kakamfo – so that this would seem to place the opening of the war after Afonja's death in or about 1824. In the absence of other evidence, however, it seems reasonable to suppose that Afonja's rebellion led the Alafin (or, if it happened at the end of the possibly long interregnum, the Oyo Mesi) to replace him during his lifetime (though Law considers it more likely that Johnson simply errs in describing Toyeje as Kakamfo at this time). Secondly, if the dates suggested above are correct it is somewhat surprising that Clapperton and Lander apparently heard nothing of the southern war and its depredations during their journeys to Oyo Ile. But sufficient explanation of this may be found in that their route took them well to the west of the area in which the war was fought and also of the Egba forest in which the subsequent operations were conducted.

Suggested chronology (main sources in brackets)

1774	Alafin Abiodun overthrows Basorun Gaha (Dalzel)
1783	Oyo defeated by Borgu (Law (1973e), Akinjogbin (1965))
1789	Death of Alafin Abiodun (Akinjogbin (1965)); accession of Alafin Awole. Afonja a disappointed claimant
1790	Oyo defeated by Nupe (Dalzel)
c. 1796	Mutiny of Afonja and other chiefs at Iwere; Awole's suicide after reign of seven years (Crowther)
	Egba revolt under Lishabi during short regency of Bashorun Ashamu (Bada of Shaki)
c. 1796–*c.* 1799	Short reigns of Alafin Adebo and Maku (S. Johnson (1921)), with the usual interregnum under the Bashorun's regency. Afonja asserts independence at Ilorin and defeats Ojo Agunbambaru
c. 1797–*c.* 1802	Interregnum of five years (Crowther)
c. 1802	Accession of elderly (S. Johnson (1921)) Alafin Majotu (= 'Mansolah'?)
c. 1810	Opening of Owu war: Ife–Owu phase
c. 1811–*c.* 1814	Ife army at Adunbieye (S. Johnson (1921))
c. 1814	Opening of Owu war, second phase: Ijebu–Owu
c. 1817	Afonja recruits slave army (Ali Eisami) and consolidates independence at Ilorin
1820	Fall of Owu after a six-year war (Osifekunde) and five year siege (S. Johnson (1921)); war extended to the Egba forest (King; Barber)
c. 1824	Hausa–Fulani *coup* at Ilorin (Clapperton); Afonja killed; Abdussalami becomes Emir of Ilorin; (Gwandu letter)
1826	Clapperton and Lander visit Oyo
	Overrunning of Egba Gbagura by Oyo freebooters (Barber; Irving)
1827	Lander returns through Oyo
c. 1828	Foundation of Ibadan
1830	Lander's last visit to Oyo
c. 1830	Foundation of Abeokuta (Biobaku (1957)); occupation of Ijaye by Kurunmi
c. 1831	Amodo succeeds Majotu as Alafin; sacking of Oyo by Ilorin; Shitta succeeds Abdussalami as Emir of Ilorin
c. 1833	Oluewu succeeds Amodo as Alafin
c. 1834	Battle of Gbodo (Crowther)
c. 1835	Battle of Ilorin; Oluewu killed (or taken captive and executed in Ilorin?); Oyo Ile abandoned
c. 1836	Accession of Atiba as Alafin; capital re-established at Ago Oja, re-named Oyo
c. 1838	Battle of Oshogbo (Crowther)

The ruin of Oyo was of tragic moment for the whole Yoruba country, involving the other kingdoms as well as Oyo itself. The sequence of events had been complex. First, the rulers of the populous and prosperous towns of Oyo, especially those in the vicinity of the capital, took advantage of the weakening of the Alafin's government to assert their independence, and then fell to prosecuting against their king and among themselves a civil war from which only the enemies of the kingdom could profit. Then the warriors of the Fulani jihad established their strong base at Ilorin, south of the Niger and in the heart of the kingdom. Finally, the ancient state of Oyo had collapsed, ending, it seemed, all possibility of unity among the Yoruba in the face of dangers from without: the Fulani on the north, the Dahomeans on the west, and, as the nineteenth century wore on, the British on the coast. The history of these years is a terrible one; the tale of the repeated treachery of the Alafin's chiefs is almost beyond bearing, and the breakdown of morale apprehended by Lander on his last visit to the doomed capital seems the decisive factor among all those making for the downfall of the kingdom.

The ruin was complete. The empire had long since fallen away; the tributary Nupe and Borgu and the Egba provinces had all thrown off their allegiance to Oyo some half-century ago, and by 1826 a town only a few miles from the capital had passed under the control of the ruler of Kaiama.[57] The Dahomeans under their warrior king Ghezo (?1818–58) repudiated the tribute which they had rendered to the Alafin since 1730 (a step which Akinjogbin considers was taken between 1821 and 1825,[58] and which in any case probably preceded the fall of Oyo). Now, too, the dependence on Oyo of other parts of Yorubaland ceased. Owu, Oyo's loyal vassal in the south, had been razed to the ground by the allied Ijebu and Ife, while in Egbado, that once-prosperous area through which ran Oyo's trade route to the sea, the local rulers rose against each other until their country became a battlefield for Ijebu, Egba, and Dahomean invaders. To the north, the Fulani had occupied or overrun most of the Yoruba Proper, and their cavalry continued to raid in all directions. But the forests of the south proved as great an obstacle to their progress as the regrouped remnants of the Yoruba armies. Thus it was southwards, towards these forests, that many of the inhabitants of northern Oyo fled for shelter.[59] The towns in this area became *ilu asala*, 'towns of refuge', expanding their sites and their farmlands to accommodate the newcomers. One of these was Oshogbo in the Ijesha kingdom, where the influence of refugees was so great as to give it the character and allegiance of an Oyo town. The site of its rival and neighbour, Ede, was moved south across the Oshun River for greater security. New towns were also founded, of which an interesting example is Modakeke, established for the Oyo by the Oni of Ife alongside his own town in order to end the hostility between his own subjects and the refugees. Of these new towns, three were to rank above all others and to emerge as successors to the greatness of Oyo, dominating much of Yorubaland within and beyond the old kingdom as well as the refounded capital of the Alafin at New Oyo: these were Ibadan, Abeokuta, and Ijaye.[60]

NOTES

1. See Allison (n.d.), Bascom (1960), and Morton-Williams (1964a).
2. Clapperton was told at 'Puka' (Ipokia, near Badagry) that Oyo was thirty days' journey from there (p. 4), information which proved to be entirely reliable. The direct distance of about 200 miles must have been considerably more on the forest tracks.

3. Quoted by Hodgkin, pp. 171–2. This report has never been confirmed.
4. Clapperton (1829); R. L. and J. Lander (1832).
5. Clapperton, p. 13; Hodgkin, p. 223.
6. R. L. and J. Lander (1832), p. 76. 'Chaadoo' is unidentified and presumably one of the numerous towns and villages which were abandoned in the wars. It was about a day's journey south-west of Shaki.
7. Clapperton, pp. 13–14, 26–7 (Hodgkin, p. 223); for Kushu see also Smith (1965a), p. 65.
8. R. L. and J. Lander (1832), pp. 61, 71.
9. Clapperton, pp. 4, 39, 56.
10. Clapperton, pp. 35–6, 48, 58–9.
11. Lander (1830), pp. 197–9.
12. See Smith and Williams (1966), p. 60, n. 1, and Williams (1974), Chapter 23 *passim*, p. 285; for Oyo pottery, see Willett (1960a). Shaw (1973), p. 237, suggests that the Tsoede bronzes along the Niger may have been 'left behind after the end of Old Oyo's control of this stretch of the river bank'. It has been suggested that the numerous stone figures at Esie, near Ilorin, were brought from Oyo Ile (see p. 50 above).
13. Clapperton, pp. 24–5.
14. Clapperton, p. 31; R. L. and J. Lander (1832), p. 80.
15. Akinjogbin (1965), especially pp. 27–9; (1966b), especially p. 458; Morton-Williams, (1967), especially pp. 36, 43; Law (1971), pp. 36, 43. For a more theoretical approach, see Atanda (1971) and Smith (1971a), both *passim*.
16. Lloyd (1971), p. 48.
17. Law (1982), p. 387 and *passim*.
18. Johnson, pp. 188–268.
19. This has been identified by Law (1972) as the village of Iwere about ten miles west of Oke Iho in the hill-country of the upper Ogun.
20. Akinjogbin (1965), pp. 34–5.
21. Sulu, p. 3. The only Iworo mentioned by Kenyo (p. 45) is in the Awori area.
22. The identification is made in S. Johnson (1921) (p. 210). Lander (1832) confirms that the same man was Alafin in 1830 as in 1826 and 1827 (p. 92). Akinjogbin (1966a) writes (p. 82) that 'there is no basis at all yet known, either in linguistics or in tradition, for equating Majotu with "Manshola" ' – the latter being the name given to the ruler of Oyo by Lander, though he spells it 'Mansolah'. Yet both Akinjogbin's and Law's chronologies support the identification, which does seem to fit best with other known facts. It has been suggested to the present writer that 'Manshola' represents the Yoruba phrase *ma s'ola*, 'continue to exercise your majesty'. Chief Ojo, Bada of Shaki, has suggested, however, that it was either Amodo, Majotu's successor, or Oluewu who was on the throne when Clapperton visited Oyo (*Iwe Itan Oyo*, pp. 77–8; *Short History of Ilorin*, p. 297). Clapperton (p. 49) writes that 'the last king' had been 'murdered by one of his own sons: not the present king'. S. Johnson (1921) suggests (p. 87) that Abiodun was poisoned by his Aremo, and it would be possible for Majotu to have been a younger son and successor of Abiodun were it not for the intervening reign of Awole who seems more likely to have been Majotu's father. Majotu, according to S. Johnson (1921) p. 216, was remarkable for having died a natural death, as the result of an influenza-type epidemic, which seems to rule out the identification of Amodo as 'Mansolah'.
23. S. Johnson (1921), pp. 199–200.
24. Crowther (1852), pp. iv–vii.
25. Curtin (1967), p. 212.
26. S. Johnson (1921), p. 197.
27. S. Johnson (1921), p. 199; Martin, pp. 20–7.
28. It is uncertain when and how the official recognition of the Emirate took place – whether the flag, the symbol of recognition, was bestowed first on Abdussalami, whether this was bestowed by the ruler of Sokoto or of Gwandu, and in which year this took place. But it is clear that Ilorin belonged to the Gwandu, or

western, side of the Fulani empire. See Hogben and Kirk-Greene, pp. 122, 292, 294.

29. S. Johnson (1921), pp. 206–12.
30. The site of the Owu capital besieged in this war was located by Mabogunje and Omer-Cooper as Owu Ipole or Ago Owu, south-east of Apomu, but Law (1973d) adduces reasons for preferring the site near Ibadan known as Owu Ogbere. Mabogunje and Omer-Cooper also speculate that the original capital of the Owu may have been in the north of Yorubaland. See note 28 to Chapter 6 above.
31. S. Johnson (1921), p. 223; Biobaku (1957), pp. 13–14. See also the narrative of the former slave Joseph Wright in Curtin (1967), pp. 317–33.
32. For Crowther's narrative, see Curtin (1967), pp. 289–316. For Kurunmi's presence at the overrunning of Oshogun, see Oguntomisin, pp. 98–9, based on Crowther's Journal for March 1855: CMS, CA2/031, Oguntomisin argues that if Kurunmi's claim to be there were correct, then Afonja's supporters at this time included non-Muslim as well as Muslim Oyo.
33. S. Johnson (1921), p. 217.
34. It is probable that it was from a horse-fair in this town that the Oyo cavalry obtained their mounts; see Smith (1967), p. 90, n. 13. The village marked on maps as 'Ogudu' on the Niger twenty miles below Jebba may well be the same place, but see Elphinstone, p. 24.
35. S. Johnson (1921), pp. 260–1. But Ojo (n.d.,b), O.S. pp. 22–3, ascribes the victory to the warriors of Shaki in combination with the Borgu.
36. The term may possibly be a Yoruba word for 'king'; cf. 'Elewe'. The Borgu ruler who welcomed the exiled Alafin Onigbogi into his country is also described as 'Eleduwe' (p. 31 above). For the connection with Nikki, see Hogben and Kirk-Greene, pp. 290, 580.
37. The inhabitants of modern Otefan, who moved from New Oyo to a site adjacent to their old town in *c.* 1947, affirm that they know nothing of battles fought there in the nineteenth century.
38. S. Johnson (1921), 262–3.
39. S. Johnson (1921), pp. 266–8; Hogben and Kirk-Greene, p. 580.
40. S. Johnson (1921), p. 287.
41. See Smith (1965a), pp. 64, n. 23 and 72.
42. See Akinjogbin (1966a), p. 86; Law (1970), *passim.*
43. Schön and Crowther (1842), pp. 317–18; Crowther (1852), Introductory Remarks; Curtin (1967), pp. 199–216, 217–88.
44. Clapperton, pp. 20–1.
45. Clapperton, pp. 24–5, 28. Robin Law has identified 'Enkoosoo' as Onisokiso.
46. In Curtin (1967), p. 212.
47. Clapperton, pp. 39, 41.
48. R. L. and J. Lander (1832), pp. 87, 91–2. A letter written by the Emir of Gwandu in July 1829 to the Emir of Ilorin, of which a copy is preserved in Gwandu, combined with the chronology of the Emirs of Ilorin in the 'New Arabic History' of that town (Martin (1965)), supports the date 1823/4 for the Hausa–Fulani coup in Ilorin and the recognition of Abdussalami as first Emir there.
49. R. L. and J. Lander (1832), p. 79, make a much greater error in writing that 'Bohoo' (Igboho) ceased to be capital of Oyo only 'about half a century ago', whereas the Alafin had returned from there two centuries or more before 1830.
50. Schön and Crowther (1842), pp. 317–18; Crowther (1852), pp. v, vi.
51. Akinjogbin's dating of Abiodun's death as 1789 (Akinjogbin (1967a), p. 175, note 1)) is based on a reference in a French officer's letter to the death of the 'Roy des Ailliots'. Morton-Williams (1967), p. 66, adheres to 1810 as the approximate date of the Alafin's death and suggests that the 1789 reference may be to Abiodun's Bebe or jubilee celebration. See also Law (1977), p. 247.
52. Akinjogbin (1966a), p. 82.
53. S. Johnson (1921), pp. 207, 209.

54. In Curtin (1967), pp. 237, 247.
55. The date of the fall of Kesi derives from Rev. Thomas King, an Egba member of the Church Missionary Society, Journal, 7 April 1850, CMS Archives, CA2/061a, and that of Ikereku from the journal of the missionary Irving, in the *Church Missionary Intelligencer*, ii (1856), p. 70. Irving's informant was a 'Mr Barber, native catechist at Ibadan'. Barber had taken part in the siege of Ikereku and remembered it as having occurred in the year before he was liberated from slavery at Sierra Leone, which he knew to be 1827.
56. S. Johnson (1921), p. 206.
57. Clapperton, pp. 61–2.
58. Akinjogbin (1966a), p. 84. See also Argyle, p. 38. Dahomean tradition records that an Oyo invasion at this time included a strong horsed contingent. This was possibly the last use of cavalry by the Oyo. See Law (1975), p. 14.
59. See Lloyd (1960c), p. 26. The main influx from the northern Oyo was to a belt on the edge of the rain-forest, lying between Ogbomosho to the north and Ibadan to the south.
60. Oko Iho, a fusion of some eleven former towns, and Ogbomosho, are other examples of 'towns of refuge' in the Oyo kingdom.

After this book went for setting, the writer was able to obtain a copy of the late Abdullahi Smith's essay, 'A Little New Light on the Collapse of the Alafinate of Yoruba' in G.O. Olusanya (ed.) *Studies in Yoruba History and Culture* (Ibadan, 1983). This advances a number of somewhat contentious points, and is largely based on the history of Ilorin written in 1912 in Arabic by Ahmad b. Ali Bakr Kokoro. In particular: (1) The reigns of Abd al-Salam (Abdussalami) and of Shi'ta as Emirs of Ilorin are dated respectively as 1823 to 1836 and 1836 to 1861; (2) it is claimed that Afonja's unruly followers were mostly non-Muslim pastoral Fulani rather than jihadist Fulani, and that these followers later played a major role in the anarchy in Yorubaland as clients of rebel Yoruba chiefs; (3) there was a wide and peaceful spread of Islam among the northern Yoruba in the first half of the nineteenth century which began before the onset of the Sokoto jihad. The article concludes that it is this peaceful Islamic influence which should be examined 'rather than the weapons of the Ilorin Fulani'.

ELEVEN

THE WARS AND THE NEW STATES

The Yoruba country had now been plunged into a state of warfare which lasted almost continuously until the imposition of peace by the British in 1893.[1] But this was a time not merely of conflict but of political, social, and economic change, partly engendered by the wars and partly by the opening of the country to European influence on a large scale and in different forms. New states arose out of the wreckage of Oyo, and older states, previously overshadowed by Oyo, asserted their independence. Firearms, first the primitive muskets and finally modern rifles, played an increasing part in the wars. Fighting became for many a profession, among both the leaders and their followers, the marauding 'war boys', a factor which contributed to the prolongation and spread of the wars. European slave traders, dealing through African middlemen, were gradually replaced by (or transformed into) the buyers of palm oil and other produce of the interior. Christian missionaries blazed a trail inland, establishing themselves first at Badagry and then at Abeokuta, Lagos, and Ijaye, setting up a chain of stations designed to reach into the Muslim north. The way had been prepared, both for their religious doctrines and for the new-style education which they brought, by the Christian recaptives (former slaves liberated by the ships of the British anti-slavery patrol and taken to Freetown) and their descendants, who from 1839 onwards were returning to their homeland.

One result of these changes, and in particular of the coming of the Europeans, is the great increase in the amount of material, especially written material, which is available for the writing of history. The missionaries and traders were keen observers of the political and economic scene, and the archives of the missionary societies and trading houses yield much information; the missionaries, indeed, though often identifying themselves too zealously for objectivity with the interests of the town where their station was situated,[2] wrote reports to their superiors which were sometimes almost on the level of diplomatic despatches. With the opening of a British consular post at Lagos in 1851, followed by the Sardinian consulate in 1856, and then in 1861 the establishment of the colonial administration, professional observation began, and statistics of trade, health, and similar matters make their appearance. For the Yoruba themselves, Christianity and literacy went together, and local histories, biographies, and collections of family papers begin to throw light on events. Samuel Crowther's historical introduction to the Yoruba language appeared in 1843, though it was not until some twenty to thirty years later that Yoruba historiography began to flourish.[3] The first newspaper, the fortnightly *Iwe-Irohin* (in Yoruba, but from 1860 with an English supplement) was produced by the C.M.S. in Abeokuta in 1859, and in 1863 a locally produced newspaper, the *Anglo-African*, appeared in Lagos. The missionaries also led the way in the study of the Yoruba language and its reduction to writing.

Although the activities of the Europeans were to have ever more important consequences, in a history of the Yoruba states in this period the warfare which plagued the country for almost a century demands first attention. Its origins lay in the breakdown of Oyo and in the holy war of the Fulani, but these issues were largely settled by 1840, when new political groupings had emerged and the south-ward thrust from Ilorin had been held. Why, then, was Yorubaland destined to suffer a further half-century of war? The explanation seems to lie in two main factors, one economic and the other political: the first, the demand for slaves, which could always be met most readily from captives taken in war; the second, and probably the more important, the struggle for power among the states, both new and old, which were attempting to fill the vacuum left by the collapse of Oyo.

It was a tragic paradox that the success achieved in the first part of the nine-teenth century for the Abolitionists' policy of encouraging 'legitimate trade', mainly in the products of the oil-palm which grows wild in southern Nigeria, led to a greatly increased demand for domestic slaves as carriers between the markets and the coast. Burton drew the attention of the 1865 British Parliamentary Select Committee on Africa to this unexpected result of the humanitarian policy,[4] and since then the Yoruba wars of this century have usually been dismissed as slaving expeditions to feed the markets of Lagos and Dahomey.[5] Certainly many, prob-ably a majority, of those taken captive in these wars must have been sent to the slave markets,[6] and a number of the fifty or so 'wars' which Johnson describes in the period were probably little more than slave raids.[7] Nevertheless, there were other, and still more profound, issues in the wars, and slave raiding and trading were as much a consequence as a cause of the long unsettlement.

'Politics cannot be divorced from power,' E. H. Carr has written,[8] and these West African wars illustrate this maxim no less clearly than the fevered interlude in Europe between the two German wars. The issues between the Yoruba states in the nineteenth century were complex and shifting, but all concerned questions about power: first, which among them was to succeed to the hegemony of Oyo? Then, when Ibadan had established its ascendancy, though by too narrow a margin for stability, how was the threat to the independence of the rest to be countered? And again, but a question all too often lost to sight among local rivalries, whose was the responsibility for withstanding the triple threat to all from the Fulani at Ilorin, the Dahomeans on the western borders, and the British at Lagos?

Each of the new states represented in one way or another a break with the tradi-tional Yoruba concepts of government. Thus Ibadan retained throughout the century the character of a military foundation; secure at home on its high ridge of hills, surrounded by forest and ever sending its armies to the field, it was nick-named *idi ibon*, 'the butt of a gun'. The government was vested in separate lines of chiefs, civil and military. The titles of these chiefs were not hereditary but bestowed for service, generally military service, to the town. Nevertheless, they constituted an aristocracy, membership of which was confined to those who had fought in the Gbanamu war, the first engagement of the Oyo Ibadan, or who had 'entered Ibadan on horseback', and their descendants. The leading chief was known as the Bale, the relatively modest title used by the rulers of the minor towns and villages of the Oyo kingdom and illustrating here the nominal subordination of Ibadan to the Alafin. He attained his office by promotion through both the civil and military grades of chieftaincy.[9]

Plate 13 Ibadan in the mid-nineteenth century. A missionary drawing, probably showing the view from the Church Missionary Society compound at Kudeti.

In its earliest days Ibadan had been a composite town, containing Ife, Ijebu, and Egba refugees, and leadership had devolved at first on Okunade, the Maye, an Ife chief. Within a short time, however, the Oyo rose against the Maye and drove him and his followers from the town. This led to a series of short, sharp wars, but with the help of their kinsman Kurunmi of Ijaye the Oyo succeeded in establishing their supremacy. Under their great leader Oluyole (who received from the Alafin the high title of Bashorun, which had been held at Oyo by Yamba, his grandfather), Ibadan emerged as a leading power in the land,[10] and as success in war increased the numbers of slaves employed on the farms, an ever more professional army was maintained. Its military importance soon began to be matched by its rising commercial· importance as a market and collecting point for palm oil from the surrounding region. So rapid was its growth that it soon exceeded in population all other Yoruba towns, while its independence and its republican character were recognized in the traditional description of its people as 'destroyers of crowns' (*omo ayade*).

The foundation of Abeokuta was made when a group of Egba led by Shodeke of Iporo (known by his military title as the Seriki) left Ibadan, where they had become unwelcome, and joined a small party of Egba hunters whom they found living under an outcrop of rocks near the east bank of the Ogun, then on the edge of Egbado country. This took place about 1830, and during the next twenty years there must have been a steady movement into the new settlement of other Egba from towns destroyed or abandoned in all parts of the forest. Unlike Ibadan, organized around its war chiefs, Abeokuta did not grow into a single community but consisted of a federation based on the three former provinces and their former towns, with the Owu, many of whom were allowed to settle here, as a fourth section. Again in contrast to Ibadan, Abeokuta had a plenitude of oba, although, as had been the custom (of all but the Gbagura) in the days when the Egba were scattered through the forest, election was not confined to candidates from specific royal houses. The office of Alake, the leading oba, had been vacant since the death of Okikilu in the Agbaje war, but in 1854 Townsend, the Anglican missionary in the town, persuaded the chiefs to elect a successor.[11] The move did not have the expected result of strengthening the central government, as the Alake continued to be strictly bound by the constitutional rules of former times, and Burton described Abeokuta at this time as 'a weak constitutional monarchy, blighted by the checks and limits which were intended to prevent its luxuriance'.[12] The real rulers of the town and its dependencies were the war chiefs, the Ologun, overshadowing the Ogboni, who had been the highest authority in the former provinces.[13] A number of military titles of Oyo origin were now adopted among the Ologun. These referred to the Egba as a whole, instead of to the individual component towns of Abeokuta, and thus to some extent offset the federalism which was a weakness in the new state.

Although to a lesser extent than the Ibadan, the Egba of Abeokuta under the leadership of their Ologun soon embarked upon a policy of expansion. In the early 1830s their army overran much of neighbouring Egbadoland, destroying the towns of Ilaro, Ilobi, Erinja, and Eyo, among others. Refugees from these places came together to form a new settlement across the River Yewa to the west. This, known as Okeodan, was organized on strictly military lines and by the mid-1840s already had a population of some 20,000.[14]

Ijaye, the third in the triumvirate of new states, followed a different pattern of government from either Ibadan or Abeokuta, yet equally exemplified a departure from Yoruba tradition. Here the warrior Kurunmi, who obtained from the Alafin the title of Are Ona Kakamfo, established on the site of a former Egba Gbagura town (whose inhabitants were now settled in Abeokuta) an autocracy in which 'He was king, judge, general, entertainer, sometimes also executioner'.[15] Not only did the town itself grow and proper but the iron rule of the Are was exercised over a state stretching northwards through the upper Ogun almost to Shaki, though it was circumscribed in the south and south-west by Ibadan and Abeokuta, which were also extending their influence over the surrounding countryside.

The foundation of these three new states preceded by a few years the final abandonment of the old capital of Oyo; indeed, the leaders of Ibadan and Ijaye, Oluyole and Kurunmi, were present on the fatal field of Ilorin, and their support (in return for the titles of Bashorun and Are Ona Kakamfo respectively) contributed to the choice of Atiba as successor to Alafin Oluewu. Before the coronation

Plate 14   An Abeokuta chief. Engraved from a sketch by Dr E.G. Irving, R.N. From the *Church Missionary Gleaner*, 1862.

members of the Oyo Mesi who had taken shelter in the strong northern towns of Kishi and Igboho sent messengers to urge the new Alafin to return to Oyo Ile, but Atiba was determined to establish his capital in his adopted town of Ago Oja ('the camp of Oja', a refugee chief from Oyo), in the south of the old kingdom and on the edge of the Egba forest. Here, some 80 miles from the old capital, a new Oyo was refounded, and a conscious attempt was made to re-create the glories of the old capital and to preserve the rituals of its kingship. Atiba transported the inhabitants of neighbouring towns and villages to swell the population; he revived the former offices and titles of the court and government; a double wall was built around the town, and in the centre, incorporating the palace of Oja, the former ruler, rose a new Afin, covering a large area and constructed on the plan of the Afin at Oyo Ile, while the compounds of the Aremo and the great officers of the Oyo Mesi radiated round the royal demesne. About a mile from the palace a new Bara, or royal mausoleum, was built between the inner and outer town walls. It is sometimes said that Atiba re-interred here the body of Oluewu, his predecessor, but it is unlikely that this was in fact recovered from the Fulani.[16]

The building of the new capital was accompanied by the enunciation of a new administrative and military policy. Under this the kingdom was formally redivided into two 'provinces', apart from the capital; the first, Ibadan, was charged with the protection of the north and north-east of the kingdom, and whenever possible was to extend its boundaries in the direction of Ijesha and Ekiti, while Ijaye, the second province, was to watch the west and to attempt to reassert the rule of the Oyo over Shabe and the coast. By this system of palatinates (to use Biobaku's term), the Ibadan would be principally concerned with the threat from the Fulani and the Ijaye with that from Dahomey, while for the future the Alafin was no longer to take the field in war but should confine himself to religious and political leadership. Oyo itself retained under its control a small area between the two provinces, and a number of towns in the north, such as Kishi and Igboho, were to be directly subject to the Alafin. These decisions preserved the formal pre-eminence of the Alafin among the Oyo, whose territory now extended southwards into the former Gbagura, offsetting to some extent the loss of Ilorin. At the same time it took account of the reality of the situation by allotting the major responsibilities to the new military towns; indeed, Johnson describes the arrangements as 'a compact . . . arrived at between the Alafin and his principal chiefs'.[17]

Already the actions of Gbodo and Otefan had shown that the warriors of Ilorin were not invincible. The relief of Oshogbo and the defeat there of a large army under Ali, the Hausa Balogun, in 1838/9 by an Ibadan army under Balogun Oderinlo was an event of even greater importance.[18] It demonstrated the unsuitability to forest warfare of the Fulani cavalry and vindicated the Yoruba withdrawal to the south. The redisposition of the resources of the shattered kingdom by Atiba and his supporters had proved a success, and the Ibadan, triumphantly fulfilling the role assigned to them, emerged as a symbol of hope, offering a prospect of restored security and stability in the land. But this decisive check to the southward drive of the Ilorin by no means meant the end of the internal wars; indeed, by abating the external pressure from one direction it tended to sharpen local issues, and from now on 'the Fulani were less a common enemy than a convenient ally to one or other side'.[19]

Thus the victory at Oshogbo was not followed by any concerted attempt to win back the lost north-eastern lands of the Oyo kingdom. Instead, the Ibadan were drawn by the ambition of their leader, Oluyole the Bashorun, into the Batedo war against their co-palatinate Ijaye. This was concluded after two years by a truce arranged by the Alafin. Then an appeal for help from the leading Ekiti town of Otun (on the former Benin–Oyo border), which was engaged in a feud with Efon Alaye, opened up prospects of further expansion for the restless Ibadan. They responded by sending a large army under Balogun Oderinlo, the victor of Oshogbo, while the Alaye sought help from Ilorin. In the ensuing battle the Ilorin not only failed to raise the Ibadan siege of Otun but were again soundly defeated in the field.[20] The extension of Ibadan influence over the Ekiti country continued to be contested by the Ilorin until in 1854 in the Ara campaign an Ibadan army under Balogun Ibikunle won a victory so decisive that the whole of Ekiti soon passed under their control.[21] Then, as they pressed still further east, into Afenmai and Akoko, the Ibadan came into contact with the armies both of Benin and of the Nupe.

In this way began the building-up of the 'Ibadan empire', a tract of country which at its greatest extent, after the absorption of a large part of former Ijaye territory, stretched from Ekiti westwards for some 200 miles, with a north-to-south depth varying from forty to eighty miles.[22] It consisted of towns and their districts which were either conquered in the endemic warfare of these years, like Ilesha and Akoko, or which voluntarily accepted Ibadan's protection, like Iwo and Ede, thereby virtually recognizing that it was the Ibadan and their chiefs who were the true successors of Oyo Ile rather than the Alafin at New Oyo. This empire was loosely administered by a system of ajele based on that of Oyo. But whereas the Oyo ajele had been supervised by the ilari, those touring representatives of the Alafin of the old kingdom, the subject towns of Ibadan were each allotted to the care of one of the chiefs in the capital, the babakere, who drew a revenue in taxes and tolls from his town or group of towns and represented its interests at Ibadan, while the ajele (who was not necessarily a man of Ibadan or Oyo) conversely represented Ibadan in the town.[23]

But though the rapid creation of the Ibadan empire had been achieved in part by the voluntary adhesion of weaker towns and afforded stability and protection to a wide area, it also exacerbated the internal rivalries of the Yoruba. At this time power in the south-west of the country was divided between the new states: Ibadan and Ijaye, the heirs of the military and administrative traditions of the old Oyo kingdom, and the reconstituted and concentrated Egba state at Abeokuta. Despite the careful dispositions of Alafin Atiba, it soon became clear that the situation hardly allowed room for the co-existence of three such close and ambitious neighbours. As early as 1832, the Egba at Abeokuta had almost suffered extinction when they were attacked by the Ijebu in alliance with the Ibadan (who were only able to contribute a small contingent to this campaign). They had been saved by Oba Adele of Lagos, who had recently regained his throne with Egba help and who now sent firearms and gunpowder up the Ogun River and himself led troops to reinforce the Egba on the banks of the Owiwi. Three years later the Egba inflicted a decisive defeat on the Ibadan (who were allied this time with the Ijaye) in the Arakonga war. Abeokuta was thus established as a leading power in the land and was soon encroaching on the territory of its Egbado neighbour). Yet in the event it was Ijaye which seemed to offer the major obstacle to Ibadan expansion, and this factor underlies the Ijaye war of 1860–5, which dominates the history of this period.[24]

The outbreak of war between Ibadan and Ijaye followed some twenty years of tension between the two towns, and had been preceded by the Batedo war (in 1844, according to Johnson). In 1855 C. M. S. missionaries reported that a peace conference was being held at Ibadan with Oyo and Ijaye. Then in 1859 occurred the death of Alafin Atiba, 'the revolutionary prince turned conservative king' as Ajayi calls him.[25] In his place his son, the Aremo Adelu, was elected to the throne, a breach with tradition in which all acquiesced except for Kurunmi of Ijaye, who protested that Adelu should have followed his father to the grave. Relations between Kurunmi and the new Alafin worsened when Adelu tried to reassert Oyo rule over the country west of the upper Ogun which had been annexed by Ijaye, and turned for support in this to Ibadan. The first phase of the ensuing war in 1860 consisted of a series of engagements in the wooded country between Ijaye and Ibadan, followed by the almost two-year-long siege of Ijaye. Meanwhile the Egba of Abeokuta had continued to increase in power and confidence; in particular, by their destruction of Aibo in 1857–8 they had almost completely subjugated Egbadoland.[26] Then, soon after the opening of the siege of Ijaye a strong army was sent from Abeokuta to aid the hard-pressed town. This resulted in the now aged and ailing Are becoming virtually the prisoner of his Egba allies, and his death in mid-1861 only emphasized the true character of the war as essentially a contest between Ibadan and Abeokuta. Finally, in March 1862, after many privations had been suffered by its citizens, Ijaye was abandoned by the Egba army (needed at home to contain a renewed Dahomean menace) and then by the Ijaye themselves, most of whom succeeded in reaching Abeokuta. But this was not the end of the war, and in the next phase the Ibadan had to face a coalition between their former allies and trading partners, the Ijebu, and the Egba. While the Ibadan secured their command of the upper Ogun, the allies occupied bases in the recalcitrant and pro-Ibadan Remo province of Ijebu, and here the last battles of the war were fought. At last peace was concluded in August 1864 through the mediation of Alafin Adelu.

The Ijaye war confirmed the position of Ibadan as the leading power in Yorubaland, and at the same time seemed to demonstrate that this new power was not only, or even primarily, concerned with the defence of the Oyo and other Yoruba against their external enemies and with weaker towns against the strong, but was animated by the restless ambition characteristic of a military state. The Egba and Ijebu, equally anxious to profit from the troubled situation, were alerted to the danger, and Oyo, too, strengthened by the addition of former Ijaye territory in the upper Ogun (except for Ibarapa, which Ibadan had kept), began to draw apart from its over-mighty vassal. Meanwhile, one of the issues which had come to the fore in the war but had been ignored in the peace settlement assumed first importance for all parties: this was the control of the 'roads' or tracks along which trade flowed in the interior of the country and between the interior and the coast (especially the harbour at Lagos). As states bordering on the lagoon, both Ijebu and Abeokuta occupied key positions, while for the inland states, especially Ibadan and other Oyo Yoruba, free movement on the roads and between the markets was vital, both for the provision of food and for the import of guns, ammunition, and gunpowder (purchased now by the sale of local produce rather than by slaves). So far as war material was concerned, the importance of communications had increased greatly with the use of firearms, which became widespread about 1840; this factor had been demonstrated in the Owiwi war and again, rather ludicrously, on the Arakonga when the Ibadan, running out of gunpowder, were reduced to pelting the Egba with gourds gathered on the battlefield.[27]

The struggle for power between the Yoruba states, together with the ever-present menace of the Fulani at Ilorin, constituted a situation which was complicated and worsened by the aggression of the western neighbours of the Yoruba, the dreaded Dahomeans under their kings Ghezo (?1818–58) and Glele (1859–89). After their final refusal of the annual tribute to Oyo, apparently during the 1820s, the Dahomeans carried out several major expeditions and innumerable raids into the Egba and Egbado countries, and though it was Ijaye which had been designated by Alafin Atiba as guardian of the west, in the event it was Abeokuta which bore the brunt of the Dahomean attacks and was the involuntary shield of the whole Yoruba against the western danger.

The pursuit of war was one of the principal characteristics of the Dahomey kingdom from its beginnings.[28] Campaigns were undertaken every dry season, a main objective being the taking of captives, most of whom were then either sold to slave traders for export, bringing in large revenues for the monarchy, or retained by their captors as domestic slaves. Yet even for the Dahomeans, warfare cannot be explained as simply undertaken for the supply of the slave market. It was that and much more. Having been the essential element in the building-up of this West African Prussia, warfare remained equally a central factor in the maintenance of its political structure and its religion. It provided, for example, the human sacrifices to the ancestors on which the continuation of the kingdom's prosperity was held to depend.[29] Expeditions were mounted in all directions from Abomey, but it was against the Yoruba, and in particular the Egba, that the two great warrior kings mainly directed their aggressions. One major reason for this specific hostility between the Dahomeans and the Egba was their rivalry for control over the Egbado territory lying between them. Dahomey already exercised control over the slave trade from Whydah and Porto Novo, and was always anxious to block the Egba policy of opening a route from Abeokuta via Ado to the coast at Badagry.

The first major clash between the Egba and the Dahomeans seems to have taken place in 1844. Two years earlier the Egba had annexed the Awori town of Otta and had then continued their westward expansion by besieging Ado, inland from Badagry. During this long siege (1842–53) a Dahomean army led by Ghezo, and including, it is said, a contingent of women soldiers (the first record of these redoubtable Amazons[30]), marched to the help of Ado, a town which they regarded as subject to their ally the King of Porto Novo who was aiding them with arms and ammunition. On this occasion they were defeated in the field by the Egba and driven off with great loss. Ghezo himself had a narrow escape from capture, leaving his state umbrella, stool, and war charms in the hands of the Egba. Then in 1851, perhaps in revenge for this humiliation, a strong and determined attack was launched on Abeokuta itself. But after a fierce battle along the walls (in which the European missionaries in the town played some part), the Dahomeans were forced to retreat.[31] A few years later they succeeded in bringing about an anti-Egba coalition in which they were joined by Ijaye, Ibadan, Ijebu, and the exiled King Kosoko of Lagos (now installed at Epe in Ijebu territory); this, however, proved abortive, partly as a result of the intervention of Consul Campbell at Lagos, to whom the Egba had sent an urgent appeal. Ghezo was killed by a Ketu musketeer while he was returning from a military expedition against the northern Egba in 1858,[32] but this did not abate the Dahomean threat to the Yoruba. After attacks on Ishaga and Ibara in 1862 and 1863 respectively, another large-scale and determined assault was made on Abeokuta in 1864. Again the walls were held and the enemy driven back. On this occasion, unlike that of 1851, the Dahomean army suffered far heavier loses than the Egba and was unable to make an orderly retreat. But the hope that after this failure the Dahomeans would desist from their attacks was unfulfilled and their armies continued to raid westwards up to the end of the century. In 1873 and 1874, for example, they encamped outside Abeokuta, pillaging nearby towns and villages.[33] They also sent expeditions against Okeodan in Egbado and, farther north, against Ketu and Shabe. Ketu was captured in 1883 during the absence on campaign of its army, and was attacked again in 1886. On the second occasion it was destroyed and abandoned, though in 1893 the refugees were able to return to the site and rebuild their town.[34] Thus the Yoruba of the far west passed first under Dahomean and then French rule. Meanwhile the upper Ogun and Ibarapa country continued to undergo Dahomean raids down to the 1890s.

While northern and western Yorubaland contended with the invasions of the Fulani and the Dahomeans, the kingdoms of the east were suffering from a renewal of Benin's westward expansion. This apparently began in the early years of the nineteenth century during the reign of Oba Obanosa. First, part of the Owo kingdom was once again brought under obedience to Benin. Then, in the reign of Oba Osemwede of Benin, Akure was reconquered and Ekiti overrun. The Benin forces for a time established a base at Otun, and a new Deji of Akure was appointed 'to watch over the interests of Benin in the Ekiti country'. About this time the Ado waged an unsuccessful war against the Bini and the Ikere (the traditional allies of Benin in Ekiti), which resulted in the abandonment for some years of their town and the diminution of the Ewi's territory. Soon after mid-century the brief resurgence of Benin's military power came to a halt, and much of Ekiti (including Ado, in 1874) was then subjected to Ibadan. Yet, according to Egharevba, the Ekiti paid tribute to Benin up to the British occupation of the area in 1897, while payments from Lagos were maintained until about mid-century. Even after the establishment of the British administration, the authority of Benin was respected in eastern Yorubaland, and as late as the reign at Benin of Eweka II (1914–33) the chiefs of Ondo looked to that Oba for his ruling in land and succession disputes.[35]

Further to the north-east, the people of Akoko and the Kabba district were being harassed by those old enemies of the Oyo, the Nupe, whose government and armies had been reinvigorated by their new dynasty of Fulani rulers. This extension of the jihad began in the 1820s in the form of slave raids,[36] but after the establishment of a new Nupe capital at Bida it was prosecuted more deliberately. Despite strong resistance by these isolated Yoruba, whose hill-top defences and poisoned arrows enabled them to beat off cavalry attacks, Nupe hegemony spread over the area. Resident agents of the Bida government, called *ajele* or *ogba*, collected tribute in cowries and agricultural produce, a form of colonialism which continued to meet resistance until it was ended by the advent of the Royal Niger Company in 1896.[37]

Finally, from the 1840s an inter-Yoruba war had been devastating the kingdom of Ondo as a result of an invasion by the Ife. During the course of the war the Ondo were forced to desert their capital and to resort to guerrilla tactics. Hostilities ended only with the intervention of the Goldsworthy peace mission sent by Glover, the British Administrator of Lagos, in 1872.

The collapse of Oyo Ile was followed within twenty years by the establishment of the British consular regime in Lagos, overshadowing the monarchy there, and within a further ten years by the annexation of the town as a crown colony. Already the importance of this island kingdom was becoming apparent. The first half of the nineteenth century had seen the steady growth of its slave market. Captain Adams noted the existence of the trade there at the turn of the century, but it does not seem to have reached large proportions until the decay of Porto Novo, which followed the first Anglo-Portuguese anti-slave-trade treaty of 1810, and the increase in the supply of slaves due to the interior wars. The population was becoming more mixed; apart from the original Awori, the numerous slaves, often brought from far off in the interior, and the Portuguese and Brazilian slave dealers (white and half-caste), from the 1830s there had been a flow of immigrants, or 'repatriates', from the former slaves in Sierra Leone, Brazil, and Cuba. The education and background of the Sierra Leonians, or Saro as they were called, and the Brazilians or Amaro (or Aguda), enabled them to play a prominent part as middlemen between the British administration and the traditional authorities, especially at Lagos and Abeokuta. Meanwhile, at the head of the town the Oba of the line established by Benin still ruled. By now there was probably no attempt by Benin to impose its authority in Lagos, even though the traditional tribute continued to be paid. The power of the Oba may in consequence have somewhat increased, but he was always subject to the constitutional restraints characteristic of the Yoruba kingdoms (and also of Benin), and especially to the influence of the chief known as the Eletu Odibo. During the 1830s troubles broke out over the kingship which led to the deposition and subsequent reinstatement of Oba Adele and then to a feud between the party supporting first Oba Oluwole and then his successor Akitoye, to which the Eletu adhered, and that of Akitoye's nephew Kosoko, an ambitious young prince and claimant to the throne, who was the son and brother of previous Oba.[38]

It was this dynastic dispute which provided the occasion for the British intervention in Lagos of 1851. Kosoko, after being forced into exile, had engaged in the slave trade at Porto Novo and Whydah, where he gained the support of the Portuguese and Brazilian merchants. In 1845 he was allowed by the mild and kindly Akitoye to return to Lagos, and within a few months he succeeded in replacing his uncle on the throne. Akitoye took refuge at Badagry, where he became the protégé of the missionaries and repatriates in the town. Soon his partisans were urging the British that they should restore Akitoye and thereby wipe out the notorious slave market at Lagos. Samuel Crowther was sent to London to point out also that 'if Lagos were under its lawful chief . . . an immense extent of country, abounding with cotton . . . would be thrown open to commerce'.[39] The British government hesitated, and the naval commander in West Africa advised caution. But their Consul for the Bights of Benin and Biafra, who had been appointed to this post in 1849 as its first holder, was John Beecroft, determined equally to stamp out the slave trade and to extend British influence in his area,[40] and he did not scruple to commit the home authorities. Kosoko had already refused to sign an anti-slave trade treaty with the British, and after a second refusal Beecroft decided on a show of force. In November 1851 the Consul entered Lagos lagoon with a naval escort, but after a sharp exchange of fire the party was repulsed. The attack was renewed in greater force at Christmastide a month later, and on 28 December Akitoye landed in the town with his British and other supporters and resumed his throne. On New Year's Day 1852 he signed a treaty with the British representatives in which he agreed to abolish the slave trade and expel the slave traders, to trade freely with British subjects, and to protect the missionaries.

The British assertion that they bombarded and brought Lagos under control in 1851 in order to put an end to the slave trade there has in recent years been questioned.[41] Ajayi, for example, has written:

> The anxiety of Britain to intervene in Lagos was not just the philanthropic desire to destroy the slave trading activities of the Portuguese and Brazilians there, but also the economic desire to control the trade of Lagos from which they had hitherto been excluded and from where they hoped to exploit the resources of the vast country stretching to and beyong the Niger.[42]

Explanation in history is rarely simple, and in this case the interests and ambitions of traders, missionaries, and government agents who were pressing for action against Kosoko had become inextricably mixed, and after agreeing that selfish motives alternated and mingled with altruistic ones, it seems impossible to determine which were uppermost. The soundness of the doctrine that 'legitimate trade' must be encouraged as a substitute for the export of slaves had been demonstrated on this coast, even though it had unexpectedly increased the domestic demand. Incontestably, an immediate result of the action taken in 1851 was the abatement of the export of slaves. The establishment of the British Consulate was quickly followed by the arrival in the town of the palm-oil factors and the Christian missionaries.[43] The British, in their several manifestations as supporters of commerce, Christianity, and sound government, had now become a part of Yoruba country, and their presence at Lagos was a portent of even greater moment than that of the Fulani at Ilorin.

The consular period in Lagos lasted only ten years, and was almost covered by the career there of Consul Benjamin Campbell, who was appointed in 1853 and died at his post in 1859. The policies and preoccupations of the British administration up to 1893 quickly became apparent: the ending of the slave trade in the town and its vicinity, together with the regulation of domestic slavery and a 'gradual approach' (to use Oroge's phrase[44]) to its elimination; the development of legitimate trade, in palm produce above all else, with its consequential emphasis on the opening of the interior and the maintenance of free and secure movement on the roads, aims and interests which, for rather different reasons, were shared by the Ibadan; the protection of newly introduced rights over land; the ending of the war in the interior, a purpose which for a time in the post-consular period seemed to the British administrators best able to be achieved by supporting the extension of Ibadan's influence, which in turn involved a clash with the missionary party at Abeokuta; and in general the spread of European ideas of ethics and conduct. But for this programme the consular regime could not provide adequate means. The end of Campbell's life saw the trade routes closing all round as the Ijaye war drew near, and a revival of the slave trade at Porto Novo and Whydah. Finally, a marked display of French interest in Lagos and its neighbourhood as a source of 'contract labour' aroused misgivings in Whitehall. It was in these circumstances that Palmerston, the British Prime Minister, acceded to the promptings of his government's agents on the coast and gave permission for the annexation of the town in 1861: an acquisition which was regarded as a 'deadly gift from the Foreign Office' by the officials at the Colonial Office who rightly anticipated that, like the other West African possessions, it would require the support of a Parliamentary grant-in-aid.[45] In August 1861, under the guns of H. M. S. *Prometheus* anchored in the lagoon, Oba Dosumu agreed to cede his kingdom to the British. Sir Richard Burton (the recently appointed Consul for the Bights) sardonically observed the scene as the Union Jack was hoisted, the guns of the *Prometheus* fired a salute, a choir of missionary boys sang a hymn, and forty-four officials and traders sat down to dine on the quarter-deck of the warship.[46]

The new Governor, Freeman, arrived with instructions from the Colonial Office to restrict his activities to defence of the local inhabitants and to putting down the slave trade. But the colony was from its beginning involved in the politics of the interior, since the only means of defraying the cost of its administration was by the imposition of customs duties, a device with which West Africans were familiar, but which in Lagos proved to require the control of commerce with the hinterland by extending the boundaries east and west along the coast. The full development of the commerce of the colony depended moreover on the opening of the 'roads' through the interior to direct trade, as opposed to that through the markets set up for external trading by the middlemen states of Egba and Ijebu; in this, the interests of Lagos were soon seen to coincide with those of Ibadan. Thus, despite attempts to apply the brake by the Colonial Office in London, bewildered by events yet approving the financial principle, Freeman and his successors continued to intervene in the wars of the Yoruba and to enlarge the area subject to their administration.[47]

There now appeared on the scene the eager and evangelical Captain Glover. His first appointment at Lagos was as harbour master, but on two occasions during Freeman's leaves he acted as Governor, and in 1866, when the colony was placed under the Governor of the West African Settlements in Sierra Leone, he became Administrator.[48] He had taken part in the Niger expedition of 1857 and after the wreck of the *Dayspring* near Jebba had made three journeys overland between the Niger and Lagos, passing through Ilorin and Abeokuta. Already he had been fired by his experiences with the ambition to gain control for Britain of both the Niger highway and the port of Lagos, and despite the opposition of government and public opinion in England – expressed, in particular, by the recommendations of the 1865 Select Committee – he bent all his great energies to realizing these aims. As early as 1863 the area under British control was enlarged by the addition of the old trading settlements of Palma and Lekki; these lay on the coast to the east of the colony in territory claimed by the Ijebu and were 'ceded' by the now-tamed

Kosoko, who had been allowed by the Awujale to take refuge nearby at Epe as a sort of tenant ruler. Glover now succeeded in checking a threatened expansion by the French from their short-lived protectorate at Porto Novo and signed treaties with local rulers which brought Ado, Ipokia, Okeodan, and Badagry on the west under Lagos, a move which he followed by a boundary agreement with the French admiral. Meanwhile, towards the end of 1864 when the Ijaye war was in its final stages, the Egba and Ijebu blocked the tracks linking Ibadan with Lagos and Egba forces laid siege to Ikorodu in Ijebu Remo, the important market town at the northern corner of the lagoon which was allied to Ibadan.[49] Finally repudiating the policy of favouring Abeokuta, long urged by an influential section of the missionaries, Glover fell on the Egba at Ikorodu in March 1865 with troops from the West India Regiment and his recently formed Hausa Constabulary, firing rockets and shells, and drove them off in disorder.

Thereafter Glover continued to press for the opening of the roads. This was a policy which especially alarmed the Egba, who in 1867, in order to prevent merchants from by-passing their town, set up a customs post at Isheri on the River Ogun near its exit to the lagoon. Glover, suspicious of this attempt to extend Egba influence almost as far south as the Lagos mainland, established constables at posts on the roads as far as Otta and up the Ogun to Isheri, and he announced that Ebute Meta was Lagos territory. His action was resented at Abeokuta and was followed by the rising against Europeans in the town known as *ifole*, 'housebreaking', and their subsequent expulsion. In 1871 Glover tried to achieve the opening of the roads for direct trade by calling a conference in Lagos to which came representatives from Oyo, Ijebu, Ibadan, and at a later stage also from Ilaro, Ijo, Ketu, and even Benin. But neither the Egba nor the Ijebu (still firmly in alliance) would co-operate, and these efforts came to nothing. From his home government Glover continued to receive little support and frequent opposition, and in 1872, on the reversal of his policies by the Governor-in-Chief, Pope-Hennessy, he was recalled. As a contemporary noted, he had been in advance of his time – but only by a few years, for within two decades his policy was vindicated by the actions taken by his successors at Lagos with the approval of Whitehall.[50]

NOTES

1. See Ajayi and Smith, *passim*.
2. See Ajayi (1965), Ayandele (1966), and Phillips (1966) for missionary, especially C. M. S., involvement in Yoruba politics.
3. Law (1976a), *passim*. Law discusses the possible existence of Yoruba historical writing in Arabic (language and script or in Yoruba written in Arabic characters) before the nineteenth century. But no such work is known before ibn Kokora's history of Ilorin (1912). For Kokoro, *see* Bibliography under Martin, B. G.
4. P.P. 1865, QQ. 2165–6.
5. For example, see Burns, p. 27.
6. Ajayi and Smith, pp. 51–2. See also the controversy between Hopkins (1968) and Ajayi and Austen (1972); also, Law (1978a), *passim*, and Law (1982), p. 397.

7. For examples, see S. Johnson (1921), pp. 321–4, and Biobaku (1957), p. 34.
8. *The Twenty Years' Crisis 1919–1939*, London, 1958, p. 97.
9. For the government of Ibadan, see S. Johnson (1921), pp. 94, 636–67. For the history of Ibadan, see also Akinyele (Morgan), Parrinder (1951, 1953), Elgee, and Awe (1964a, 1965).
10. S. Johnson (1921), pp. 305–7; for Oluwole, see Biobaku in Diké (ed.).
11. Ajisafe, pp. 48–9, 102; Biobaku (1957), p. 52.
12. Burton (1863a), pp. 275–8.
13. Biobaku (1957), pp. 5–6, 21–2.
14. Folayan (1967a), pp. 78–80, 106.
15. Ajayi and Smith, p. 67. For Ijaye, see Stone (1900), Bowen (1857), and Smith (1962).
16. S. Johnson (1921), pp. 279–83; Smith (1965b), pp. 415–16, 416, n. 3; Ojo (1966b); Morton-Williams (1967), p. 45. According to Awe (1964a), p. 174, citing Hinderer, the name of the town was not changed from Ago Oja to Oyo until about 1856.
17. S. Johnson (1921), p. 282.
18. There is a graphic description of the battle in S. Johnson (1921), pp. 285–9. See also Ajayi and Smith, Part I, Chapter 5.
19. Ajayi and Smith, p. 55.
20. S. Johnson (1921), pp. 294–6.
21. S. Johnson (1921), pp. 317–21; Awe (1964b), pp. 48–50.
22. Compare maps 3 and 4.
23. Awe (1964b), *passim*. See also D. J. May, pp. 215, 221. For the Ekiti ajele, see Oguntuyi, pp. 46, 61.
24. For this war, see S. Johnson (1921), pp. 331–54; Biobaku (1957), Ch. 6; Ajayi and Smith, Part I, Ch. 8, and Part II, *passim*.
25. Hinderer to Venn, 21 Oct. 1855, CMS Archives CA2/049; Mann's Journal, Dec. 1855, CMS Archives, CA2/066; Ajayi and Smith, p. 76.
26. For the Aibo war, see Awe (1964a), p. 191; Folayan (1967a), pp. 55–62. Awe notes that the missionary Townsend 'predicted quite rightly that the Aibo war would be the prelude to a bigger conflict' (CMS Archives, CA2/085a, Townsend to Venn, 25 September 1857). Both the forgotten town of Aibo and the war await their historian.
27. S. Johnson (1921), p. 252.
28. Argyle, *passim*, and especially Ch. 5.
29. Argyle, p. 82.
30. Ajisafe, p. 82, though Argyle (p. 87) quotes Foa's suggestion that women were first used as soldiers only in 1851.
31. Ajisafe, pp. 96–7; Ajayi and Smith, Part I, Ch. 6.
32. Parrinder (1956), p. 42, citing Hazoumé (1937), *Le pacte du sang au Dahomey*, Paris.
33. S. Johnson (1921), pp. 362–3; Ajisafe, pp. 133–4.
34. S. Johnson (1921), p. 455; Parrinder (1956), Chs. 8 and 9.
35. Egharevba, pp. 44–7; Oguntuyi, pp. 36–41; S. Johnson (1921), pp. 390–1.
36. R. L. and J. Lander (1832), II, p. 315.
37. Mason (1970), pp. 193–209.
38. For Kosoko, see Biobaku in Dike (ed.); Smith (1969, 1978); Oguntomisin (1979).
39. Ajayi (1961a).
40. See Dike (1956) for an account of Beecroft, also Lynn (1982).
41. For references to earlier views and a re-examination, see Ajayi (1961a).
42. Ajayi (1961a), p. 97.
43. Newbury, Chs. III and IV. For the consular period, see Smith (1974, 1978).
44. Oroge, Chapter V, especially pp. 304–5.
45. Robinson and Gallagher, p. 36. For the importance of the closing of the roads and other interruptions to trade in the explanation of the European partition of Africa, see Hopkins (1973), p. 155. For the protection of property rights as a factor in explaining the British annexation of 1861, see Hopkins (1980), *passim*.
46. Burton (1863b), pp. 212–13 and 216–17 (Hodgkin, p. 281). Burton was appointed to his

post in March 1861, but did not sail to take up appointment until the following August, so he was not an eye-witness of this ceremony.

47. Hargreaves (1963), pp. 58–61.
48. For Glover, see Biobaku (1957), Ch. 7, and McIntyre, *passim*.
49. See Phillips (1970), who argues convincingly that Glover had inveigled the Egba into attacking Ikorodu in order to bring about a coalition against them of Lagos, Ibadan and Ijebu.
50. For the crisis of 1871–2, see Mbaeyi (1972).

TWELVE

ON THE THRESHOLD OF NIGERIA

The last quarter of the nineteenth century saw the end of the sovereignty of the Yoruba states and the beginning of their elimination as political units. In 1892–3 all were brought under British control as a protectorate administered with the colony of Lagos, with the exception of the Egba at Abeokuta who were allowed to maintain an anomalous semi-independence until 1914. In 1906 the colony and protectorate were amalgamated with the Niger Coast (formerly Oil Rivers) Protectorate and in 1914 with the Protectorate of Northern Nigeria. The colonial government, advancing from the system of informal rule typified by the consuls, extended its influence by its apparatus of Travelling Commissioners and later by Residents and District Officers posted to the major towns, a system which to some extent kept alive, and after the introduction of Lugardian indirect rule into Yorubaland from 1914 even strengthened, the identities of the kingdoms. Political independence had been lost, but in the longer term more important than the establishment of this alien rule was the absorption of all the Yoruba – Oyo, Ijebu, Egba, and the rest – into a wider grouping, that of Nigeria.

Before all this was achieved, the last quarter-century of independent Yorubaland witnessed profound changes of many kinds. In politics and warfare Ibadan's predominance, which had offered one solution to the problems posed by the decline of Oyo and the external threats, was rejected and its short-lived empire broken up. There was resurgence of vitality in some of the ancient kingdoms, especially Ijebu, and the much-divided Ekiti drew together in a military confederation against Ibadan. These were variations on old themes, but there were changes, and portents of changes, of a deeper nature. Missionaries of various churches – Anglican, Roman Catholic, and the Protestant sects – and of many lands, European and American, were penetrating the kingdoms and everywhere challenging old ways of life and thought, and wherever the missionaries went, new educational systems were introduced. Traders both followed and preceded the missionaries, and the work and influence of the two were more often complementary than antagonistic. In Lagos and Abeokuta and to a lesser degree in a few other places, a new kind of society was being created, based on westernized Yoruba who were emancipated not only from slavery but also from former ties with their towns and families. Against this background took place the political

141

movement of Europe into Africa known as the Partition of Africa – or, when the fifteen years or so of heightened activity after 1884 are considered, as the Scramble – momentous not so much because of the establishment of the colonial regimes, which nearly all proved to be ephemeral, as for the new nation states which were created after the European pattern.[1]

It is possible that the comparative richness and accessibility of the archives of the missionary societies have led to some exaggeration of the role which they played in the life of Yorubaland during this period. Their direct influence on events was often less than they realized or hoped; at Abeokuta, for example, Townsend, the Anglican agent, was constantly disappointed in his ambitions to convert the town into a peace-loving, Christian polity. Nevertheless, the missionaries were the most powerful vehicles of change, first because they were identified in the minds of the Yoruba with the material power of the British settlement at Lagos, and secondly, because of the educational and economic programme which they were determined to implement as the pre-condition, according to their theory, of the Christianization of the land and which met with a growing and enthusiastic response from those they taught. Unlike the leaders of the Muslim jihad, they could not – or would not – compromise with existing conditions and institutions. Wherever they went, a pro-missionary party sprang up around them, dedicated not so much to their dogmatic and moral teaching – the Egba, for example, remained keen slave traders almost to the end of the century, despite their numerous Christians – as to exploiting their political and economic support. This in turn was usually soon followed by the development of a party hostile to the missionaries, equally animated by political and economic motives. To a great extent, support for the missions was based on the early Western-educated Africans, the Saro or repatriates from Sierra Leone living in Lagos, Abeokuta, and (in smaller numbers) elsewhere, but such men were also found in the ranks of the anti-missionaries. Among the latter a prominent example was G.W. Johnson, the Secretary of the Egba United Board of Management which was established in 1865 as the government at Abeokuta during the regency following the death of Alake Okukenu in 1862. The E.U.B.M. was an attempt by a westernized group of repatriates to co-operate with the traditional chiefs in the modernization of Egbaland, but as it failed to obtain a stable revenue it never attained real influence. In 1898 the experiment was revived with British support as the Egba National Council, renamed in 1902 the Egba United Government, which lasted until 1914.[2]

The relations of the missionaries with the British administration varied. All missionaries continued to demand that British protection should be extended to them wherever they went, and in order to further their aims – religious, educational, and political – they usually welcomed and encouraged the establishment of British rule (despite some reservations, in particular about the annexation of Lagos in 1861). Thus in many ways they prepared the way for the extension of the protectorate over the whole of the Yoruba country; one writer has contended that the work of the missionaries was the primary factor in bringing about this extension by peaceful and gradual means.[3] There were many occasions when the missionaries strongly disapproved of the actions of the British administrators at Lagos, and especially of the restless and ambitious Governor Glover. Nevertheless, the interdependence of missionaries and officials was so strong, and so clear to all concerned, that it could not be broken by such disagreements. During the major and protracted war which broke out in 1877 it was to the missionaries, and to the British power behind them, that many among the distracted Yoruba looked for intervention and help amid their intractable rivalries.

The Sixteen Years' War (1877–93) between Ibadan and a grand coalition of other Yoruba states, allied from 1878 with the Ilorin, was on a larger scale than any of the previous wars and lasted for a longer time.[4] Essentially it arose from the widespread hostility engendered by the Ibadan, who had not only succeeded to much of the central and southern territories of the old Oyo kingdom, including a large part of the former territory of Kurunmi of Ijaye, but had also brought the Ekiti and Ijesha under their rule. More immediately, it concerned the issue of the freedom of the roads along which food and other supplies moved to the towns and Ibadan's need for access to the coast, where guns and powder could be obtained. The outbreak of war in 1877 was occasioned by the Egba who, resentful of an Ibadan expedition through their country to collect a consignment of gunpowder bought by the Alafin from Porto Novo, barred the roads to Ibadan traders. The Ibadan opened hostilities in a desultory manner by raids on Egba farms, but the war was soon extended as the Ijebu joined in a coalition with the Egba. Next, the Ekiti and their northern neighbours, the Ila, rose in revolt, murdering the Ibadan ajele in their towns, a move which brought the Ilorin, always interested in this eastern area of Yorubaland, to join in the war against Ibadan.

The extension of the war to the north-east was in part a consequence of the development of an eastern route from the coast to Ibadan, which had been advocated by Governor Glover in 1872 in order to avoid Egba and Ijebu territory. This route had two southern termini: the western one at Atijere at the eastern end of the lagoon, and the other at Aboto on the creeks in Mahin country. From these it ran northwards to Ode Ondo, whence it was known as the Ondo Road. The Ondo capital had been reoccupied in 1872 after the British mission had brought about peace with the Ife, and at Glover's suggestion the Church Missionary Society established a mission station there in 1875. From Ondo the road continued to the Ife town of Oke Igbo, where it divided, one branch running westwards to Ibadan and the other north to Ilesha.[5] The road at first served its purpose in enabling military and other supplies to reach Ibadan without interference from the Egba and the Ijebu, but it soon became a focus of dissension. In particular, the Ijesha at its northern end, who had been brought back to obedience by Ibadan after a rebellion in 1870 under their war leader, Ogedengbe, were determined to regain their independence. A group of educated repatriates formed an Ijesha Association which, though it began in 1876 as a Christian prayer group, was soon directing its activities to stirring up resistance to Ibadan, both in their own state and among the neighbouring Ekiti. They strongly supported the maintenance of the Ondo Road, since it linked them with Lagos and allowed them to import firearms and ammunition into their area. This was of special importance at this time when the southern Yoruba were replacing their muzzle-loading muskets with modern breech-loading rifles and securing thereby a marked superiority in armament over the Ibadan.[6]

The first major engagement of the war took place in 1878 at Ikirun, north of Ilesha, where the Ibadan attacked and drove off in disorder strong armies from Ilorin, Ekiti, Ila, and Ijesha encamped north of the town.[7] But Ibadan's victory in this action – known as the Jalumi or 'rush into the water' war from the drowning of

Plate 15 On the River Otin. The Ibadan were victorious in the battle of Ikirun, fought near here in 1878, and many of the fleeing enemy were drowned in this river.

many of the fleeing Ilorin in the nearby River Otin – was singularly indecisive. The Ijebu declined Ibadan's offer of alliance with them, and the Egba continued to bar the roads through their territory to the coast, while the Ekiti and Ijesha strengthened their alliance, the former (excluding the Ado) grouping themselves into the military confederation called the Ekiti Parapo, whose armies were placed under the command of Ogedengbe of Ilesha. Soon the Ibadan were fighting on three main fronts: around their own town and to the south and west against the Egba and the Ijebu; in the north against the Ilorin, who were besieging their allies the Offa, and in the north-east against the Ekiti and Ijesha on the battlefield among the hills and rocks near Oke Mesi (north of Ilesha) known as Kiriji (a word derived onomatopoeically from the report of the firearms).

Fighting continued at Kiriji for over a decade. Meanwhile, in or about 1882, a new front against Ibadan was opened up by Ife. Relations between the Ife and the Oyo refugees resettled at the contiguous town of Modakeke had never been easy, and at some period, probably about 1850, had degenerated into active hostilities during the course of which Ife had been abandoned by its inhabitants. About 1854, however, the Ibadan persuaded the Ife to return to their former homes.[8] It seems that from this time until the 1880s the ancient town and kingdom of Ife were within the Ibadan empire, paying tribute and supervised by an ajele resident in nearby Modakeke.[9] During the Sixteen Years' War the Ife were required to contribute a contingent of troops to the Ibadan forces at Kiriji. But they grew ever more restive under Ibadan rule, and were especially resentful of the imposition on them through Ibadan influence of an unpopular Oni. In 1882 these troubles came to a head, and again the Ife expressed their hostility to the Ibadan and other Oyo Yoruba by attacking their neighbours at Modakeke, and again Ile Ife was destroyed. But now the Ijesha and Ijebu sent troops to their aid, while their own soldiers under the war chiefs decamped from Kiriji and returned to help in the siege of Modakeke. Johnson writes: 'Thus stood the Ibadan lion at bay facing five fronts, with ammunition spent, yet flinching from none, at Ofa, at Kiriji, at Modakeke, and against the Egbas as well as the Ijebus at home.'[10]

Despite Ibadan's difficulties, the war was now approaching stalemate, and war-weariness was widespread. Many Yoruba, and especially the educated, looked to British intervention to bring the fighting to an end. But at this time vigorous action could hardly be expected from the Lagos administration. Between 1874 and 1886 the government of the colony was incorporated with that of the Gold Coast, an arrangement which inhibited a forward policy; Lagos, moreover, was only just beginning to pay its way and to justify its maintenance.[11] Not until pressure was applied by trading interests, for example, did the local Administrator take steps to foil the cession of Mahin beach to the Germans in 1885 by the Omopetu. In this situation it fell to the missionaries to explore the prospects for peace, a task to which they were suited since not only did they themselves regard a settlement as a matter of urgency in the interests of Christianity but also their reputation stood high with the chiefs and people of the country. A series of meetings was held in Lagos at the end of 1882, apparently on the initiative of the veteran Anglican missionary at Ibadan, David Hinderer, to which came representatives from the main kingdoms. This led to the sending of a Lagos mission to Ijebu Ode, where it was found that though Awujale Afidipote wished to continue the war against Ibadan, a strong party in the kingdom was in favour of peace and the resumption of trade. The upshot was the deposition of the Awujale and the gradual return of peace and trade between Ijebu and Ibadan, the latter being now enabled to obtain from the Ijebu, at high prices, enough new rifles and cartridges to hold their positions at Kiriji.

These efforts for peace brought about what Johnson calls a 'rift in the clouds', but on the main fronts fighting continued. In January 1884 the Reverend J. B. Wood, an influential missionary at Abeokuta, succeeded in visiting the opposing camps at Kiriji, but he failed to persuade the combatants to accept terms. Hostilities dragged on there, as also at Modakeke and Offa. Then, in January 1886, the Colony of Lagos was detached from the Gold Coast and again became self-administering. Almost at once Governor Moloney dispatched two delegations into the interior to reopen peace negotiations. Both delegations were headed by Yoruba clergymen of the Church Missionary Society, the first, to the Ibadan camp, being led by the Reverend Samuel Johnson, the historian, and the second, to the Ekiti and their allies, by the Reverend Charles Phillips of Ondo (later Assistant Bishop of Western Equatorial Africa). A cease-fire was arranged by the delegates, first at Kiriji and then at Modakeke, and a peace treaty was signed at Lagos in June 1886. By this treaty Ibadan recognized the independence of the members of the Ekiti Parapo, and it was provided that the Oyo town of Modakeke, whose contiguity to Ife had long been a source of trouble, should be broken up and rebuilt on Ibadan territory between the Oshun and Oba rivers; by implication the treaty also severed the formal dependence of Ibadan on Oyo.[12] Special Commissioners were named, this time two officials of the Lagos administration, who proceeded to Kiriji and supervised the firing and evacuation of the war camps there at the end of September. They went next to the Modakeke battlefield. Here, although the cease-fire was in operation, they failed to persuade either the Modakeke to comply with the Lagos treaty by quitting their homes or the Ife to leave their camp and return to their town. Nevertheless, fighting was not resumed there.

The wars in Yorubaland had now been brought to an end and peace restored, even though precariously, with an important exception: the contest between Ibadan and Ilorin continued, centring on the siege by the Ilorin of Offa, once their vassal town and now Ibadan's ally in the north. The Ilorin, commanded by Karara, the fierce and intransigent Balogun of the Gambari (general of the Hausa population of Ilorin), had rejected the peace proposals brought to them by Phillips and had no part in the Lagos treaty, though they did agree to carry on negotiations with the Ibadan. But during the next year (1887) the latter, wearied of hostilities and nervous about the isolated position of their army at Offa, withdrew from the besieged town, after rescuing its ruler, the Oloffa, and returned to their base at Ikirun. Karara now entered Offa, which for so long and so obstinately had resisted him behind its five walls. Its remaining chiefs came at his summons to do homage, and while they lay prostrate before him at the palace gate he gave the order for them all to be slaughtered on the spot. Yet the fall of Offa did not end the war, and desultory fighting continued between the Ibadan at Ikirun and the Ilorin encamped at Yanayo for a further six years.

Ibadan's attempt to assume the mantle of Oyo had now decisively failed. This was mainly due, Mrs Awe has written, to its lack of a 'traditional heritage' and its consequent inability to command the loyalty of the former Oyo towns,[13] but it was bound up too with the difficulties arising from the control of the roads by its enemies, and especially in obtaining the newer types of firearms. Meanwhile the Egba, who since 1879 had taken little part in the war, were split by a religious dissension reminiscent of the Franza–Ingleza troubles in Uganda. One party, which included most of the chiefs, supported the extension of French influence in the town, for which the way had been prepared by the Roman Catholic missionaries who had been working in Abeokuta since 1880, while a Protestant party, led by Wood, the Anglican missionary,[14] looked to Lagos for protection. In 1888 a young French trader named Viard, who claimed to represent the French government, visited Ilaro, the leading Egbado town, and then moved on to Abeokuta, where he persuaded the chiefs to enter into a treaty of trade and friendship. It was also reported that the French would build a railway from Porto Novo via Ilaro and would recognize domestic slavery. Wood and his party immediately raised the alarm. The Colonial Office in London realized that this French penetration threatened the main source of Lagos trade, and the issue was taken up with the French government through diplomatic channels. In 1889 the British and French governments signed a treaty settling what was to be Nigeria's western frontier on a line well to the west of Abeokuta and Ilaro. Against the background of these events Governor Moloney hastily concluded a treaty (in July 1888) with Oyo by which the Alafin agreed to cede no territory without the consent of the Lagos government,[15] and he made renewed attempts to bring the Ilorin war to an end. After Moloney's departure in 1891 the Acting Governor, Denton, hoisted the British flag in Ilaro and other parts of Egbadoland. This action, taken at the instance of the chiefs of Okeodan and other towns, brought relief to the Egbado, hard-pressed as they were between the Fon and Aja on their west and the Egba to the east,[16] while from the British point of view it served to divert Egbado trade towards Lagos and away from Porto Novo. Naturally, however, the annexation incurred the indignation of the Egba, who retaliated as usual by closing the roads and the River Ogun.

The Anglo-French clash of interests in Abeokuta was one facet of the Scramble for Africa. The Berlin Conference of 1884–5 is conveniently, but rather misleadingly, held to have partitioned Africa; in fact, the famous provision in its Final Act that international recognition of territorial acquisitions in Africa must be preceded by an effective occupation of the area concerned was specifically confined in its application to the coastal districts, most of which had already been brought under control by the European powers, and left the boundaries between the spheres of influence of the powers in the interior undefined. Thus it was fortunate for the British, and in the long run for the Yoruba, that Viard's treaty with Abeokuta in 1888 so stirred the Protestant party there that, as a result of their pressure, the British government exerted themselves in time to secure an agreement with the French under which most of the Yoruba country fell to the east of the demarcation line – though the Ketu, Shabe, and other western Yoruba were left to be incorporated eventually into the French colony of Dahomey, and are still separated by an international frontier from the Yoruba in Nigeria. But the treaty had done nothing to clarify the position in the area east of the line and within the British sphere. Only in 1891, when the scholarly Moloney was replaced as Governor at Lagos by Carter, was a vigorous forward policy undertaken, and it was not until Chamberlain came to the Colonial Office in 1895 that the old informal system of rule was finally discarded.

When Carter arrived in Lagos in September 1891 three major obstacles remained to the extension of British rule within the limits determined by agreement among the European powers: the Ilorin–Ibadan war in the north and the recalcitrance of the Egba and the Ijebu in the south, which all hindered free movement and the flow of trade between Lagos and the interior. Carter dealt first with the problem presented by the determinedly independent Ijebu. Denton had already visited the Awujale and had been ill received. Carter now demanded an apology for the insult to the Acting Governor, and at a meeting in Lagos in January 1892 he secured both this and a 'treaty' under which the Ijebu promised to open the roads through their country to all. The validity of this treaty was somewhat doubtful, since the members of the Awujale's delegation, pleading illiteracy, refused to sign it, though they allowed its signature on their behalf by two Ijebu residents of Lagos. In any case, its terms were soon broken when the Awujale picked a quarrel with Ibadan, demanding the execution of two missionaries there (one a Yoruba and the other English) whom he accused of having brought Europeans and their goods into his territory without permission, and threatening to close the roads. Carter now received permission by telegraph from the Colonial Secretary to take coercive action, and in May 1892 he sent a military expedition against the Ijebu. The force was under the command of Colonel Scott of the Gold Coast Constabulary and consisted of some 450 men from the West India Regiment, the Lagos and Gold Coast Hausa, and a contingent of Ibadan warriors, with fourteen British officers. They sailed down the lagoon in a small flotilla and landed at Epe, whence after two days' preparation they marched on Ijebu Ode. The Ijebu, who had expected the landing at Itoiki nearer their capital, were taken by surprise, but they resisted the advance with determination in the thick forest through which the Lagos force was making its way. A particularly fierce engagement was fought at the crossing of the Yemoji River, but after two and a half hours' fighting there the invaders, with their rockets, Maxim gun, and three seven-pounders, prevailed over the Ijebu with their Sniders, and seven days after setting out from Lagos they entered the Ijebu capital. After a further ten days the main force withdrew, leaving behind a detachment of the Lagos Constabulary under a British officer.[17]

Carter's decision to attack the Ijebu rather than the Egba, who had caused the greater inconvenience in closing the interior roads, has been attributed in a recent study to the influence of the Anglican and Protestant missionaries, who had met with continuous rebuffs in their attempts to extend their missions to Ijebu from the Awujale and his chiefs, strong conservatives intent on maintaining the traditional isolation of their state.[18] The missionaries were right in their assessment of the potential importance of Ijebu to their cause. After 1892, as Ayandele shows, Ijebu supplanted Abeokuta as the leading centre of missionary activity among the Yoruba.[19]

Politically and economically, the Ijebu expedition transformed the whole situation in the interior. Not only was the northern shore of the lagoon now brought under British control but, as Johnson writes, 'a shock of surprise and alarm' was felt throughout the land.[20] The Egba (unaware that the Colonial Office in London were demurring at proposals from the War Office that operations should next be mounted against them) reopened the Ogun to the traders' canoes and barges and invited the Governor to visit Abeokuta. Encouraged by these developments, Carter set out at the beginning of 1893 on his trek through Yorubaland, accompanied by a posse of local soldiers.[21] He went first to Abeokuta, where he signed a treaty of trade and friendship with the Egba. But the chiefs there successfully resisted proposals for posting a Resident to their town and for cessions of land for a railway linking Lagos with Ibadan, and also obtained the inclusion in the treaty of a clause guaranteeing their independence (which, in the event, was revoked in 1914). From Abeokuta Carter continued to Oyo, where he again made a treaty, here less favourable to the local authorities, and thence to Ilorin, where he interviewed the Emir. Turning south, the Governor had a series of meetings near the Otin River with the leaders of the opposing war camps of the Ilorin and the Ibadan, at which he succeeded in obtaining their recognition of the Awere stream (near Erin, between Ikirun and Offa) as the boundary between the territories of the two towns and their agreement to the breaking-up of the camps. By the end of March the Ibadan army had returned to its town. Carter followed in its wake to Ibadan, where he was disappointed in his hopes of obtaining a treaty providing for the posting there of a Resident. He then returned to Lagos, to receive the plaudits of the merchants for his successful pacification of so wide an area. A few months later, in August 1893, the Ibadan chiefs reopened negotiations with the Governor and, after assurances that no interference with their government was intended, agreed to a treaty with the British. Under this their town was recognized as the administrative centre of the larger part of the old Oyo kingdom and the chiefs now agreed to provide land for the construction of a railway and to accept a British Resident.[22]

Thus ended the Sixteen Years' War, and also the history of the Yoruba states as independent political units. There remained the two problems of Ilorin and of French infiltration into an area which, although still undemarcated, clearly belonged under the Anglo-French agreements to the Lagos hinterland. Despite Carter's visit and the Emir's protestations of friendship, the Ilorin continued to harass the countryside, and in 1894 Captain Bower, the Travelling Commissioner (and later Resident) at Ibadan, established a camp on the River Otin a little north of Ikirun in order to protect the area and to demarcate the boundary between Ilorin and Ibadan. But still the Ilorin were hostile, treating Bower roughly on a visit he paid to their town and launching attacks during his absence in 1896 on the camp at Odo Otin. Ilorin now fell within the territory of the Royal Niger Company, the chartered trading company which preceded the establishment of the Protectorate of Northern Nigeria. Carter sent many protests to London about the Company's supine attitude over the Ilorin situation, but until it was pressed by the Colonial Office to take action the Company showed little interest in asserting its rule in this part of the huge area assigned to it. At last, in January 1897, Goldie, the Governor of the Company, led out his troops from Lokoja. Having first conquered Bida, the Nupe capital, he continued to Ilorin. After overcoming a brief resistance the troops entered the ruins of the city, which they had shelled and set on fire. The Emir signed a treaty, agreeing to accept a frontier with Lagos 'as the Company shall decide'. Even now the Company did not have the resources to bring about proper control of the area, but for the future the Lagos government was able to complain about the behaviour of the Ilorin not to the Company alone but more effectively to the West African Frontier Force. This had been established in 1897 under Lugard in order to check the French, one of whose expeditions from Dahomey in January 1897 had for a time even occupied Kishi in the extreme north of Yorubaland.[23]

The settling of the Ilorin–Lagos boundary resulted in a large number of Yoruba in the north-east corner of the old Oyo kingdom and also most of the Igbomina and Kabba peoples to the north of the Ijesha and Ekiti coming under the rule of the Royal Niger Company and being included, from 1900, in the Protectorate of Northern Nigeria. In the First Republic of independent Nigeria they constituted a sort of irredenta in the Northern Region (at least from the point of view of the Western Region), but since the administrative rearrangements of May 1967 they have belonged to the Kwara State with its capital at Ilorin.

In 1893 the inhabitants of the Yoruba states stood on the threshold of a wider polity and wider loyalties were offered them. Though the ending of the Sixteen Years' War, in shattering Ibadan's attempt to impose its own form of unity on the country, had restored for a few years the independence of the eastern kingdoms, this independence lost its meaning in the new situation created by the peace which British rule brought about. Shielded by foreign arms and power from the incursions of the Dahomeans (whose capital was occupied by the French in this same year) and the Fulani, and forbidden to engage in their own internecine wars, the Yoruba were free to discover a cultural unity within the new political unity imposed upon them, and in a few years were invited to share in an even wider identification as Nigerians, fellow-citizens with the Hausa, Kanuri, Igbo, Ijo, Edo, and the rest of Nigeria's many different peoples. Within a half-century this was to engender among the educated a sense of belonging to a nation, the most populous and one of the most important in Africa. It also led to the assertion, within this wider context, of the linguistic, cultural, and political ties which give unity to the Yoruba of the different kingdoms, the diverse 'children of Oduduwa', who, as a result of the demographic and other changes in the nineteenth century, had grown closer to each other both physically and in sentiment. Time must show which of these concepts, the national and the tribal, unhappily often in rivalry, will prevail.

The British peace was paid for by a loss of political independence which lasted for sixty-four years. But in the history of the Yoruba kingdoms the colonial period, and the longer period covered by European penetration, are but a fraction, though an important one. The dangers and uncertainties of the present can be understood only by a study of the past which both takes account of the rapid changes of the last hundred years and goes beyond them to the earlier centuries when these kingdoms flourished as the political framework within which the ancestors of the Western Nigerians of today lived their lives from generation to generation.

NOTES

1. For the missionary role in the creation of Nigeria, see Coleman (1958), Ch. 4, Ajayi (1965) and Ayandele, *passim*. For the partition of West Africa, see Robinson and Gallagher (1961), especially Ch. XIII, and Hargreaves (1963). The latter includes the part played by the European and other traders, which has otherwise been somewhat neglected. Western education quickly led to the emergence of Yoruba historiography: see Law (1972).
2. See Phillips (1969) and Pallinder-Law (1974).
3. Ayandele, p. 29.
4. For this war, see the detailed account in S. Johnson (1921), Chs. XXIII–XXXIV, and also Awe (1965), *passim*, and Ayandele, Ch. 2.
5. Governor Glover's sketch map of the trade routes to the interior from Lagos is reproduced in Biobaku (1957) as map 4. For the Ondo Road, also see Ayandele, pp. 33–5, and numerous references in Akintoye (1971). The southern end of the road was the scene of fierce fighting with the 'Biafrans' in August 1967.
6. S. Johnson (1921), pp. 415–16.
7. S. Johnson (1921), pp. 427–36; Ajayi and Smith, Part I, Ch. 8.
8. S. Johnson (1921), pp. 232–3.
9. Akintoye (1971), p. 53.
10. S. Johnson (1921), p. 478.
11. Robinson and Gallagher, p. 387, n. 2.
12. For the text of the treaty, see S. Johnson (1921), pp. 527–32.
13. Awe (1965), p. 230.
14. The use of the term 'Protestant' to include Anglicans seems regrettably unavoidable in this context.
15. For the text of this treaty, see S. Johnson (1921), pp. 574–6. Johnson was himself a witness to both this and the 1886 peace treaty.
16. Folayan (1967a), Chapters IV, V.
17. See Smith in Crowder (1971), pp. 170–204.
18. Ayandele, pp. 54–68.
19. Ayandele, pp. 68–9.
20. S. Johnson (1921), p. 623.
21. The Lagos Constabulary, often called the 'Lagos Hausas', who provided this escort,

descended from the force raised in 1863 by Glover from the runaway slaves who had sought his protection in Sierra Leone in 1858 and later that year accompanied him on his return march from Lagos to Jebba. Probably not all those with Glover were Hausa and of the forty 'Hausa' Constables who accompanied Lugard in 1894–5, ten were in fact Yoruba (Lugard, ed. Perham and Bull, Vol. 4, p. 96).

22. For the texts of these 1893 treaties with Abeokuta, Oyo, and Ibadan, see S. Johnson (1921), Appendix A.

23. For the subjugation of Ilorin and the aftermath, see Flint, Chs. 10, 11, and 13. The West African Frontier Force was composed of units from Britain's four West African colonies.

APPENDIX I
CROWNED OBA

The Oni of Ife visited Lagos in 1903 at the invitation of the Governor, Sir William MacGregor, to give his ruling to the Governor and the members of his Central Native Council (a body mainly representative of Lagos and the Colony) on the complaint of the Akarigbo of Ijebu Remo against the wearing of a crown by the Elepe, another ruler in Ijebu Remo. Sitting with his back to the Council, the Oni stated that only the following oba were entitled to the crowns with beaded fringes which were conferred by his predecessors at Ife and which usually denote membership of the house of Oduduwa:

1. Alake of Abeokuta
2. Olowu of Owu (Abeokuta)
3. Alafin of Oyo
4. Oba of Ado (Benin?)
5. Oshemawe of Ondo
6. Awujale of Ijebu Ode
7. Alara of Ara (Ekiti)
8. Ajero of Ijero (Ekiti)
9. Orangun of Ila
10. Owa of Ilesha
11. Alaye of Efon (Ekiti)
12. Olojudo of Iddo (Ekiti)
13. Olosi of Osi (Ekiti)
14. Ore of Otun (Ekiti)
15. Akarigbo of Ijebu Remo (Ofin, now in Shagamu)
16. Alaketu of Ketu
17. Elekole of Ikole (Ekiti)
18. Olowo of Owo
19. Ewi of Ado (Ekiti)
20. Oloko (or Oshile) of Oko (Abeokuta)
21. Alagura (or Agura) of Gbagura (Abeokuta)

A notable omission in the list is the Onishabe of Shabe, perhaps because his kingdom lay outside Nigeria, or perhaps because it was believed in Nigeria to be extinct. The order in the list follows that given in the report of the meeting of the Council.[1]

The British policy of 'indirect rule' when applied in Yorubaland greatly accelerated the demand by rulers for crowns.[2] The total of twenty-one titles in this list of 1903 compares with forty-one claimants in 1966 to titles conferred by Ife, recorded on the map in Ojo's *Yoruba Culture*[3] which omits number 4, the 'Oba of Ado' (presumably a reference by the Oni to Benin). In 1977 it was reported that the government of Oyo State had recognized no fewer than sixty-seven oba in that state alone who were entitled to wear beaded crowns. These included the Olubadan of Ibadan and the Soun of Ogbomosho.[4]

NOTES

1. Editor, *JRAS*, 2, no. VII (1903).
2. Asiwaju (1976b), *passim*.
3. P. 125.
4. *Daily Times* (Lagos), 16 May 1977.

APPENDIX II
A SUMMARY OF LINGUISTIC EVIDENCE

Although Yoruba is recognizably a single language (or 'dialect continuum'), spoken Yoruba varies considerably in phonetics, vocabulary, and grammar in the different parts of the country. The geographical arrangement of kingdoms adopted in Chapters 2 to 6 of this book corresponds only partially to this variation. An alternative arrangement might be based on a classification of Yoruba dialects recently proposed by Abiodun Adetugbo.[1] This distinguishes three main dialect areas in south-western Nigeria. Unfortunately it does not include Yoruba speakers in the far west (that is, in the modern republic of Bénin, formerly Dahomey) or in Kwara State to the north.

I. *North-West Yoruba*	II. *South-East Yoruba*	III. *Central Yoruba*
Oyo	Ondo	Ife
Owo	Ijesha	Oshun
Ibadan	Ikale	Ekiti
Egba	Ilaje	Akure
Egbado	Ijebu	Akoko
Awori		

(It will be noticed that Adetugbo's geographical descriptions are in some cases inappropriate.)

Adetugbo has pointed out that resemblances in dialect between the peoples in each of the three groups are paralleled by resemblances in social and political organization, which in turn reflect what is known of the history of these areas. Thus, in North-West Yorubaland, much of which was comprised within the kingdom and empire of Oyo, lineage and descent are patrilineal and traditional government is divided between civil and military chiefs. Among the South-East Yoruba, many of whom were subject at times in the past to Benin, lineage and descent tend to be multi-lineal and the division between civil and military chiefs is less common. Age-group associations (*egbe*) are found in the South-East and Ekiti but not elsewhere. Adetugbo has concluded that 'both Central Yoruba and South-East Yoruba dialects preserve an earlier stage of Proto-Yoruba than North-West Yoruba' and that the linguistic evidence suggests that settlement in the North-West is more recent than in the other two areas.

155

Recent work on the classification of Nigerian languages by Carl Hoffman[2] has provided further evidence of interest to the historian. The 'Yoruba group' is now held to comprise: (a) Yoruba, Itsekiri, and Igala; (b) the Northern Akoko 'cluster'. Thus, the languages most similar to Yoruba and presumably stemming from Proto-Yoruba are concentrated in North-East Yorubaland and its adjacent areas.

These findings tend to support the view that the migrations recorded in Yoruba tradition took place over only relatively short distances within that part of West Africa lying west of the Niger–Benue confluence, were from the grassland into the neighbouring forests, and were generally in a westerly and also southerly direction. They might also support the tradition that Ife was a dispersal centre for an important section of the migrants were it not that, according to Adetugbo, the influence of Ife on the other dialects of Yoruba seems to have been small.[3]

NOTES

1. In Biobaku (1973), pp. 176–204, and also in a University of Ife seminar paper (n.d.), 'Towards a Yoruba Dialectology'.
2. *The Languages of Nigeria by Language Families*, Department of Linguistics and Nigerian Languages paper, University of Ibadan, 1974. The significance of this distribution for the origins of the Yoruba was pointed out by Mr H. A. Obayemi in a seminar at the University of Ibadan in February 1975.
3. The writer thanks Professors Ayo Bamgboshe and Kay Williamson for their comments on this Appendix.

SOURCES AND BIBLIOGRAPHY

A. Books

Abiola, J. D. E., and others (1932). *Iwe Itan Ijesa*. Lagos.

Adams, Captain J. (1823). *Remarks on the Country Extending from Cape Palmas to the River Congo*. London.

Ademakinwa, J. A. (1958). *Ife, Cradle of the Yoruba*. Lagos.

Adewoye, O. (1977). *The Judicial System in Nigeria, 1854–1954*. London.

Ajayi, J. F. A. (1965). *Christian Missions in Nigeria, 1814–1891*. London.

Ajayi, J. F. A. and Crowder, M., (ed.) (1971, 1974; 1976). *History of West Africa*. Two vols. London.

Ajayi, J. F. A. and Smith, R. S. (1964, 2nd edn., 1971). *Yoruba Warfare in the Nineteenth Century*. Cambridge.

Ajisafe, A. K. (alias E. O. Moore) (1924). *A History of Abeokuta*. London.

Akerejola, G. B. (1973). *The History of Ogori*. Ibadan.

Akindoju, S. A. and Olagundoye (1962). *History of Idanre*. Ibadan.

Akinjogbin, I. A. (1967a). *Dahomey and its Neigbhours, 1708–1818*. Cambridge.

Akintoye, S. A. (1971). *Revolution and Power in Yorubaland, 1840–1893*. London.

Akinyele, I. B. (1950). *Iwe Itan Ibadan*. Exeter. (See also Morgan.)

Argyle, W. J. (1966). *The Fon of Dahomey*. Oxford.

Asabia, D. O. and Adegbesan, J. O. (1970). *Idoani Past and Present*. Ibadan.

Ashara, Chief M. R. (1951). *The History of Owo*. Owo.

Asiwaju, A. I. (1976a). *Western Yorubaland under European Rule*. London.

Atanda, J. A. (1973a). *The New Oyo Empire: Indirect Rule and Change in Western Nigeria, 1894–1934*. London.

Avoseh, T. O. (1938). *A Short History of Badagry*. Lagos.

Avoseh, T. O. (1960). *Short History of Epe*. Epe.

Ayandele, E. A. (1966). *The Missionary Impact on Modern Nigeria*. London.

Barbot, J. (1732). *A Description of the Coasts of North and South Guinea*. London.

Barrett, S. R. (1977). *The Rise and Fall of an African Utopia*. Ontario.

Beier, U. (1959). *A Year of Sacred Festivals in One Yoruba Town*. Lagos.

Biobaku, S. O. (1957). *The Egba and their Neighbours, 1842–1872*. Oxford.

Biobaku, S. O. (ed.)(1973). *Sources of Yoruba History*. Oxford.

Bosman, W. (1705). *A New and Accurate Description of the Coast of Guinea*. London.

Bovill, E. W. (1958). *The Golden Trade of the Moors*. Oxford.

Bowen, T. J. (1857). *Adventures and Missionary Labours in Several Countries in the Interior of Africa from 1849 to 1856*. Charleston.

Bowen, T. J. (1858). *Grammar and Dictionary of the Yoruba Language*. Washington.

Buchanan, K. M. and Pugh, J. C. (1955). *Land and People in Nigeria*. London.

Burns, Sir A. (1947). *A History of Nigeria*. London.

Burton, Sir R. F. (1863a). *Abeokuta and the Cameroons Mountain*. London.

Burton, Sir R. F. (1863b). *Wanderings in West Africa*. London.

Burton, Sir R. F. (1864). *A Mission to Gelele, King of Dahomey*. London.

Clapperton, H. (1829). *Journal of a Second Expedition into the Interior of Africa from the Bight of Benin to Soccattoo*. London.

Clarke, W. H. (ed. Atanda, J. A.)(1972). *Travels and Explorations in Yorubaland (1854–1858)*. Ibadan.

Coleman, J. S. (1958). *Nigeria: Background to Nationalism*. California.

Cornevin, R. (1962). *Histoire de Dahomey*. Paris.

Crowder, M. (1966 revision). *The Story of Nigeria*. London.

Crowder, M. (ed.) (1971). *West African Resistance*. London.

Crowder, M. and Ikime, O. (ed.) (1970). *West African Chiefs*. Ife.

Crowther, S. A. (1852). *A Grammar and Vocabulary of the Yoruba Language*. London.

Curtin, P. D. (ed.) (1967). *Africa Remembered*. Wisconsin and Ibadan.

Dalzel, A. (1793). *The History of Dahomey, an Inland Kingdom of Africa*. London.

Dapper, O. (1686). *Description de l'Afrique*. Amsterdam.

Delany, E. and Campbell, R. (1860, 1969 edn.). *Search for a Place*. Michigan.

Diké, K. O. (ed.) (1960). *Eminent Nigerians of the Nineteenth Century*. Cambridge.

Douglas, M. and Kaberry, P. M. (ed.) (1969). *Man in Africa*. London.

Duncan, J. (1847; 1967 reprint). *Travels in Western Africa*. London

Eades, J. S. (1980). *The Yoruba Today*. Cambridge.

Echeruo, M. J. C. (1977). *Victorian Lagos*. London.

Egharevba, J. U. (3rd edn., 1960). *A Short History of Benin*. Ibadan.

Elgee, C. H. (1914). *The Evolution of Ibadan*. Lagos.

Ellis, A. B. (1894). *The Yoruba-speaking Peoples of the Slave Coast of West Africa*. London.

Elphinstone, K. V. (1921). *Gazetteer of Ilorin Province*. London.

Fabunmi, M. A. (1969a). *Ife Shrines*. Ife.

Fadipe, N. A. (ed. Okediji, F. O. and Okediji, O. O.)(1970). *The Sociology of the Yoruba*. Ibadan.

Fage, J. D. (1978). *A History of Africa*. London.

Fagg, W. (1963). *Nigerian Images*. London.

Flint, J. E. (1960). *Sir George Goldie and the Making of Nigeria*. Oxford.

Forde, D. (1951). *The Yoruba-speaking Peoples of South-Western Nigeria*. London.

Forde, D. and Kaberry, P. M. (1967). *West African Kingdoms in the Nineteenth Century* (also cited as Morton-Williams (1967)).

Gbadamosi, T. G. O. (1978). *The Growth of Islam among the Yoruba*. London.

Geary, W. N. M. (1927). *Nigeria under British Rule*. London.

George, J. O. (1895?). *Historical Notes on the Yoruba Country and its Tribes*. Lagos.

Hargreaves, J. D. (1963). *Prelude to the Partition of West Africa*. London.

Hermàn-Hodge, H. B. (1929). *Gazetteer of Ilorin Province*. London.

Hinderer, Anna (1872). *Seventeen Years in the Yoruba Country*. London.

Hodgkin, T. (1960; 1975). *Nigerian Perspectives*. Oxford.

Hogben, S. J. and Kirk-Greene, A. H. M. (1966). *The Emirates of Northern Nigeria*. Oxford.

Hopkins, A. G. (1973). *An Economic History of West Africa*. London.

Idowu, E. B. (1962). *Olodumare – God in Yoruba Belief*. London.

Ikime, O. (ed.) (1980). *Groundwork of Nigerian History*. Ibadan.

Jacolliot, L. (n.d.). *Voyage aux Pays Mystérieux*. Paris.

Johnson, S. (1921). *The History of the Yorubas*. Lagos.

Jones, A. (1983). *German Sources for the West African History 1599–1669*. Wiesbaden.

Kenyo, E. A. (1964). *Yoruba Natural Rulers and their Origin*. Ibadan.

Kopytoff, J. H. (1965). *A Preface to Modern·Nigeria*. Wisconsin.

Lander, R. L. (1830). *Records of Captain Clapperton's Last Expedition to Africa*. 2 vols. London.

Lander, R. L. and J. (1832). *Journal of an Expedition to Explore the Course and Termination of the Niger*. London. References are to the edited and abridged edition by R. Hallett (1965), London.

Law, R. (1977). *The Oyo Empire, c. 1600–c.1836*. Oxford.

Law, R. (1980a). *The Horse in West African History*. Oxford.

Leigh, J. A. (1917). *History of Ondo*.

Lloyd, P. C. (1971). *The Political Development of Yoruba Kingdoms in the Eighteenth and Nineteenth Centuries*. London.

Lloyd, P. C., Mabogunje, A. J. and Awe, B. (1967). *The City of Ibadan*. London.

Losi, J. B. (1914). *History of Lagos*. Lagos.

Lucas, J. O. (1948). *The Religion of the Yoruba*. Lagos.

Lugard, Lord (ed. Perham, M. and Bull, M.) (1963). *The Diaries*. Vol. 4.

Mabogunje, A. L. and Omer-Cooper, J. (1971). *Owu in Yoruba History*. Ibadan.

McCall, D. F. (1964). *Africa in Time-perspective*. Boston, U.S.A.

Morgan, K. (n.d.). *Akinyele's Outline History of Ibadan*. Parts 1, 2. Ibadan.

Morton-Williams, P. (1967). 'The Yoruba Kingdom of Oyo', in Forde and Kaberry.

Newbury, C. W. (1961). *The Western Slave Coast and its Rulers*. Oxford.

Nigerian Museum (1955). *The Art of Ife*. Lagos.

Norris, E. G. (1978). *Wirtschaft und Wirtschaftspolitik in Abeokuta, 1830–1867*. Wiesbaden.

Norris, R. (1789). *Memoirs of the Reign of Bossa Ahadee King of Dahomey*. London.

Odutola, O. (1946). *Itan Ijebu*. Ijebu-Ode.

Oguntuyi, A. (1957). *A Short History of Ado-Ekiti*. Akure.

Ojo, G. J. A. (1966a). *Yoruba Culture*. London.

Ojo, G. J. A. (1966b). *Yoruba Palaces*. London.

Ojo, O. S. (Bada of Shaki) (n.d., a). *Short History of Ilorin*. Oyo.

Ojo, O. S. (Bada of Shaki) (n.d., b). *Iwe Itan Oyo*. Oyo.

Ojo, O. S. (Bada of Shaki) (n.d., c). *Iwe Itan Saki*. Oyo.

Okubote, B. M. (1937). *Iwe Itan Ikereku ati Ijebu*. Ibadan.

Olafinmikan, J. B. (1950). *Iwe Itan Offa*. Offa.

Oliver, R. and Fage, J. D. (1962). *A Short History of Africa*. London.

Olugunna, D. (1959). *Oshogbo*. Oshogbo.

Olunlade, E. A. (ed. Beier, U.; trans. Akinjogbin, I. A.) (1961). *Ede, A Short History*. Ibadan.

Olusola, J. A. (1968). *Ancient Ijebu-Ode*. Ibadan.

Oyerinde, N. D. (1934). *Iwe Itan Ogbomoso*. Jos.

Parrinder, G. (1953). *Religion in an African City*. Oxford.

Parrinder, G. (1956). *The Story of Ketu*. Ibadan.

Payne, J. A. O. (1893). *Table of Principal Events in Yoruba History*. Lagos.

Pereira, Duarte Pacheco (ed. R. Mauny, 1956). *Esmeraldo de Situ Orbis*. Bissau.

Robertson, G. A. (1819). *Notes on Africa*. London.

Robinson, R. and Gallagher, J. (1961). *Africa and the Victorians*. London.

Ryder, A. F. C. (1969). *Benin and the Europeans*. London.

Schön, J. F. and Crowther, S. A. (1842). *Journals*. London.

Sertorio, G. (1967). *Struttura sociale-politica e ordinamento fondiario Yoruba*. Como.

Shaw, T. (1964). *Archaeology and Nigeria*. Ibadan.

Shaw, T. (1978). *Nigeria: Its Archaeology and Early History*. London.

Smith, R. S. (1978). *The Lagos Consulate, 1851–1861*. London.

Snelgrave, W. (1734). *A New Account of Some Parts of Guinea and the Slave Trade*. London.

S. O. A. Authority (1958). *The Happy City, Aiyetoro*. Lagos.

Stevens, P. (1978). *The Stone Images of Esie*. Ibadan.

Stone, R. H. (1900). *In Africa's Forest and Jungle or Six Years among the Yoruba*. Edinburgh.

Talbot, P. A. (1926). *The Peoples of Southern Nigeria*. London.

Temple, O. (ed. Temple, C. L.)(1919; 1965 reprint). *Notes on the Tribes, Provinces, Emirates and States of the Northern Provinces of Nigeria*. London.
Thorp, Ellen (1950). *The Swelling of Jordan*. London.
Thorp, Ellen (1956). *Ladder of Bones*. London.
Whitford, J. (1877; 1967 reprint). *Trading Life in Western and Central Africa*. London.
Willett, F. (1967). *Ife in the History of West African Sculpture*. London.
Williams, D. (1974). *Icon and Image*. London.

Two works which came to the writer's attention too late for consideration in this edition, but which are recommended, are: D. Laitin (1986), *Hegemony and Culture: Politics and Religious Change among the Yoruba*, Chicago, and J. Vansina (1984, 1987), *Art History in Africa*, London.

B. Articles

Abimbola, W. (1967). 'Ifa Divination Poems as Sources for Historical Evidence', *L. N. R.*, I, 1.
Adegoriola I, Ogoga of Ikerre (n.d.). 'A Note on the Administration of Ikerre before the Advent of the British', *Odu*, 3.
Aderemi, Oni of Ife (1937). 'Notes on the City of Ife', *Nigeria Magazine*, no. 12.
Aderibigbe, A. B. (1962). 'The Ijebu Expedition 1892: An Episode in the British Penetration of Nigeria Reconsidered', *Proceedings of the Leverhulme Inter-Collegiate History Conference, 1960*.
Adewale, T. J. (1956). 'The Ijanna Episode in Yoruba History', *Proceedings of the Third International West African Conference*, Lagos, 1949.
Agiri, B. A. (1972). 'The Ogboni among the Oyo Yoruba', *L. N. R.*, III, 2.
Agiri, B. A. (1975). 'Early Oyo History Reconsidered', *History in Africa*, 2.
Agiri, B. A. (1976). 'When was Ogbomoso Founded?', *Transafrica Journal of History*, V, 1.
Agiri, B. A. (1977). 'A Reconsideration of the Chronology of Ogbomoso History before the Colonial Period', *Odu*, (n.s.), XV.
Ahmad b. Abi Bakr (alias Abu Ikokoro). *Ta'lif akhbar al-qurun min 'umara bilad Ilorin*. See Martin (1965).
Ajayi, J. F. A. (1960). 'How Yoruba was Reduced to Writing', *Odu*, 8.
Ajayi, J. F. A. (1961a). 'The British Occupation of Lagos', *Nigeria Magazine*, 69.
Ajayi, J. F. A. (1961b). 'Nineteenth Century Origins of Nigerian Nationalism', *J. H. S. N.*, II, 2.
Ajayi, J. F. A. (1964a). 'Samuel Johnson, Historian of the Yoruba', *The Historian*, I, 1.
Ajayi, J. F. A. (1964b). 'Professional Warriors in Nineteenth Century Yoruba Politics', *Tarikh*, I, 1.
Ajayi, J. F. A. and Austen, R. A. (1972). 'Hopkins on Economic Imperialism in West Africa', *Econ. Hist. Review*, 2nd series, XXV, 2.
Ajuwon, B. (1980). 'The Preservation of Yoruba Tradition through Hunters' Funeral Dirges', *Africa*, 50, 1.
Akinjogbin, I. A. (1963). 'Agaja and the Conquest of the Coastal Aja States, 1724–30', *J. H. S. N.*, II, 4.
Akinjogbin, I. A. (1965). 'The Prelude to the Yoruba Civil Wars of the Nineteenth Century', *Odu* (n.s.), I, 2.
Akinjogbin, I. A. (1966a). 'A Chronology of Yoruba History', *Odu* (n.s.) II, 2.
Akinjogbin, I. A. (1966b). 'The Oyo Empire in the Eighteenth Century', *J. H. S. N.*, III, 3.
Akinjogbin, I. A. (1967b). 'Ife: The Home of a New University', *Nigeria Magazine*, 92.
Akintoye, S. A. (1969a). 'The Ondo Road eastwards from Lagos, c. 1870–95', *J. A. H.*, X, 4.
Akintoye, S. A. (1969b). 'The North-eastern Yoruba Districts and the Benin Kingdom', *J. H. S. N.*, IV, 4.

Allison, P. (n.d.). 'The Last Days of Old Oyo', *Odu*, 4.

Anene, J. C. (1963). 'The Nigeria–Dahomey Boundary', *J. H. S. N.*, II, 4.

Anon. (1955). 'Idanre', *Nigeria Magazine*, 46.

Anon. (1963). 'Igogo Festival', *Nigeria Magazine*, 77.

Asiwaju, A. I. (1973). 'A Note on the History of Sabe', *L. N. R.*, IV.

Asiwaju, A. I. (1974). 'Anti-French Resistance Movement in Ohori-Ije (Dahomey), 1895–1960', *J. H. S. N.*, VII, 2.

Asiwaju, A. I. (1976b). 'Political Motivation and Oral Historical Tradition in Africa: the Case of Yoruba Crowns, 1900–1960.', *Africa*, XLVI, 2.

Asiwaju, A. I. (1979). 'The Aja-Speaking Peoples of Nigeria: Origin, Settlement and Cultural Adaptation up to 1945', *Africa*, 49, 1.

Atanda, J. A. (1971). 'The Fall of the Old Oyo Empire: A Reconsideration of its Cause', *J. H. S. N.*, V, 4.

Atanda, J. A. (1973b). 'The Yoruba Ogboni Cult: Did it Exist in Old Oyo?', *J. H. S. N.*, VI, 4.

Awe, B. (1964b). 'The Ajele System: A Study of Ibadan Imperialism in the Nineteenth Century', *J. H. S. N.*, III, 1.

Awe, B. (1965). 'The End of an Experiment: The Collapse of the Ibadan Empire, 1877–1893', *J. H. S. N.*, III, 2.

Awe, B. (1974a). 'Praise Poems as Historical Data: The Example of the Yoruba Oriki', *Africa*, XLIV, 4.

Babayemi, S. O. (1968). 'Oyo Ruins', *African Notes*, V, 1.

Babayemi, S. O. (1971). 'Upper Ogun: An Historical Sketch', *African Notes*, VI, 2.

Ballard, J. (1971). 'Historical Inferences from the Linguistic Geography of the Nigerian Middle Belt', *Africa*, XLI, 4.

Barker, H. (1972). 'The Accuracy of Radiocarbon Dates', *J. A. H.*, XIII, 2.

Bascom, W. (1960). 'Lander's Routes through Yoruba Country', *Nigerian Field*, XXV, 1.

Beier, H. U. (n.d.). 'Before Oduduwa', *Odu*, 3.

Beier, H. U. (1956a). 'The Oba's Festival, Ondo', *Nigeria Magazine*, 50.

Beier, H. U. (1956b). 'Obatala Festival', *Nigeria Magazine*, 52.

Beier, H. U. (1956c). 'Olokun Festival', *Nigeria Magazine*, 49.

Beier, H. U. (1960). 'Oshogbo, Portrait of a Yoruba Town', *Nigeria Magazine*, Independence issue.

Bertho, J. (1949). 'La Parenté des Yoruba aux Peuplades de Dahomey et Togo', *Africa*, XIX, 2.

Biobaku, S. O. (1956a). 'The Problem of Traditional History with Special Reference to Yoruba Traditions', *J. H. S. N.*, I, 1.

Biobaku, S. O. (1956b). 'Ogboni, the Egba Senate', *Proceedings of the Third International West African Conference*, Lagos, 1949.

Bivar, A. D. H. and Hiskett, M. (1962). 'The Arabic Literature of Nigeria to 1804: A Provisional Assessment', *Bulletin, S. O. A. S.*, XXV.

Bradbury, R. E. (1959). 'Chronological Problems in Benin History', *J. H. S. N.*, I, 4.

Bridges, A. F. B. (1936). 'Idanre', *Nigerian Field*, V, 4.

Dike, K. O. (1956). 'John Beecroft, 1790–1824', *J. H. S. N.*, I, 1.

Duckworth, E. H. (1952). 'Badagry – its Place in the Pages of History', *Nigeria Magazine*, 38.

Editor, *Journal of the Royal African Society* (1902–3). 'Native Crowns.'

Eluyemi, O. (1976). 'Egbejoda Excavations, Nigeria, 1970', *W. A. J. A.*, 6.

Eluyemi, O. (1977). 'A Note on Egbejoda Terracotta Sculpture', *Odu*, 16 (n.s.).

Eyo, E. (1974). 'Odo Ogbe Street and Lafogido: Contrasting Archaeological Sites in Ile-Ife, Western Nigeria', *W. A. J. A.*, 4.

Eyo, E. (1976). 'Igbo Laja, Owo', *W. A. J. A.*, 6.

Fabunmi, M. A. (1969b). 'Notes on Ile-Ife', *Nigeria Magazine*, 100.

Fagg, W. and Willett, F. (1960). 'Ancient Ife, An Ethnographical Survey', *Odu*, 8.

Flight, C. (1973). 'A Survey of Recent Results in Radiocarbon Chronology of Northern and Western Africa', *J. A. H.*, XIV, 4.

Folayan, K. (1967b). 'Egbado to 1832: The Birth of a Dilemma', *J. H. S. N.*, IV, 1.

Garlake, P. S. (1974). 'Excavations at Obalara's Land, Ife: An Interim Report', *W. A. J. A.*, 4.

Garlick, J. P. (1962). 'Blood Group Maps of Africa, *J. A. H.*, III, 2.

Gbadamosi, G. O. (1972). 'The Imamate Question among Yoruba Muslims', *J. H. S. N.*, VI, 3.

Gleave, M. B. (1963). 'Hill Settlements and their Abandonment in Western Yorubaland', *Africa*, XXXIII, 4.

Goddard, S. (1965). 'Town-Farm Relationships in Yorubaland: A Case-Study from Oyo', *Africa*, XXXV, 1.

Herbert, E. W. (1973). 'Aspects of the Use of Copper in Pre-colonial West Africa', *J. A. H.*, XIV, 2.

Hill, P. (1966). 'Notes on Traditional Market Authority and Market Periodicity in West Africa', *J. A. H.*, VII, 2.

Hodder, B. W. (1962–3). 'Badagri: Slave Port and Mission Centre', *N. G. J.*, V, 2; VI, 1.

Hopkins, A. G. (1960). 'A Report on the Yoruba, 1910', *J. H. S. N.*, V, 1.

Hopkins, A. G. (1968). 'Economic Imperialism in West Africa'. *Econ. Hist. Review*, 2nd series, XXI, 3.

Hopkins, A. G. (1972). 'A Rejoinder', *Econ. Hist. Review*, 2nd series, XXV, 2.

Hopkins, A. G. (1980). 'Property Rights and Empire Building: Britain's Annexation of Lagos, 1861', *J. Econ. Hist.*, XL, 4.

Ibigbami, R. I. (1977). 'The Sacred Images of Ogun in Ire Ekiti', *Odu*, 16 (n.s.).

Johnson, M. (1970), 'The Cowrie Currencies of West Africa', *J. A. H.*, XI, 1, 3.

Law, R. (1968a). 'The Dynastic Chronology of Lagos'. *L. N. R.*, II, 2.

Law, R. (1968b). Review of I. A. Akinjogbin, *Dahomey and its Neighbours*, *J. H. S. N.*, IV, 2.

Law, R. (1969). 'The Fall of Allada: An Ideological Revolution', *J. H. S. N.*, V, 1.

Law, R. (1970). 'The Chronology of the Yoruba Wars of the Early Nineteenth Century: A Reconsideration', *J. H. S. N.*, V, 2.

Law, R. (1971). 'The Constitutional Troubles of Oyo in the Eighteenth Century', *J. A. H.*, XII, 1.

Law, R. (1972). 'Iwere', *J. H. S. N.*, VI, 2.

Law, R. (1973a). 'The Heritage of Oduduwa: Traditional History and Political Propaganda among the Yoruba', *J. A. H.*, XIV, 2.

Law, R. (1973b). 'Anthropological Models in Yoruba History', *Africa*, XLIII, 1.

Law, R. (1973d). 'The Owu War in Yoruba History' (review article), *J. H. S. N.*, VII, 1.

Law, R. (1973e). 'The Oyo Kingdom and its Northern Neighbours', *Kano Studies*, 1 (n.s.).

Law, R. (1975). 'A West African Cavalry State: The Kingdom of Oyo', *J. A. H.*, XVI, 1.

Law, R. (1976a). 'Early Yoruba Historiography', *History in Africa*, 3.

Law, R. (1976b). 'Horses, Firearms, and Political Power in Pre-Colonial West Africa', *Past and Present*, 72.

Law, R. (1978a). 'Slaves, Trade, and Taxes: the Material Basis of Political Power in Precolonial West Africa', *Research in Economic Anthropology*, I.

Law, R. (1978b). 'The Career of Adele at Lagos and Badagry, c. 1807–c. 1837', *J. H. S. N.*, IX, 2.

Law, R. (1980b). 'Wheeled Transport in Pre-Colonial West Africa', *Africa*, L(3).

Law, R. (1982). 'Making Sense of a Traditional Narrative: Political Disintegration in the Kingdom of Oyo', *Cahiers d'Etudes Africaines*, XXII, 3–4.

Law, R. (1983). 'Trade and Politics behind the Slave Coast: The Lagoon Traffic and the Rise of Lagos, 1500–1800', *J. A. H.*, XXIV.

Law, R. (1984). 'How Truly Traditional is our Traditional History? The Case of Samuel Johnson and the Recording of Yoruba Oral Tradition', *History in Africa*, 11.

Law, R. (1985a). 'Human Sacrifice in Pre-Colonial West Africa', *African Affairs*, 84, 334.

Law, R. (1985b). 'How Many Times Can History Repeat Itself? Some Problems in the Traditional History of Oyo', *International J. African Hist. Studies*, 18, 1.

Law. R. (1986). 'Early European Sources Relating to the Kingdom of Ijebu (1500–1700): A Critical Survey', *History of Africa*, 13.

Lewis, H. S. (1966). 'The Origins of African Kingdoms', *Cahiers d'Etudes Africaines*, VI, 3.

Lloyd, P. C. (1959). 'Sungbo's Eredo', *Odu*, 7.

Lloyd, P. C. (1960a). 'Sacred Kingship and Government among the Yoruba', *Africa*, XXX, 3.

Lloyd, P. C. (1960b). 'Osifakorede of Ijebu', *Odu*, 8.

Lloyd, P. C. (1960c). 'Yoruba Towns', *Ibadan*, 12.

Lloyd, P. C. (1961). 'Installing the Awujale', *Ibadan*, 12.

Lynn, M. (1981). 'Change and Continuity in the British Palm Oil Trade with West Africa, 1830–55', *J. A. H.*, XXII, 3.

Lynn, M. (1982). 'Consuls and Kings: British Policy, "the Man on the Spot", and the Seizure of Lagos, 1851', *J. Imperial and Commonwealth Hist.*, X, 2.

Mabogunje, A. L. and Oyawoye, M. O. (1961). 'The Problems of Northern Yoruba Towns: The Example of Shaki', *N. G. J.*, IV, 2.

McIntyre, W. D. (1963). 'Commander Glover and the Colony of Lagos, 1861–73', *J. A. H.*, IV, 1.

Martin, B. G. (1965). 'A New Arabic History of Ilorin', *Research Bulletin*, Centre of Arabic Documentation, University of Ibadan, I, 2.

Mason, M. (1969). 'Population Density and Slave Raiding in the Case of the Middle Belt of Nigeria', *J. A. H.*, X, 4.

Mason, M. (1970). 'The Jihad in the South: An Outline of the Nineteenth Century Nupe Hegemony in North-Eastern Yorubaland and Afenmai', *J. H. S. N.*, V, 2.

May, D. J. (1860). 'Journey in the Yoruba and Nupe Countries in 1859', *Journal of the Royal Geographical Society*, XXX.

Mbaeyi, P. M. (1972). 'Lagos and the British, 1871–1874', *Ikenga*, I, 1.

Morton-Williams, P. (1960). 'The Yoruba Ogboni Cult in Oyo', *Africa*, XXX, 4.

Morton-Williams, P. (1964a). 'The Oyo Yoruba and the Atlantic Trade, 1670–1830'. *J. H. S. N.*, III, 1.

Morton-Williams, P. (1964b). 'An Outline of the Cosmology and Cult Organization of the Oyo Yoruba', *Africa*, XXXIV, 3.

Moulero, R. P. (1964). 'Histoire et légende de Chabe (Save)', *Études Dahoméenes*.

Munoz, L. J. (1978). 'La Ciudad Ceremonial Yoruba, Mecanismo de Tradicion', *Africa* (Rome), XXXIII, 2.

Ogunba, O. (1964). 'Crowns and *Okute* at Idowa', *Nigeria Magazine*, 83.

Ogunba, O. (1965). 'The Agemo Cult in Ijebuland', *Nigeria Magazine*, 86.

Ogunkoya, T. (1956). 'The Early History of Ijebu', *J. H. S. N.*, I, 1.

Olajubu, O. (1964). 'Obokun', *The African Historian*, I, 2.

Omer-Cooper, J. D. (1964). 'The Question of Unity in African History', *J. H. S. N.*, III, 1.

Oyediran, O. (1973). 'The Position of the Ooni in the Changing Political System of Ile-Ife', *J. H. S. N.*, VI, 4.

Ozanne, P. (1969). 'A New Archaeological Survey of Ife', *Odu*, 3rd series, 1.

Pallinder-Law, A. (1974). 'Aborted Modernization in West Africa? The Case of Abeokuta', *J. A. H.*, XV, 1.

Parratt, J. K. (1969). 'An Approach to Ife Festivals', *Nigeria Magazine*, 100.

Parrinder, G. (1947). 'Yoruba-speaking Peoples in Dahomey', *Africa*, XVII, 2.

Parrinder, E. G. (1951). 'Ibadan Annual Festival', *Africa*, XXI, 1.

Phillips, E. H. (1969). 'The Egba Abeokuta: Acculturation and Political Change, 1830–1870', *J. A. H.*, X, 1.

Phillips, E. H. (1970). 'The Egba at Ikorodu, 1865: Perfidious Lagos?', *African Historical Studies*, III.

Posnansky, M., and McIntosh, R., 'New Radiocarbon Dates for Northern and Western Africa', *J. A. H.*, XVII, 2.

Ryder, A. F. C. (1965). 'A Reconsideration of the Ife–Benin Relationship', *J. A. H.*, VI, 1.

Shaw, T. (1971). 'Africa in Pre-history: Leader or Laggard?', *J. A. H.*, XII, 1.

Shaw, T. (1973). 'A Note on Trade and the Tsoede Bronzes', *W. A. J. A.*, 3.

Smith, R. S. (1962). 'Ijaiye, the Western Palatinate of the Yoruba', *J. H. S. N.*, II, 3.

Smith, R. S. (1964). 'Erin and Iwawun, Forgotten Towns of the Oke Ogun', *Odu* (n.s.), I, 1.

Smith, R. S. (1965a). 'The Alafin in Exile', *J. A. H.*, VI, 1.

Smith, R. S. (1965b). 'The Bara, or Royal Mausoleum, at New Oyo', *J. H. S. N.*, III, 2.

Smith, R. S. (1967). 'Yoruba Armament', *J. A. H.*, VIII, 1.

Smith, R. S. (1969). 'To the Palaver Islands: War and Diplomacy on the Lagos Lagoon, 1852–1854', *J. H. S. N.*, V. 1.

Smith, R. S. (1971a). 'Event and Portent: The Fall of Old Oyo, a Problem in Historical Explanation', *Africa*, XLI, 3.

Smith, R. S. (1971b). 'A Note on Two Shirts of Mail in the Palace at Owo in South-Western Nigeria', *Odu*, 3rd series, 5.

Smith, R. S. (1974). 'The Lagos Consulate, 1851–1861: An Outline', *J. A. H.*, XV, 3.

Smith, R. S. and Williams, D. (1966). 'A Reconnaissance Visit to Old Oyo', *Odu* (n.s.), III, 1.

Soper, R. (1975). 'Some Comments on the Site of Old Oyo', *The Archaeologist*, 2.

Soper, R. (1978). 'Carved Posts at Old Oyo', *Nigerian Field*, 43, Pt. 1.

Stevens, P. (1966). 'Orisha-Nla Festival', *Nigeria Magazine*, 90.

Tylecote, R. F. (1975). 'The Origin of Iron Smelting in Africa', *W. A. J. A.*, 5.

Verger, P. (1959). 'Notes on Some Documents in which Lagos is Referred to by the Name "Onim" . . .' *J. H. S. N.*, I, 4.

Walsh, M. J. (1948). 'The Edi Festival at Ile-Ife', *African Affairs*, 47.

Wescott, R. W. (n.d.). 'Did the Yoruba Come from Egypt?', *Odu*, 4.

Willett, F. (1958). 'The Discovery of New Brass Figures at Ife', *Odu*, 6.

Willett, F. (1960a). 'Investigations at Old Oyo, 1956–57; An Interim Report', *J. H. S. N.*, II, 1.

Willett, F. (1960b). 'Ife and its Archaeology', *J. A. H.*, I, 2.

Willett, F. (1960c). 'Discoveries in Ilesha', *Odu*, 8.

Willett, F. (1966). 'On the Funderal Effigies of Owo and Benin and an Interpretation of the Life-size Bronze Heads from Ife, Nigeria', *Man* (n.s.), I, 1.

Willett, F. (1971). 'A Survey of Recent Results in the Radiocarbon Chronology of Western and Northern Africa', *J. A. H.*, XII, 1.

Williams, D. (1964). 'The Iconology of the Yoruba *Edan Ogboni*', *Africa*, XXXIV, 2.

Williams, D. (1965). 'Lost Wax Brass-casting in Ibadan', *Nigeria Magazine*, 85.

Williams, D. (1967b). 'Bronze Casting Moulds, Cores and the Study of Classical Techniques', *L. N. R.*, I, 1.

Wrigley, C. (1960). 'Speculations on the Economic Pre-history of Africa', *J. A. H.*, I, 2.

Wrigley, C. (1962). 'Linguistic Clues to African History', *J. A. H.*, III, 2.

C. Unpublished material

Aderibigbe, A. B. (1959). *The Expansion of the Lagos Protectorate*, Ph.D. thesis, University of London.

Agiri, B. A. (1966). *The Development of Local Government in Government in Ogbomoso, 1850–1950*. M. A. thesis, University of Ibadan.

Arifalo, S. O. 'An Analysis and Comparison of the Legends of Origin of Akure'. University of Ife, Original Essay, B. A. Special Honours in History, 1966.

Awe, B. A. (1964a). *The Rise of Ibadan as a Yoruba Power in the Nineteenth Century*. D.Phil. thesis, Oxford.

Awe, B. (1974b). 'Notes on the Institution of the Iyalode within the Traditional Yoruba Political System'. Paper presented to the 20th Annual Congress of the Historical Society of Nigeria.

Ayantuga, O. O. (1965). *Ijebu and its Neighbours, 1851–1941*. Ph.D. thesis, University of London.

Babayemi, S. O. (1974). 'The Structure of Administration at Oyo Atiba'. Paper presented to the 20th Annual Congress of the Historical Society of Nigeria.

Brown, S. H. (1964). *A History of the People of Lagos, 1852–1886*. Ph.D. thesis, Northwestern University, U.S.A.

Egbeola, Z. A. 'Egbado History'. University of Ife, Original Essay, B. A. Special Honours in History, 1966.

Folayan, K. (1967a). *Egbado and Yoruba–Aja Politics, 1832–1894*. M. A. dissertation, University of Ibadan.

Folayan, K. (1976). 'Aspects of Pre-Colonial Patterns of Government in the Frontier Zone of South-Western Yorubaland'. Seminar paper, University of Ife.

Hodder, B. W. (1964). *Markets in Yorubaland*. Ph.D. thesis, University of London.

Law, R. (1973c). 'The Horse in Yorubaland'. Typescript.

Leslie, R. M. (1944). *A History of Ilorin*. Rhodes House, Oxford, mss. Afr. r.63.

Obayemi, U. H. M. A. (1969). 'Oral Evidence as an Introduction to the Early History of the North-East Yoruba-speaking People'. Paper presented to the Fifteenth Annual Congress of the Historical Society of Nigeria.

Ogunremi, G. O. (1973). *Pre-Colonial Transport in Nigeria*. Ph.D. thesis, University of Birmingham.

Oguntomisin, G. O. (1979). *New Forms of Political Organization in Yorubaland in the Mid-nineteenth century: A Comparative Study of Kurunmi's Ijaye and Kosoko's Epe*. Ph.D. thesis, University of Ibadan.

Oroge, E. A. (1971). *The Institution of Slavery in Yorubaland with Particular Reference to the Nineteenth Century*. Ph.D. thesis, University of Birmingham.

Oyerinde, N. D. (1964). 'Notes on the History of Ogbomoso'. Seminar paper, University of Ife.

Phillips, E. H. (1966). *The Church Missionary Society, the Imperial Factor and Yoruba Politics, 1842–1873*. Ph.D. thesis, University of South California.

Schwab, W. A. (1962). *The Political and Social Organization of an African City (Osogbo)*. Ph.D. thesis, University of Pennsylvania.

Soper, R. (1973–77). *Annual Reports* on 'Archaeological Work at Old Oyo'. Department of Archaeology, University of Ibadan.

Sulu, M. (1951). *History of Ilorin*. Rhodes House, Oxford, mss. Afr. s.1210.

Williams, D. (1967a). 'Iron and the Gods: A Study of the Sacred Iron Figurines of the Yoruba', seminar paper, University of Lagos.

INDEX

Abdussalmi (Abd al-Salam), Emir of Ilorin, 114–6

Abeokuta, Egba capital, 94, 125, 141, 146; foundation of, 67, 121; Dahomean attacks on, 105, 128, 133; army of, 100, 103; ifole riots at, 138; British treaty with (1893), 141, 148

abidagba (sons born to a reigning king), 65, 92

Abiodun, Alafin, 38–9, 69, 71, 111, 119

Abipa, Alafin 32, 83

Abiri, near Ife, 23

abobaku (those who must die with an Alafin), 71

Abomey, capital of Dahomey, 4, 6, 55

aborigines, 15, 30, 43, 46–7, 51, 53, 56, 57, 65

Abweila, Oni, 18

Adams, Captain J., 63, 73, 74, 135

Adebo, Alafin, 113

Adele, Oba of Lagos, 74, 131

Adelu, Alafin, 132

Ademakinwa, J.A., 16

Adeyemi, M., 30

Adimu, 16, 81

Ado (Egbado), 37, 71, 138; siege of (1842–53), 133

Ado Ekiti, town and kingdom, 45–6, 92, 134

Adunbieye, near Iwo, Ife army at, 119

Afenmai people, 45, 48

Afidipote, Awujale, 145

afin, see palaces

Afonja, Kakamfo, 96, 113–4

Africa, partition of, Scramble for, 7, 142, 147

Agaja, king of Dahomey, 36, 57

Aganju, Alafin, 30, 31

Agbadaye, ruler of Igbadaye, 43

Agbaje war, 70, 128

Agbanla council, Ilesha, 95

Agbolaje, Alafin, 38, 66

age groups, 96

Agemo cult, 65

Agiri, B.A., 30, 36

Ago Iwoye, 63

Ago Oja, *see* New Oyo

Agura, ruler of Egba Gbagura, 68

Aibo, destruction of (1857–8), 132

Airo, Oshemawe, 52

Aiyetoro community, 53

Aiyetoro, Egbado, 71

Aja, people, 35, 72, 147

Ajagbo, Alafin, 35, 66

Ajaka, Alafin, 30

Ajaka (Ajibogun, Obokun), founder of Ijesha kingdom, 42

Ajalake, first Alake, 68

Ajalorun, oba of Ijebu Ife, 63

Ajapada, *see* Deji

Ajashe, 39, 41

Ajashe, Igbomina, 48

Ajashe Ipo, *see* Porto Novo

Ajayi, J.F.A., 132, 136

ajele, Oyo and Ibadan officials, 37, 40, 47, 69, 131, 144

Ajiboyede (Shopasan), Alafin, 32–3

FORTHCOMING

ALSO BY
Robert S. Smith

Warfare & Diplomacy in Pre-Colonial West Africa

SECOND EDITION

This is a new edition of this well-known innovative study of the relations of the peoples of West Africa in the precolonial period. It covers a period of some four or five hundred years up to the last decades of the nineteenth century.

The author takes a wide range of examples from the histories of those peoples whose levels of political organisation entitle their societies to be called 'states'.

Arrangements for the exercise of power differed greatly but in broad terms there were states where the power to make decisions about war and peace were concentrated in the hands of one man or an oligarchy and those states where the power was diffused between members of the community.

While he takes account of outside contributions the book is directed primarily to examining what happened between the states before the partition of the area and the establishment of colonies.

'This book . . . makes the link between war and diplomacy which is the stuff of much of European history. There are lots of works of scholarship on such subjects as slavery but this subject has been missed in African history except by Professor Smith.' – Michael Crowder, Visiting Professor, Amherst College

Contents Peace & War – Peaceful relations – West African Wars: Their causes & consequences – Armies & canoe fleets – Arm and armour – Static warfare & fortifications – Strategy, tactics and the battle – A summing up – Appendix: The Battle of Musfeia 1823 – Illustrations – Bibliography – Index